Advance Praise for
In the Path of Abraham

"Jason Greenblatt served the United States of America with distinction during his time at the White House. He played a significant role in helping establish my historic policies and achievements regarding our Middle East allies, including those relating to Jerusalem and the Abraham Accords. Read Jason's book to learn about his essential work and to understand how the Trump Administration created peace in the Middle East."

— President Donald J. Trump

"Jason Greenblatt played a pivotal role in our efforts to recognize Jerusalem as the capital of Israel and in establishing a future for peace and prosperity with the Abraham Accords. There are few people better positioned to reflect on those accomplishments and contemplate the possibilities of future successes in the name of peace and opportunity in the Middle East."

— Vice President Mike Pence

"The Abraham Accords will stand the test of time. Read Jason Greenblatt's book to learn about the work that led to these historic peace deals and how standing with our allies and friends is an essential complement to diplomacy. Jason writes with the same power and clarity he showed working for America and its relationship with Israel."

— Mike Pompeo, former US Secretary of State

"The Abraham Accords were historic and will go down as an amazing legacy for a small group of people, including Jason Greenblatt. Jason's work toward Middle East peace is remarkable, inspiring, and well worth reading about."

— Ambassador Nikki Haley, former US
Ambassador to the United Nations

"While working at the White House, Jason Greenblatt did a tremendous job helping to create President Trump's economic and political vision for a long-sought peace in the Middle East. He is an American patriot, devoted to Israel, a diplomat who understands today's Middle East and he continues to build peace between Israel and its Arab neighbors. This book is a must-read for anyone seeking to understand the Trump Administration's efforts to chart a new course for the Middle East."

— Jared Kushner, former Assistant to the President
and Senior Advisor to President Donald J. Trump

"Jason Greenblatt's work as Middle East Envoy at the White House improved dramatically the relationship between the United States and our allies in the Middle East and fostered an historic new dynamic between Israel and some of its Arab neighbors. What we now know as the Abraham Accords would not have been possible without Jason's empathetic nature and selfless commitment to foster peace and prosperity for all the peoples of that troubled region. This is a story that must be told, and Jason is the right person to tell it. Anyone interested in how the Trump Administration made progress on what many described as a fool's errand and want to know what might be possible in the future must read this book."

> — Lieut. Gen. (ret.) H.R. McMaster, 26th National Security Advisor and author of *Battlegrounds: The Fight to Defend the Free World.*

"From when I met Jason Greenblatt in early 2017, I knew I was talking to a man with a sincere devotion to achieving peace. While Jason and I have different views about certain issues, including the best route to a just and peaceful settlement for the Palestinian people, he and I share common ground in our passion to help make the world a better place. His book charts his account of his remarkable journey working at the White House and should be read by all who are interested in the Middle East."

> — Sheikh Mohammed Bin Abdulrahman Al Thani Deputy Prime Minister & Foreign Minister of the State of Qatar

"During his eventful tenure in the Trump Administration, Jason Greenblatt worked tirelessly to strengthen the alliance between Israel and the United States, defend Israel at the United Nations and advance peace by helping lay the foundations for the Abraham Accords. An insider's account from a first-class mensch, Jason's book is sure to be a must read for anyone interested in one of the most consequential periods in the history of US-Israel relations."

> — Ambassador Ron Dermer, former Israeli Ambassador to the United States of America

"Jason Greenblatt, together with his colleagues, created something historic that continues to lead to new economic opportunities and demonstrated to the world the possibilities and potential of peace. I highly recommend reading about Jason's historic journey throughout the Middle East, which ultimately led to the signing of the Abraham Accords and the dawn of a new era in the Middle East."

> — His Excellency Yousef Al Otaiba, United Arab
> Emirates Ambassador to the United States

"Jason Greenblatt, an outsider to traditional Washington D.C. and diplomatic circles, approached his role of achieving peace between Arab nations and Israel with zeal, passion and sincerity. The work that he and his colleagues did to achieve the historic Abraham Accords has without a doubt changed the landscape of the Middle East forever. Jason's book about his time in the White House is an important read for anyone who wants to better understand today's Middle East."

> — His Excellency Shaikh Abdulla Bin Rashed
> Al Khalifa, Ambassador of the Kingdom of
> Bahrain to the United States of America.

IN THE PATH OF
ABRAHAM

*How Donald Trump Made Peace
in the Middle East—and How to
Stop Joe Biden from Unmaking It*

JASON D.
GREENBLATT

WICKED SON

A WICKED SON BOOK
An Imprint of Post Hill Press
ISBN: 978-1-63758-309-8
ISBN (eBook): 978-1-63758-310-4

In the Path of Abraham:
How Donald Trump Made Peace in the Middle East—and How
to Stop Joe Biden from Unmaking It
© 2022 by Jason D. Greenblatt
All Rights Reserved

Cover Design by Tiffani Shea

Post Hill Press
New York • Nashville
posthillpress.com

Published in the United States of America
1 2 3 4 5 6 7 8 9 10

To my incredible wife Naomi and my amazing children: I am deeply indebted to you for allowing our family to take the wondrous journey of seeking peace. To my dear Noah, Julia and Gabe, Anna and Eric, Sophia, Avery and Vera—may you always strive to bring peace and tranquility to all people of the world. With all my love and devotion, Abba.

*"For the LORD shall comfort Zion:
He will comfort all her waste places; and
he will make her wilderness like Eden, and
her desert like the garden of the LORD;
joy and gladness shall be found therein,
thanksgiving, and the voice of melody."*

Yesha'yahu—Isaiah 51:3

CONTENTS

A NEW WAY AROUND
OLD OBSTACLES

This is a different kind of book about diplomacy. Most books like this are written by professional politicians or longtime Washington insiders. I am neither of those. What I *am* is an impossibly fortunate husband, a proud father of amazing children, a grateful American, an observant Jew, and a passionate supporter of Israel.

Although I wear my support and sympathy for Israel on my sleeve, that does not mean that I am opposed to the Palestinians. Far from it. That each of them—man, woman, and child—may one day soon live in peace and prosperity, realizing their full potential, is, quite literally, my daily prayer.

As White House Envoy to the Middle East during Donald Trump's administration, it was my honor and privilege to have served as one of the chief architects of the Peace to Prosperity Plan between Israel and the Palestinians. It was ultimately, though not unexpectedly unsuccessful, at least at the time. It did play a significant role in creating the infrastructure, developing the relationships, and helping shape the mindset for what became the Abraham Accords, between Israel and its Arab neighbors, which proved far more fruitful. These agreements, as the name suggests, were named after the biblical figure Abraham to emphasize the shared origin of belief between Judaism, Islam, and Christianity.

Thus far, the United Arab Emirates, the Kingdom of Bahrain, Sudan, and the Kingdom of Morocco have agreed to normalized relations with Israel. Each of these agreements is another step toward peace and greater economic opportunities for Israel and its neighbors, and a step back from the murderous conflicts that have, for far too long, characterized this region of the world. I believe our work in the Trump Administration demonstrates conclusively that the Abraham Accords are a useful template that can be applied successfully, nation by nation, to forge a more peaceful and prosperous Middle East between Israel and its Arab neighbors.

Such progress is neither inevitable nor permanent. The hard truth is, so much of the critical momentum that the Abraham Accords has accomplished thus far can sputter and stall unless the current and future administrations decide to remain actively engaged in encouraging it. The stakes could not be higher—and time is not on our side.

When I first began to think about writing this book, I watched on TV as several hundred pro-Palestinian demonstrators in Brooklyn, roughly twenty miles from my home, were blocking traffic and making their murderous intentions toward Israel known to all.

In an outrage no doubt borne of social media misinformation and an educational system that has utterly failed to acquaint them with the history of the Israeli-

Palestinian conflict, they loudly cheered for new intifada uprisings against the Jewish State. Organized by a group calling itself "Within Our Lifetime—United for Palestine," these deeply delusional demonstrators proudly marched behind three large banners: "Globalize the Intifada," "Zionism is terrorism," and "We will free Palestine within our lifetime."

For those who aren't familiar with the word, *intifada* is of Arabic origin and literally means "shaking off." It's the name given to a violent uprising or rebellion. There have been two such intifadas directed against Israel. The First Intifada raged from 1987 to 1993. During the Second Intifada from 2000 to 2005, Palestinian terrorist groups, including Hamas, Palestinian Islamic Jihad, and some affiliated with Fatah—among those Israel is supposed to negotiate a "peace plan" with—carried out hundreds of terrorist attacks against Israeli civilians and security personnel.

During the Brooklyn rally, marchers chanted, menacingly, "We don't want two states, we want all of it," a reference to the so-called "two-state solution" that has formed the basis of many failed Israeli-Palestinian peace proposals. Other slogans were no less provocative: "If we don't get justice, then they don't get peace." And this: "From the river to the sea, Palestine will be free." This rhyme was originally used in the 1960s by Palestinian nationalists who called for the elimination of Israel.

After the Oslo Accords were signed in 1993, some Palestinian groups stopped using it, since under the agreement, the Palestine Liberation Organization (PLO) recognized Israel. But old habits die hard. The sanguinary phrase remains popular with Hamas and other Islamist groups. The marchers were thus, knowingly or unknowingly, the mouthpieces of bloodthirsty terrorists.

Holding aloft Palestinian flags and firing red, green, and black flares—the colors of that flag—they held up oversized photos of Palestinians they claimed had been killed by the Israeli military. Of course, photos of innocent Israelis, killed by past intifadas or other terror attacks over what are now decades, were nowhere in evidence.

And so it goes. Another day, another outrageous attack on the only functioning democracy in the entire Middle East—and America's greatest ally in the region.

Since the 1967 Arab-Israeli War, the world's memory of Israel being attacked, time and again, has faded. With that war itself largely forgotten, the world has increasingly focused on how Israel administers the very territories that still contain those who once tried their best to murder them, and those who still dream of doing so today.

But more than half a century later, that actual *history* has been replaced by an alternative *narrative*. It is one carefully contrived, and repeatedly advanced and fostered by the Palestinian leadership and Hamas, some in the United States, as well as the United Nations and our European allies. They strive to perpetuate an alternative story, to wit: that this essentially defensive act of Israeli governance, which was thrust upon it as a result of war, is now an unlawful "occupation" that has, as its sole purpose, the wholly unwarranted daily degradation and subjugation of the Palestinian people. Meanwhile, the original aggression that caused it has evanesced into the mists of memory, leaving Israel to shoulder the responsibility for what others in the region—themselves—initiated.

Judging from those marching in Brooklyn, the idea that Israel and its people—many of whom have survived the Holocaust, two full-scale wars, and almost daily terror attacks from the moment their nation was born—are not villains, but victims, was obviously inconceivable.

As for Israel's reluctance to peremptorily withdraw from so-called "occupied territories," is it paranoid to want to protect yourself from further mayhem and murder? Is it immoral to simply want to live?

Of Israel's inherent vulnerability, former US Secretary of Defense Donald Rumsfeld once summed it up nicely by observing that "If you have a country that's a sliver and you can see three sides of it from a high hotel building, you've got to be careful what you give away and to whom you give it." Wiser words were never spoken.

For decades now, the Palestinian leadership has continued the public pretense that all of their misfortunes are the result, not of their own making, but of Israel's unilateral and unprovoked actions. According to their account, the long-suffering Palestinian people have never been offered a state of their own. But that is demonstrably untrue. In fact, the idea of a "Palestinian State" actually predates the identification of "Palestinians" as a distinct people.

Yes, that's right. At the risk of making the heads of those pro-Palestinian protesters in Brooklyn explode, here's a bit of history that might prove useful. Until the twentieth century, the name "Palestine" had never been anything other than an exclusive reference to the ancient homeland of the Jews. Up until that time, no one argued about the supposed rights of the "Palestinians" for the simple reason that they did not exist as a separate people at that point.

The Turks, the Druze, the Kurds, the Circassians, and the Arabs who lived in the region were known as Turks, Druze, Kurds, Circassians, and Arabs—for so they were. All of these different peoples understood that they were living in an area that was part of southern Syria.

According to the 1910 edition of the *Encyclopedia Britannica*, an overview of "Palestine" lists no less than nineteen foreign ethnicities other than the Jews. "Palestinian" is not among them. Why? Once again, because the Arabs who lived there did not identify as "Palestinian" then or ever before. By contrast, it was scarcely remarkable to anyone that the scattered nation of Israel, exiled for so long, in so many distant lands, would wish to return and thereby re-establish their national life in this place.

Following swiftly on the heels of World War I, the Allied powers signed the Treaty of Versailles. This treaty established President Woodrow Wilson's League of Nations, the forerunner of today's United Nations, and enshrined Wilson's concept of "self-determination." It meant that a nation—a group of people with similar political ambitions, such as the Jews—should be free to seek the creation of its own independent government or state.

The Treaty of Versailles and the series of conferences that were created from it also produced a political template of sorts that was predicated on the principle that distinct national groups were entitled to form countries of their own choosing.

This, for example, is how Czechoslovakia and Hungary, once merely a part of the Austro-Hungarian Empire, became nations unto themselves. This was how Poland, which had been divvied up among Austria, Prussia, and Russia, became a country in its own right. This was how Canada, Australia, and South Africa were, for the first time, recognized as sovereign countries, as well as Albania, Armenia, Georgia, Latvia, Lithuania, and so on.

Among this dizzying list of "new" nations that are now familiar to people the world over, there is just one that a dedicated core of fanatical enemies has made into an international fetish of hatred and abuse: Israel. Why is Israel regarded as the sole illegitimate state among so many others? Why don't the Palestinians have a state? The first is obviously about anti-Semitism; the second would appear to be just plain stubbornness.

As the late Abba Eban, Israel's longtime ambassador to the United States and its first permanent representative to the United Nations once archly observed, "The Arabs never missed an opportunity to miss an opportunity" when it comes to rejecting statehood. Notice, if you will, that Ambassador Eban said "Arabs," not "Palestinians," for the very simple reason that "the State of Palestine" was a proposed political construct, not the recognition of a preexisting set of people calling themselves by that name.

The Palestinian leadership considered the Trump administration's Peace to Prosperity Plan dead on arrival when it was unveiled in January 2020. However, we were only the latest in a long, long line of similarly rebuffed "olive branches"—so many, in fact, that they would now make a considerable tree, a tree whose roots stretch back for nearly a century.

The Arabs said "no" to the 1937 Peel Commission that proposed a partition plan and the creation of an Arab state. They said "no" again to the 1939 British White Paper that proposed an Arab state; it was "no" again to a 1947 United Nations plan that would have created an even larger Arab state as part of an overall partition plan. In the nearly two decades from 1948 to 1967, when Israel did not control the West Bank, the Arabs could have, again, demanded an independent state from Jordan, which did control it, but they never did.

In 1979, during the Israel-Egypt peace negotiations, Palestinians were again offered autonomy, which would have inevitably led to full independence, but again, they refused. In 1993 there was, and technically still is, the Oslo agreement, but it was never followed, much less implemented. And in 2000, then-Israeli Prime Minister Ehud Barak offered to create a Palestinian State, but then-Chairman of the Palestinian Liberation Organization Yasser Arafat rejected it.

In 2005, Israel gave up all of its settlements in the Gaza Strip and several more in the northern part of Samaria, a "land for peace" deal that produced nothing but Hamas terror attacks in return. In 2008, Israel offered to give up nearly 94 percent of the so-called "West Bank," but the Palestinian leadership rejected that, too.

After so many decades of repeatedly rejected peace offers from Israel, the so-called "Palestinian cause" that was once widely hailed by its advocates as a compelling, even tragic, one in urgent need of a solution, has succeeded in one sense. It's begun to make more than a few countries in the Arab world experts on the ultimate futility of appeasing the Palestinian leadership.

In fact, in so many ways, Palestinian President Mahmoud Abbas is quickly starting to resemble the Imperial Japanese officer, Hiroo Onoda, who refused to surrender in August 1945 when World War II ended. He stubbornly held on in the jungles of the Philippines for another 29 years, until 1974. Like Lt. Onoda, Abbas is in danger of becoming an irrelevant relic of an era that no longer has a purchase on the political sensibilities or the realities of a new Middle East.

In my nearly three years at the White House, almost no one ever mentioned Abbas's predecessor, Arafat, other than a handful of people who called him a terrorist or a fool for missing so many opportunities. Essentially, he was, and remains, an irrelevant figure when it came to a potential solution for the conflict, or any form of positive future for the Palestinians. I think President Abbas has it within him not to suffer that same fate, but the question is: Does he have the courage to leave a lasting legacy? I don't know the answer to that question. But sadly, more and more, I think the answer is no.

That doesn't make resolving the Israeli-Palestinian conflict meaningless, but it does serve to place that conflict in perspective.

Before President Trump arrived in Washington, it had been popular to refer to the resolution of the Israeli-Palestinian conflict as the "Middle East Peace Process." Unfortunately, for far too many, it still bears that political branding. But that name is a colossal misnomer.

The Israeli-Palestinian conflict is just one of a multitude in the region, and I knew that solving it would not put an end to other conflicts, such as the Islamic State in Iraq and Syria, terrorists in the Sinai Desert in Egypt, the tragic civil war in Syria, the war in Yemen and the Iran-sponsored Houthi terrorists there, Hezbollah—a terrorist organization sponsored by Iran—in Lebanon, instability in Libya, and last but certainly not least, an Iranian regime that oppresses and kills thousands of its own people and foments terrorism around the world on a staggering scale.

One of the things that the Abraham Accords demonstrated is that the path to better relations between Israel and many of its Arab neighbors does not depend on finding the proverbial "Goldilocks" solution for the ultimate contours of a Palestinian State, especially when the political "porridge" never seems to be "just right" to the Palestinian leadership.

The Abraham Accords confounds the conventional wisdom that Israel has to accept the creation of a Palestinian State—on the unyielding terms of the Palestinian leadership—to have warm relations with other nations in the region. Among other things, it demonstrates conclusively that former US Secretary of State John Kerry was completely wrong when he repeatedly claimed that peace between Israel and its Arab neighbors in the Middle East was impossible without Israel abandoning its settlements and accepting the geostrategic straitjacket of what some claim are its former, pre-1967 borders, but which are in fact nothing more than armistice lines, not actual borders, no matter how many times and how many people claim otherwise.

The Biden administration, and future ones, would be wise to follow our lead in this respect. Until approximately September 2021, they were reluctant to even call the Abraham Accords by their name—referring to them obliquely as "normalization of relations agreements." Whether this reflected mere political optics and an aversion to giving credit where credit is due, or opposition to the process that has already amply proven itself, is difficult to discern. For the sake of those countries which are part of the Abraham Accords, and for the sake of a safer and more stable Middle East, I sincerely hope it is the former rather than the latter.

I not only actively encourage the pursuit of more such agreements, but I also remain deeply concerned that America's failure to attend to these practical expressions of political cohesion could undo the progress we began, making the Middle East a more volatile, more dangerous, place.

Power is a relative thing, and nature abhors a vacuum. If the Biden administration, as it would seem, is anxious to reduce its footprint in the Middle East to confront a more bellicose China, America's relative absence will have consequences—for Israel, for the Middle East, and for America itself.

For Israel, this could mean that all the hard work it has put into building relationships with the Sunni Muslim countries around it may begin to fray as America looks for an exit ramp from the region, and a newly emboldened Iran looks to make even more murderous mischief than before. For that matter, Iran is scarcely keeping a low profile now.

As this book is being written, the office of the US Attorney in Manhattan has announced kidnapping conspiracy charges against an Iranian Intelligence Officer and members of an Iranian intelligence network who that office says plotted to kidnap an American journalist off the streets of New York City for rendition to Iran. And that's apparently just the tip of the proverbial iceberg. Such a plot is, of course, an egregious violation of fundamental international norms. That the kidnapping was planned to silence a US citizen exercising her free speech rights to criticize Iran is all the more outrageous. The State Department confirmed the charges and said it remains aware of "ongoing interest in targeting yet other American citizens, including current and former US officials."

Such operations are nothing new. Iranian Intelligence Services have previously lured other Iranian dissidents from France and the United States for the purposes of capturing and imprisoning Iran's critics, and have publicly claimed responsibility for these capture operations. And this is the regime that President Biden dreams of signing a new nuclear deal with?

Iran likely already has more than enough enriched uranium for a nuclear bomb. It also has amply demonstrated that it has long-range missile capability for delivering such a bomb. Unless *something* or *someone* derails that program, the murderous mullahs who run Iran will one day—and soon—have nuclear weapons. By that time, no "deal" that any American president can dream up will tempt them in the slightest to give them up. By then, there simply won't be a carrot or a stick big enough to entice or dissuade them from realizing their ambitions.

And what are those ambitions? They're certainly not a secret. First and foremost, Iran wants to destroy Israel, to wipe it from the map and from the memory of man. Nuclear weapons will give them the means and the ability to do so. But for all the horror of that doomsday scenario for Israel, that's just the start, not the end, of the Iranian regime's evil, destructive ambitions. For that matter, Iran doesn't care about the Palestinians or their Arab neighbors, either. They're in as much danger as Israel is from the nuclear terror from Tehran.

A nuclear Iran would set off an arms race in the Middle East that would make previous conflicts there look like a spat in a sandbox. If you think the Middle East looks unstable now, consider for a hot second or two what multiple countries with multiple nuclear warheads aimed at one another would mean to the possibility of a peaceful future in that part of the world—in a place through which a majority of the world's oil is located and distributed.

Would there even *be* a future?

It's readily apparent that the Biden administration wants to "do a deal" with Iran, thus giving it the fig leaf of an excuse to disengage from the Middle East and concentrate on other, apparently more important things. So far, the president doesn't seem to be having much luck with that.

Is America's disastrously managed withdrawal from Afghanistan a preview of an even greater tragedy-in-waiting in the Middle East? Sadly, that seems increasingly likely. Here's something else to think about: For Iran, Israel is merely the "Little Satan." After Tehran has tasted the delicious appetizer that is the destruction of the Jewish State, it will no doubt direct its attention and appetite toward the feast of all feasts—the destruction of the "Great Satan," the United States. We can stop Iran now—or later. To paraphrase President Harry S.

Truman, the buck stops here, with us. No other nation on Earth has the power—and perhaps just as important—the willingness to do so.

Peace is a precious thing—and we were well on the path to achieving it in meaningful portions of the Middle East—both for Israel and a growing number of its Arab neighbors. But it wasn't a matter of luck or timing, although both those things certainly played a part.

As history shows all too clearly, peace is often an uneasy equilibrium between wars, not an active force in its own right. Peace isn't easy. It isn't a matter of "consensus" or thinking good thoughts about your enemies.

Peace is hard, but the consequences of its alternative are harder still. Moreover, peace doesn't come by blurring the essential differences between people or groups. Rather, it comes from bringing those differences into sharper relief, sharper focus. It doesn't depend on adhering to a silly diplomatic "two-side-ism" that attempts to attach equal blame to both right and wrong, but to identify right *from* wrong—and taking the side of right against that wrong—no matter how many others counsel against it.

The Trump administration's approach to the Middle East challenged the myth that America has to be an "honest broker"—that is, indifferent to the fate of its chief ally, Israel—in negotiations with its Arab neighbors.

Rather, our approach showed that America's willingness to be stalwart in support of a key ally is respected, not reviled, and that Israel's acceptance lies not in the extent of the concessions it is willing to make, but in the inherent value it has to its neighbors, both technologically and militarily. When America is perceived as a weak sister, that weakness is exploited. When it pressures an ally to sacrifice its sovereign interests in the name of peace, as the previous administration did, it doesn't win new friends but merely encourages old foes, while harming its ally, besides.

Consider this passage from President Barack Obama's much-lauded Cairo Speech on June 4, 2009. It's a model of the "honest broker" approach so dear to the political left, a warped world where Palestinian terrorism, aided and abetted by Iran and Syria, is no more problematic than Israeli settlements. The delusion that Palestinian terrorism will cease once Israel makes suicidal settlement concessions is a kumbaya compromise that not even a kindergarten class would regard as plausible. Here is what President Obama said:

> So let there be no doubt: the situation for the Palestinian people is intolerable. And America will not turn our backs on the legitimate Palestinian aspiration for dignity, opportunity, and a state of their own.

> For decades, there has been a stalemate: two peoples with legitimate aspirations, each with a painful history that makes compromise elusive. It's easy to point fingers—for Palestinians to point to the displacement brought about by Israel's founding, and for Israelis to point to the constant

hostility and attacks throughout its history from within its borders as well as beyond.

But if we see this conflict only from one side or the other, then we will be blind to the truth: the only resolution is for the aspirations of both sides to be met through two states, where Israelis and Palestinians each live in peace and security. That is in Israel's interest, Palestine's interest, America's interest, and the world's interest. That is why I intend to personally pursue this outcome with all the patience that the task requires.

President Obama's unwillingness, or inability, to judge right from wrong here is both astounding and disturbing. It's "easy to point fingers," he says, as he wags his own finger at anyone with the temerity to actually identify the cause of the conflict, and the address of the aggressor. He goes on to breezily equate Israel's construction of houses, hospitals, and schools with Palestinian terror attacks. His patronizing tsk-tsking is deliberately designed to create an illusionary, even obfuscating, balance between perpetrator and victim, between right and wrong. One can easily imagine him speaking about World War II with the same affected amorality: "The Japanese attack on Pearl Harbor was a regrettable incident to which America overreacted."

The message that Israel had been trying to deliver to the Palestinians for decades was that violence was not going to make them give up land upon which they

depended for their safety and security. Instead of joining Israel in that message, President Obama signaled his
desire to get everyone back to the negotiating table as
quickly as possible. If that meant Israel would have to
deliver its settlements up on a silver platter to Palestinian
President Mahmoud Abbas, no matter the consequences
to Israel, so be it.

Of course, this magical thinking had already been
tried by Israel before Obama showed up in Cairo to ped-
dle this political prescription. It was a "solution" he and
his coterie of admirers seemed to regard as something
new under the sun. It wasn't. "Land for peace" in Gaza
had ended with Israel merely allowing Hamas and other
terrorist groups to get closer than ever before to launch
rockets and mortars and loose suicide bombers into its
communities.

Here, again, the Trump presidency provides a template for a way forward in the Middle East that relies on
two main observations, or principles, upon which our
approach was predicated.

First, we recognized not only the futility, but the
danger—both to Israel and the region—by continuing to
allow the Palestinian leadership a virtual veto on Israel's
ability to form relationships with other Arab countries,
as well as effectively paralyzing any real hope for progress and a brighter future for the Middle East generally.

Although we tried our level best to construct a plan
we thought resonated with reality, the Palestinian leadership saw it otherwise and walked away long before

they even saw any portion of the peace plan. It would appear, after previous offers of a Palestinian State have been made by Israel—and summarily dismissed as inadequate by the Palestinian Authority—that there is no longer any point in attempting to negotiate with the Palestinian leadership who, quite literally, refuse to negotiate.

Issuing unrealistic demands is not negotiating; it is a temper tantrum, and it shouldn't be tolerated, much less encouraged. That's a shame for the Palestinians, and especially those suffering under the oppressive yoke of Hamas in Gaza, but it is not the business of Israel or of the United States—or indeed of other Arab countries in the region—to help leaders who refuse to be helped.

For now, at least, and perhaps for many years to come, a Palestinian State should be put on the diplomatic back burner. That is, until or unless the political leadership in Ramallah finally decides it wants to actually construct a functioning state, as opposed to merely complaining that they don't have the "perfect" state their daydreams are made of. And even a "perfect" peace deal with Ramallah doesn't begin to address the problem of Hamas in Gaza. Why should Israel make hard compromises for peace with a Palestinian leadership that doesn't actually represent all of the Palestinians? Why conclude a "peace deal" that conspicuously excludes Hamas? This closes one door, only to open another one.

The second principle that the Trump administration was focused on in the Middle East did not originally proceed from the first, but the failure of the Palestinian leadership to step up to the plate to honestly engage in negotiations gave it added urgency.

That principle was based on our repeated experiences with Arab leaders who, while still championing a Palestinian State, were nevertheless interested in a closer relationship with Israel. Hearing this, we were determined to, in White House Senior Advisor Jared Kushner's words, "align the different countries in the region around their common interests, as opposed to focusing on historical grievances."

While those common interests ran the gamut from greater ease of travel and tourism to technology exchanges and other business opportunities, perhaps the most pressing and critical one was a shared realization that Iran is the real threat to the entire region. While many of our European allies and practically the entirety of the United Nations commonly considered the Israeli-Palestinian conflict to be the core problem in the Middle East, we saw very quickly that the proverbial elephant in the room was no elephant at all, but the terrorists from Tehran.

Designated as a "State Sponsor of Terrorism" in 1984, Iran has continued to live up—or down, as it might more accurately be stated—to its well-deserved reputation. The list, which is an ever-lengthening one, reads like a history of terrorism itself.

Iran has long supported Hezbollah, Palestinian terrorist groups in Gaza, and various terrorist groups in Syria, Yemen, Iraq, and others throughout the Middle

East. Iran also used the Islamic Revolutionary Guard Corps-Qods Force (IRGC-QF) to provide support to terrorist organizations, provide cover for associated covert operations, and create instability in the region. Iran has acknowledged its involvement of the IRGC-QF in the Iraq and Syria conflicts. It is Iran's primary mechanism for cultivating and supporting terrorists abroad.

Iran has also provided hundreds of millions of dollars in support of Hezbollah and trained thousands of its fighters at camps in Iran. Hezbollah fighters have been used extensively in Syria to support the Assad regime. In Bahrain, Iran has continued to provide weapons, support, and training to local Shia militant groups, including the al-Ashtar Brigades. In Yemen, Iran has provided weapons, support, and training to the Houthi terrorists, who have engaged in terrorist attacks against regional targets, including Saudi Arabia and the United Arab Emirates. Lest people think Iran confines its malign activity to the Middle East, they are active elsewhere as well—in the Moroccan Sahara, for example.

Iran views the Assad regime in Syria as a crucial ally, and Syria and Iraq as vital routes through which to supply weapons to Hezbollah, Iran's primary terrorist proxy group. Through financial or residency enticements, Iran has facilitated and coerced primarily Shia fighters from Afghanistan and Pakistan to participate in the Assad regime's brutal crackdown in Syria.

Iran-supported Shia militias in Iraq have also committed serious human rights abuses against primarily Sunni civilians. Iranian forces have directly backed militia operations in Syria with armored vehicles, artillery, and drones. Since the end of the 2006 Israeli-Hezbollah conflict, Iran has supplied Hezbollah with thousands of rockets, missiles, and small arms.

The United States Department of State has issued reports that identify Iran as supplying Hezbollah with advanced weapons systems and technologies, as well as assisting the group in creating infrastructure that would permit it to indigenously produce rockets and missiles to threaten Israel from Lebanon and Syria.

Iran provides ongoing support to Hamas and other designated Palestinian terrorist groups, including the Palestinian Islamic Jihad and the Popular Front for the Liberation of Palestine–General Command. These groups have been behind numerous deadly attacks originating in Gaza and the West Bank, including attacks against Israeli civilians, as well as in the Sinai Peninsula. The Iranian government also maintains a robust offensive cyber program and has sponsored cyber-attacks against foreign governments and private sector entities.

Of all the terrorists in all the world, President Biden wants to make a deal with these thugs? Wasn't watching his old boss do the first deal with Iran instructive? Did he miss the message?

The proverbial clock is ticking here. Even if Iran agreed to a second "nuclear deal," do President Biden and his team really believe that they are doing anything other than allowing Tehran to run out that clock? Does the President truly think that some "over the horizon capability" on America's part—the monitoring of terrorist activity from halfway around the globe—will be sufficient to keep Israel and our other friends and allies in the Middle East—the Gulf Cooperation Council, Jordan, Egypt, and others—safe from Iran's evil intentions?

Obama's old political calculus was that by doing a nuclear deal with Iran, he would have greater leverage with Israel to curb its settlements. As usual, Obama's strategy revealed just how far down the rabbit hole he had fallen, and how utterly biased against Israel he was. He didn't see Iran's ever-expanding role in terrorism as the problem. Instead, he saw the settlements as the problem. If Israel would just give those up, the President promised to "contain" Iran's nuclear program.

Such invincible ignorance of the Middle East and its history, combined with the equally credulous belief that evil simply melts away in the glow of diplomatic "engagement," is risible. As privately held beliefs, they are merely unfortunate, but they are fatal as the basis for, and the conduct of, American foreign policy. From this unique mix of nonsense and naivete would flow eight years of some of the most damaging policies that region has seen in modern times.

Speaking of damaging policies, in that same speech in Cairo, President Obama pledged to offer talks with Iran with absolutely no preconditions, a proposal he appeared to regard as something new under the diplomatic sun. Many in the media, both in America and abroad, swooned over this "bold outreach" as well, but there was nothing new here.

Since the days of the Iranian hostage crisis, American administrations had sought any number of public or back-channel ways to encourage communication with the rogue regime, from Carter to George W. Bush. Iran's response was always the same. Cold silence. But President Obama, as always, was vocationally cheerful about the power of a tête-à-tête to turn a terrorist's heart:

> Rather than remain trapped in the past, I've made it clear to Iran's leaders and people that my country is prepared to move forward. The question, now, is not what Iran is against, but rather what future it wants to build. It will be hard to overcome decades of mistrust, but we will proceed with courage, rectitude and resolve. There will be many issues to discuss between our two countries, and we are willing to move forward without preconditions on the basis of mutual respect.

Of course, it was not, and is not, a dialogue that Iran's leaders want with us, but rather our death. This has been true since 1979 when they overthrew the Shah and seized the American embassy and took fifty-two members of its staff as their hostages. They only returned those hostages when Ronald Reagan was sworn in as president. They recognized a strong leader when they saw one, and they reacted accordingly. But their long-term strategy has remained the same: death to Israel, and death to the United States.

Obama's stated goal of rapprochement with the rogue regime in Tehran, and especially the Joint Comprehensive Plan of Action—an agreement on the Iranian nuclear program reached in Vienna on July 14, 2015, between Iran and the P5+1 (the UN Security Council's five permanent members (the P5); namely China, France, Russia, the United Kingdom, and the United States; plus Germany) together with the European Union—was quite possibly the most dangerous deal ever entered into by an American president.

What was billed by President Obama and his supporters as a way to "contain" Iran's nuclear program was really an exercise in self-delusion. With the usual winks and nods, we pretended to believe that these terrorist leaders would actually abide by their word and not continue to develop offensive nuclear weapon capability. For this, we delivered on tens of billions in previously frozen assets and allowed Iran to again resume selling oil on the international markets.

President Trump withdrew the United States from the JCPOA in 2018, and was dedicated to helping form a coalition against it in the Middle East, consisting of Israel and its Arab neighbors. It was clear to him that simply trying to delay the day when Iran would have an offensive nuclear capability was not in America's interests, or those of Israel or our Arab allies in the region. The President had imposed sanctions that were really beginning to have an effect on the leadership in Tehran, but that policy has not outlived his administration, and that's a grave concern.

It would appear that Obama's understudy is now anxious to re-enter that same delusional accommodation with these murderous fanatics who talk openly of their desire for revenge against what they call the "World of Arrogance"—meaning the Western world. In a way, that description is a fitting one. It *is* arrogant to believe, against all evidence to the contrary, that the current Iranian regime will make peace with us or with our ally, Israel. President Trump knew it instinctively. It would appear President Biden does not adequately recognize the danger. I hope, for Israel's sake, and ours, that he doesn't learn that lesson too late. Making peace with terrorists may sound like the stuff that Nobel Prize dreams are made of, but the problem is, terrorists can't be relied upon to make peace with us.

Just as concerning has been the disastrous way the Biden administration left Afghanistan. Even our smugly cynical European allies were shaken by that spectacularly incompetent exit. It certainly didn't have to be that way. Every time America deserts an ally in whatever way—whether that is a vote in the United Nations that condemns Israel, or a literal sudden desertion of the American military in Afghanistan, which left American citizens and thousands of Afghans who had worked with us behind—we lose that much more credibility with our other allies, as well as those other nations that remain on the fence about partnering with us. They all naturally wonder if we will stand by them in tough times.

Both the Obama administration and the Biden administration have shown the entire world, and especially our enemies, that we won't necessarily take such a stand. Biden has actually proven to be the worse of the two leaders. In cringingly describing the Taliban in Afghanistan as "professional and businesslike," a phrase chosen to display these murderous thugs in a positive light, the Biden administration has shown that it is willing to make a deal with the devil and won't dare complain about the heat. For the most powerful nation on Earth, that's not just an embarrassment—it's deeply humiliating. The American people deserve, and should demand, more from their president. He should live up to our nation's ideals. That includes standing up for our allies and confronting our enemies.

What appears to be the Biden administration's plan— to re-engage with Iran and conclude a weak agreement that merely checks a box, but does not check Iran's nuclear weapons ambitions—is not just disappointing, but dangerous and craven. That the current administration apparently desires to simultaneously reduce America's military footprint in the Middle East at the same time will not only significantly undermine the positive steps we made toward normalization of relations between Israel and its Arab neighbors, but also will inevitably have the effect of promoting Iran, one of the most murderous regimes in history, as a regional superpower. The progress achieved thus far between Israel and the Arab world would then be stopped in its tracks, or worse, actually reversed.

If the Biden administration continues to proceed down this path, in essence creating a power vacuum in the region, it is scarcely beyond the realm of possibility that some Gulf States would begin to calculate that a strategic alliance with Iran might well be in their own self-interest. If that occurs, it is no exaggeration to observe that the peace and security of the entire Middle East would be put at grave risk, not to mention the very survival of the State of Israel. And yet it is increasingly clear that the Biden administration is willing to take that risk so that it can pivot away from the Middle East and focus the bulk of its foreign policy energy on an increasingly bellicose China. That would be a mistake of monumental proportions.

The United States must remain vigorously engaged in the Middle East, not only for the sake of its friends and allies in the region, but for the very real possibility of creating a prosperous and vital future in a place that has, for far too long, been a byword for violence and diminished expectations. For that matter, what happens in the Middle East, for good or ill, doesn't just affect that region alone. The ripples emanating from there, either positive or negative, are felt around the world.

Decades of intense diplomatic activity in the pursuit of a resolution to the Israeli-Palestinian conflict have obscured a simple, yet revelatory fact: There is a new, emerging reality in the region that doesn't depend on pie-in-the-sky rhetoric about peace and universal brotherhood, but rather down-to-earth, common-sense relationships based on mutual economic and strategic benefits.

It is that new reality, that new logic, that new language of cooperation, that the Abraham Accords both reflected and relied on to help move the Middle East in a more positive direction. It's a promising start, but only that. The Abraham Accords aren't a perpetual motion machine. Sooner or later, the Biden administration will have to put its shoulder to the wheel and push as well. The twofold question is: How hard are they willing to push, and in what direction?

Bertrand Russell once observed: "In all affairs it's a healthy thing now and then to hang a question mark on the things you have long taken for granted."

Is the continued appeasement of Iran an example of effective diplomacy, or a meek masquerade that merely emboldens an implacable foe of Israel and America? Is the Israeli-Palestinian conflict really the biggest impediment to peace in that war-torn region, or a dangerous distraction from a far more deadly adversary in Tehran?

This book is my attempt to answer these pressing questions and to chart a way forward toward a more peaceful and prosperous Middle East.

Jason D. Greenblatt

CHAPTER 1

Prelude to a Presidency

APRIL 16, 2016: 26TH FLOOR, TRUMP TOWER

It had been exactly ten months to the day since my boss of nearly twenty years descended that famous golden escalator to the garden level of his eponymous New York tower. On a June afternoon in 2015, he climbed up onto a hastily constructed stage and announced that he was running for president.

Rumors had it that many reporters did not take the announcement seriously, and in the days and weeks that followed, it became abundantly clear that much of the mainstream media considered the Donald Trump campaign little more than a sideshow in what was supposed to be a serious search for America's next president. How wrong they turned out to be.

Ten months on, that view had—albeit grudgingly—begun to change. As an initially huge field of Republican competitors with far greater political bona fides withdrew one by one from the race, or watched with dismay as their polling numbers dwindled to single digits, even those who had initially scoffed at this political neophyte's pursuit of the highest office in the land had to admit, the Trump campaign was certainly not something to laugh at. If nothing else, the Secret Service agents I saw each day at our offices in the Trump Tower, assigned to protect him around the clock, put an end to that nonsense.

I was, of course, intensely aware and interested in the progress of the Trump campaign, but I was not a part of it in any official capacity. My relationship with Trump was, quite literally, all business. Despite my frequent volunteer efforts on behalf of his electoral effort, my first and foremost duty remained The Trump Organization itself.

When Donald Trump originally hired me to be part of his staff all those years ago, he did so with the full knowledge that I was an observant Jew, including all that it entailed. Other workaholic business titans might not have hired a junior attorney who had to leave early every Friday afternoon in the fall and the winter to make it home in time to observe Shabbat, the Jewish day of rest. Others might not have tolerated a lawyer of theirs being completely unavailable for twenty-five hours per week during the Sabbath. Many bosses might have promoted others over me for missing as many as six weekdays (during which I am also completely unavailable) in the fall season to observe Jewish holidays that occur, just as everyone else is getting back to work after a slower summer season.

As my responsibilities grew over the years, all of those things could have given him even more reason to turn to others instead of me. But Donald Trump hadn't merely *tolerated* my religious observance for nearly two decades; he had *encouraged* it. He understood that my faith was a blessing, an important part of who I was, and from all the available evidence, he valued me all the more for it.

It's relatively easy to talk a good game about religious liberty; it's another thing entirely when the exercise of that religious liberty directly impacts your business in real and measurable ways. Time and again, Trump made it clear that he appreciated my unique and religiously demanding lifestyle, and he encouraged me not only to practice it, but to be proud of it.

On one occasion, long before his campaign for president, I remember feeling particularly guilty to be hurrying out of the office for a Jewish holiday in the midst of a major transaction involving hundreds of millions of dollars, something that necessarily ground negotiations to a complete halt for three full days. I was distressed about telling Trump that I had to leave for the holiday, but he put my mind at ease, saying, "Go home, go pray, and be with your family. We'll pick things up after the holiday."

Needless to say, I never took Trump's respect lightly. I would take extraordinary steps on my part to limit the times when Shabbat or holidays became an issue. There were times when I slept in my office for two nights in a row in advance of a holiday to avoid situations where I needed to leave a deal unfinished. Trump never even hinted that I should do that, but my feeling was, if he and his family were so respectful of me, I owed them the same respect in return. The point is, I was always extremely cognizant of his respect and appreciated it; I never abused it. He was a true mensch.

I know there are many who have a far different impression of Donald Trump, but his kindness to me and my family over the years and his deep regard for my religion say something important to me about the man and his sensitivity to others. I will always remember that incident, and many others, with a grateful heart. He and his three children who I worked with—Don Jr., Ivanka and Eric—were also always respectful and sensitive about my religious observance.

On previous occasions, because of my faith, Trump and I had talked privately, from time to time, about my experiences in Israel, including my year as a student in the mid-1980s at a small town not too far from Jerusalem.

When I turned 18—as with many kids in American Orthodox schools (Yeshivas)—it's customary to do a gap year and study in Israel. I had a variety of schools to choose from and the one that I chose to go to was what was called a Hesder Yeshiva. Hesder Yeshivas are generally composed of Israelis who extend their army service and combine it with the learning of Jewish texts. Many of these have an American program or a foreign program.

The one that I went to was called Yeshivat Har Etzion. It was located in what I would describe as a town, the town of Alon Shevut, although others may prefer to call it a settlement. It had Jewish foreigners from the US,

Canada, Australia, South Africa, and elsewhere. The town was in an area of Judea and Samaria, or what is popularly called the West Bank; because of that location, they had to be vigilant about their security.

The entire town was surrounded by a fence; there was a guard posted at the front gate and there were patrols and lookouts. All of us had to serve on a rotating basis, as part of the patrol and the lookout service. Sometimes, for example, I had to man the entry booth, and when people came in, we'd check IDs and that sort of thing. If necessary, we'd search a suspicious vehicle. Palestinians came in frequently, either to go shopping at the little supermarket or, oftentimes, as workers within the town. While I was there, from 1985 to 1986, it was fortunately a fairly quiet time and violent incidents were not common.

During my stay, I was assigned an adopted family in the town—as each of the foreign students was—and I became particularly close with mine. I've remained in touch with them ever since. My kids who were studying in Jerusalem a couple of years ago spent a lot of time with this family.

It's personally gratifying and heartwarming to me that, thirty-plus years later, my kids are friendly with their now-grown kids. Sadly, this same family also experienced a terrible tragedy, one unfortunately all-too common in that part of the world. Years before I joined The Trump Organization, when I was a young lawyer at a large law firm, this family's then high-school-aged son was murdered by a Palestinian drive-by shooter. He had just been hanging out with some of his friends when it happened.

There is certainly crime and violence in America, but few people here can really understand the ever-present threat that so many people face in the Middle East. I've had the unnerving experience of having missiles fly close to me twice: once in Riyadh and once in Tel Aviv. It's easy to talk about what should or should not be done in responding to violence. It's something else again for a parent to be in a bomb shelter with their kids crying beside them. In parts of the Middle East, these things happen far too frequently.

I was fortunate that, in all my time as a student at Yeshivat Har Etzion, I was never called upon to use the M-16 I carried from time to time. Still, that experience gave me an appreciation for what life was like in those communities, both their shared sense of purpose and their ever-present vulnerability to attack. After all, guarding the perimeter of your town with a rifle is not something an American teenager has to do. We take so many things in America for granted, not merely in a material sense, but in terms of our own personal safety.

That was certainly true for my parents, both refugees from Hungary. My father fled Szatmárcseke as a child in the early 1940s. My maternal grandfather was sent to a labor camp somewhere in Hungary. The rest of my mother's family was loaded onto a deportation train. Once on the train, they understood that they were being sent to be killed at the notorious death camp Auschwitz.

Miraculously the train ended up being rerouted just a few kilometers from Auschwitz, when a bridge along the route exploded. My mother's family ended up being sent to Austria and were eventually liberated by the Soviet army. After the war, my mother's family made their way back to Debrecen, Hungary, where they were reunited with my grandfather, and they continued living in Debrecen until the Hungarian Revolution, at which point they fled Hungary and moved to the United States.

That family history, my experiences as a young adult, and the trips that my own family would later take to Israel, made a deep impression on me. I was always willing to share the insights I learned whenever Trump inquired about them.

As the presidential campaign took shape and gained momentum, Trump occasionally elicited my views about Israel, the Israeli-Palestinian conflict, as well as other matters. In the same way, I helped prepare his speech to the AIPAC Conference earlier that spring, and had penned numerous opinion pieces supportive of my boss, when I thought appropriate or when asked to do so by various news outlets. I would have gladly contributed more effort to Trump, the presidential candidate, but at the time, I had my hands full as the executive vice president and chief legal officer to Trump, the businessman, and the complex, multibillion-dollar organization he led.

So, on that April afternoon in 2016, when Trump's secretary buzzed me and asked me to head down to the large conference room on the twenty-fifth floor, one floor below my office, I naturally assumed it had to do with some contract or associated business issue. It never occurred to me that I would walk into a room full of journalists from a dozen or more Jewish-interest media outlets.

Reporters shot question after question at my boss, who seemed to be handling things just fine. At some point though, Trump decided to redirect some of the barrage to me. "I rely on Jason as a consultant on Israel," he said. "Jason's a person who truly loves Israel," he added, his open hand extended in my direction. "I love to get advice from people that know Israel—from people that truly love Israel."

In that moment I was elated. Sure, I had talked with him many times about Israel, although I never considered those conversations to be more than an exchange of personal stories. But now, I had been elevated to the status of "consultant" to his campaign for president.

I recall giving him a sidelong glance as I answered a particularly sensitive question about Israeli settlements, and I remember that he was looking at me intently. It would have been lost on anyone else in the room, I'm sure, but I had worked for the man a long time, and I intimately knew his facial expressions. I thought to myself, *he's having fun with me right now. He's enjoying putting me on the spot.* And perhaps part of him was doing just that.

But I sensed that he was also doing something else: I was being interviewed for a job—one that didn't yet exist—and perhaps never would. Besides, the political intelligentsia had already confidently calculated the outcome of this contest: This was former Secretary of State Hillary Clinton's time. She had everything going for her: a popular, two-term president in her corner, an embarrassing amount of money, an organization of exceptionally-seasoned operatives, and the cachet of being the first ever female candidate for president of the United States. She was, in a word, inevitable.

ELECTION DAY: NOVEMBER 8, 2016

This day you know about, so I'll skip over it, except to say that, gratifying as the results of that election were, I did not have the luxury of giving that extraordinary political victory very much thought. As far as I was concerned, my fifteen minutes of fame as Trump's "Man on Israel"— as one newspaper put it—seemed to have run its course. Besides, I still had a full-time job as chief legal counsel for The Trump Organization.

For the greater part of the past year, Jared Kushner and his wife, Ivanka, Trump's daughter, had both been heavily involved in the campaign and there was a great deal of conjecture about whether one or both of them would consider going to work at the White House. High among the issues that were a priority for Jared was his desire to secure a lasting peace between Israel and its Arab neighbors, either as part of an Israeli-Palestinian negotiation, or separately if need be.

Jared was very keen to work on those items, and from time to time, in the weeks after election day, he had asked me if I'd be interested in helping. I, of course, said that I would. But these were only brief conversations in passing. Besides, I already had a job to do; frankly, it had been made even more intense and difficult as a consequence of the election. At that point, I was in the throes of trying to put all the necessary paperwork in place for my old boss—now the President-elect—so that he would be able to leave his company, and thus commence this hugely important new phase of his life.

My wife Naomi and I had never been "political people." I hadn't even registered as a Republican until my boss decided to run for president. Don't get me wrong. My wife and I take our responsibility to vote very seriously, but we had never closely followed the goings-on in Washington. All of that just seemed too remote, too raucous, and too irrelevant to our lives in Teaneck, New Jersey.

In the days after the election, and because I had been thrust into all the excitement of the Trump campaign, my wife and I began, as a sort of lark, to watch the Aaron Sorkin series, *The West Wing*. Ideologically, it was catnip for liberals, but it was also fun and entertaining.

After almost every episode, we would turn off the TV before we went to bed, and just look at each other and say, "We would never immerse ourselves into that crazy environment." I think we both felt somewhat thankful that the campaign was over and life seemed to be, slowly but surely, returning to its previous pace.

At least now, I remember thinking, Naomi and I could, at long last, finally take a breath and simply enjoy one another and the family we had created together.

It was a pleasant prospect. Maybe we could take the whole family for a short vacation to Washington planned around the coming inaugural in late January. Who knows, maybe we could even get a private tour of the White House. Our youngest, Vera, who was not yet five, might not appreciate it all that much, I thought, but our seventeen-year-old triplets: Noah, Julia, and Anna, our thirteen-year-old Sophia, and ten-year-old Avery would surely get a kick out of it. It couldn't take more than a couple days to hit all the major tourist sites, and then we could head back home to Teaneck and our normal life. It sounded like a plan.

DECEMBER 9, 2016: WELCOME ABOARD

Donald Trump's office, just two offices down from mine on the 26th floor of Trump Tower, is a mirror of the man. Almost every square inch of the walls is covered with awards, plaques, and dozens of framed national magazines—everything from *Time*, *Newsweek*, and the *London Economist* to *Variety*, *The New Yorker*, and *Playboy*—each with his face, now familiar the world over, on the cover. Collectively, they provide a visual history of sorts for his storied career, from a young, brash, real estate entrepreneur, to a still brash, but seasoned business titan sitting atop a multibillion empire of high-end hotels, luxury condominiums, and exclusive golf clubs. He even has his own vineyard and a winery named after him.

Trump has appeared on the cover of so many magazines, and more arrive every day, that there is literally no room left to exhibit more than a tiny fraction of them. So they sit, stacked on his desk, on side tables and bookshelves, where they compete with a veritable museum of sports memorabilia—everything from Mike Tyson's Championship belt to a monstrous, size-23 shoe that Shaquille O'Neal once took off impulsively after a game and gave to him. There are more than enough autographed helmets and jerseys to field his own football team. The distinctive, red leather chair from *The Apprentice*, which he hosted for fourteen seasons, is there as well, and so are scores of family photos behind his desk, interspersed with occasional signed "grip and grin" photos of himself and US presidents like Ronald Reagan, and foreign dignitaries from every country imaginable. But perhaps the most impressive thing about the room—aside from Trump himself—is an enormous window on the far wall, with that indescribably breathtaking and ever-changing view of Central Park.

It was a Friday in early December 2016, when the man who was now President-elect of the United States of America called me to that office. I assumed it was to talk over one or more of the myriad details concerning his handover of The Trump Organization prior to being inaugurated as President of the United States. But just as I had been wrong about the purpose of that earlier surprise, meeting with the media in April, I was mistaken about the intention of this invitation as well.

Like almost all of my meetings with Trump over the years, it was brief and to the point. He didn't waste words.

He said he had been talking to Jared and he wondered whether or not I'd be interested in coming to work at the White House. He didn't have a specific title for me in mind at the moment, but he emphasized the job would be consequential, something with a lot of responsibility. He wanted me to be one of the key point people, together with Jared, who would attempt to strengthen America's standing in the Middle East, which he believed had suffered tremendously under President Obama. And naturally, because of my intense interest in the subject, he wanted me to help strengthen the US-Israel relationship, correct many of the policy mistakes from the past when it came to Israel, and work on the Israeli-Palestinian conflict and the Israeli-Arab conflict, in particular, which he thought might potentially be ripe for a breakthrough after so many previously failed attempts.

Although I had witnessed firsthand Trump's negotiating skills hundreds of times, it suddenly struck me that this was the first time I had been on the receiving end of a "pitch" from my own boss. It was an extremely novel, yet flattering experience. Donald Trump is a deal-driven person. He thrives on the difficult, on things that are challenging. He never does anything half-heartedly. He throws his heart and soul into seeing if he can make something work. The result is—far often than not, far more times than I ever thought possible—he actually makes it work. I could tell from the tone of his voice and the look on his face that he was passionate about this.

So, when he asked me if I would consider joining his administration to work on those things, it really just took my breath away. At first, I didn't know what to say. It's not as if it came out of left field, because I had previously talked about these issues with Jared. But those were just passing conversations with a friend. This was different. This was official. The President-elect was formally asking me to join him at the White House to work on things I'd long been passionate about. Time, itself, seemed to stop, and for what seemed like an eternity, although it was probably only a few seconds, I could scarcely form the words, much less speak.

No doubt due to all those late nights of binge-watching *The West Wing*, came, completely unbidden, a flurry of disconnected scenes and the theme music from the series, all flitting around my head, as I finally managed to say, "Why, yes! It would be the honor of a lifetime!"

Trump smiled broadly and said, "Welcome aboard!"

"Donald," I said, now slightly embarrassed, "would it be okay if I checked with my wife and kids before I give you a final answer?"

He smiled and waved his hand, saying "Of course, of course." But I knew that, in his mind, "Of course" meant, "Just tell me when you're going to sign."

I called Naomi from work and shared my news with her. After talking excitedly on the phone for a couple of minutes, we agreed to wait to tell the children that evening and discuss it. That night, when we were all sitting in the reflected glow of the candles from the Shabbat table, I told them I had an important family matter for all of us to consider. I told them, briefly, of the offer that the President-elect had made to me earlier that day, and then I asked them the following question: "Is this an opportunity, a responsibility, or an obligation?"

After talking it over, they all agreed it was an obligation—something that I had to do. Their swift and excited affirmation was inspiring. After all, how often do any of us actually get a chance to not only work in the White House and not only serve our country, but potentially impact the lives of millions of people?

Looking back, Naomi and I have since joked that we never really considered all the "what ifs" that should have gone through our minds before I packed up a van and moved to Washington. We simply felt that this was an important mission, so we took comfort in that and just basically jumped off the cliff into the unknown. I sometimes still wonder whether, if someone had sat us down at the time and told us what we were going to experience, we would have made the same decision.

I'm not talking about the Israeli-Palestinian conflict, which I knew would be fraught with its own challenges. It was all the other stuff—the political divides in our country and abroad, and the vitriol against President Trump that seemed to have no bounds. There was so much anger and hatred directed at him and the administration generally, that it sometimes seemed that we were all being dragged down into a vortex of craziness.

But I was blissfully ignorant of all that at the moment. I had been given what I considered the most important mission of my life, and I was intent on trying my best to accomplish it. When I returned to work on Monday, I stuck my head in Trump's office that morning just long enough to say, "About that offer last week—it's a yes—for sure."

CHAPTER 2

No Experience Necessary

DECEMBER 27, 2016

The announcement from the Trump transition team that I had been named the administration's "Special Representative for International Negotiations" was not exactly a lead item in the evening news. Nor did my lack of experience for the job or my legal and business-world experience unduly dazzle the critics. The national media consensus seemed to be that I, much like my boss, was dangerously out of my depth. In several stories, my lack of any formal training or background in foreign policy was always front and center. One writer, in particular, seemed to go out of his way to mention that the most insightful writing I had done to date on the Middle East was a family travel guide to Israel.

These and other similar observations were certainly no boost to my ego, but I had to admit, they were true. I may have negotiated substantial and complex transactions on behalf of The Trump Organization for nearly twenty years, and I had both lived in and visited Israel extensively, but I couldn't honestly claim the slightest experience as a diplomat.

But then I began to think that might not necessarily be such a bad thing.

I don't mean to diminish the role of professional diplomats at all. Many are exceptionally skilled at what they do, and I was to learn a great deal from some of them during my time at the White House. But I also knew that, over the past seventy years, literally scores of professional diplomats and polished politicians in our country, as well as many others, had tried to bring the Israeli-Palestinian conflict to a satisfactory conclusion, and they had nothing to show for it. If experience in diplomacy and politics were the key to unlocking this long-standing crisis, why hadn't one of those professionals already solved the problem? Was the Israeli-Palestinian conflict so utterly unique, so uncommonly complex, that no human mind had yet fathomed it and formulated a solution?

The "experts" could question my lack of qualifications all they wanted, but despite their superior expertise, were they any closer to achieving peace? That question, conspicuous by its absence in any discussion of the matter, never seemed to be posed. Were those experts who put our team down confusing activity with accomplishment? "Shuttle diplomacy" had a rarified aura about it to be sure, but just as the Stone Age didn't end for lack of rocks, maybe an end to the Israeli-Palestinian conflict didn't depend on finding even more skilled diplomats to draft even more complicated peace processes. Maybe the much-vaunted "Peace Process" had become a circular and cynical end in itself. Maybe we needed a different approach. And maybe—just maybe—we could succeed where others had failed.

Meanwhile, the outgoing Obama administration seemed dedicated to making our work in the Middle East as difficult as possible, and Trump hadn't yet even been sworn in. Just four days prior to my new position being announced, the United Nations Security Council (UNSC) had adopted Resolution 2334, condemning Israeli settlements in the so-called "Palestinian territories occupied since 1967, including East Jerusalem."

The resolution passed on a 14–0 vote by members of the UNSC. Four members with veto power—China, Russia, France and the United Kingdom—voted for the resolution. It was an outrageous abandonment not only of Israel, but of the truth itself.

The United States could have easily vetoed the measure; indeed, the administration had vetoed a similar one in 2011. Had material conditions changed on the ground in the Middle East since then? No—but they had in Washington. The next occupant of the White House was not going to be a Democrat, and President Obama obviously wanted to make his displeasure with Israeli Prime Minister Benjamin "Bibi" Netanyahu as public—and politically painful—as possible.

And so, for the first time in the history of that issue, the United States conspicuously and dramatically abstained, allowing the resolution condemning Israel to pass. The document declared that Israel's settlements were a "flagrant violation of international law...with no legal validity," and it demanded that Israel stop all settlement activity. It cited the language of the Fourth Geneva Convention, which concerns the treatment of civilian populations in war zones and states that "The Occupying Power shall not deport or transfer parts of its own civilian population into the territory it occupies."

These were strong accusations, to be sure, and similar ones had been made many times before. When opponents of these Israeli communities used the seemingly innocuous or neutral word *settlement*, they actually meant it to convey a far more menacing meaning, like "thieves," people who have unlawfully occupied an uninhabited building or piece of land that is not their own.

I readily concede that it's a powerful image in a compelling narrative frame. In this moral melodrama, Israel is cast as the powerful villain of the piece, taking by force and violence that which was not rightfully theirs to take from a powerless Palestinian State. If this were a script for a movie, it would, as the saying goes, be "greenlighted" by some Hollywood producer immediately.

But the real story here ignored some significant facts. Perhaps the first and most important one is that Israel never invaded or occupied a Palestinian State—for the simple reason that an actual, functioning Palestinian State has never existed. The sovereign nation known as "Palestine" is an aspiration for some—indeed many people—but it is not an accomplished fact on the ground.

Moreover, the idea that Israel's settlement policy violated the Fourth Geneva Convention, which concerns the treatment of civilians in a war zone, was ridiculous on its face. That's not just my opinion. The late Morris B. Abram, a famed civil rights attorney who helped write the Convention, explained that what the authors had in mind were "heinous crimes" of the sort committed by Nazi Germany. Among these were the forceable eviction and transport of Jews to the death camps of Europe.

I'd like you to pause here for a moment and consider what this UN resolution was actually saying. It was daring to compare the existence of Israeli settlements to the Holocaust. To compare such unutterably monstrous and murderous acts to the construction of homes, schools, and businesses in the West Bank is cynical and wicked beyond belief. To draw an equivalence between the construction of Israeli communities and the likes of Auschwitz and Treblinka is both odious and nauseating.

On a purely practical level, it's probably worth mentioning that the last actual sovereign government in the territory now known as the West Bank was the Ottoman Empire, which relinquished it after the end of World War I. That was swiftly followed by a League of Nations recognition of a "close settlement" of Jews in what was called the British Mandate in 1922, a specific right to the land memorialized by Article 80 of the UN. That's right—the same UN that was now equating Jews with Nazis!

Both as a lawyer and as someone with a deep interest in the history of this issue, I was amazed at the fundamental ignorance of both law and history and the precedent that this UN vote revealed.

It was the Carter administration that first advanced the notion that these Israeli settlements were inconsistent with international law. Three years later, in 1981, the Reagan administration reversed that finding, concluding that the settlements were not inherently illegal. Since then, it had been the official position of the United States government that these settlements, while technically "illegitimate," are not "illegal." This may seem like a subtle, even sophistic, distinction, but it is, nonetheless, an extremely important one. It is because of this distinction that, for more than thirty-five years, the United States had, up until that very moment, always objected to any condemnatory resolutions on the issue of "settlements" whenever such attempts to discourage, denounce, or dismantle them came before the United Nations.

This decision on the part of the Obama administration was nothing short of a sea change in American policy. The fact that it came less than four weeks before a new administration took office seemed to me simultaneously both cynical and vindictive. If Hillary Clinton was not going to be the next president, the Obama administration seemed to be saying, then they were going to deliberately throw a lighted match, on their way out the door, into the gigantic can of gas that was the Middle East—just to watch us try to put out the fire.

Several of America's supposed friends at the UN, and all of our enemies, seemed similarly inclined to sit back and watch the resulting diplomatic conflagration. They knew well that the passage of this resolution was a thumb in the eye of the incoming Trump administration. Nor were they ignorant of the history of this issue. They knew that Israel, and its chief ally, America, had long maintained that the land upon which these settlements were located were not "occupied" territories, but "disputed" ones, for the very good reason that there was no "Palestine" to "occupy" within the Gaza Strip and West Bank, either before or after the Six-Day War—and also because Israel had neither officially deported nor transferred any populations in those areas.

While it's true that Jordan "annexed"—that is, captured—the West Bank during the 1948 war against Israel, no other Arab state recognized Jordan's claims of sovereignty there. In 1967, when Israel captured what was still that disputed territory in the West Bank as a result of the Six-Day War, Israel claimed it had done so as the result of a war of self-defense—a claim that was self-evidently true. At the time, the Soviet Union, which had backed the attack against Israel by Egypt, Syria, and Jordan, attempted to persuade members of the UN to condemn what it said was an "illegal occupation." Unlike today, however, members of the Security Council saw Israel as a victorious underdog and the motion failed to gain a majority of votes.

Since then, of course, claims that Israeli settlements in the West Bank are illegal have frequently been made by various bodies within the United Nations. And while the United Nations considers itself—and indeed, claims—that it is the final word on the world's affairs, such claims are only that. Simply restating them doesn't confer any particular validity on them. The UN passes a great many resolutions on a great many things, but none of those resolutions regarding the Israeli-Palestinian conflict are, in themselves, legally binding. Nor are the decisions by the equally impressive-sounding International Court of Justice, whose decisions are actually not legal as the word *court* implies, but political. Once again, this is not just my opinion. According to the US Congressional Research Service (CRS), "with the exception of 'advisory opinions,' which are non-binding, the ICJ may only resolve legal disputes between nations that voluntarily agreed to its jurisdiction."

So, let's review here: UN resolutions regarding the Israeli-Palestinian conflict aren't legally binding; the decisions of the ICJ are political, not legal; and the ICJ may only resolve legal disputes between nations that agree, in advance, to abide by its decisions. Where does this leave us? For starters, the only "nation" involved here is Israel, and Israel does not recognize the ICJ's jurisdiction on the issue of settlements. As for the "State of Palestine"—well, it doesn't legally exist.

What Israel *does* recognize and abide by are the decisions of its own Supreme Court. That court has both upheld the legality of Israeli settlements where they are consistent with government policy, while at the same time declaring others illegal, in which case the settlements and the settlers have been removed.

But let's leave aside the history of UN resolutions and the question of who has a legal claim on the West Bank. The argument that had suddenly become so compelling to the Obama administration was not about any of that. It was about the building of Israeli settlements and how their construction was a provocation without parallel. If only those horrible settlements didn't exist, the reasoning went, the Palestinian leadership would link arms with Bibi Netanyahu, peace would guide the planet, and love would steer the stars. Wouldn't it be pretty to think so?

When it comes to the issue of Israeli settlements, however, even a cursory look at history demonstrates that these communities have not been an obstacle to peace. How's that, you ask? By pointing out a simple, incontrovertible statement of historical fact, which is: If Israeli settlements are the only reason a peace deal can't be reached, then why wasn't one concluded between 1949 and 1967 when Jordan occupied the area, and by definition, Jews were prohibited from living in the West Bank altogether?

The answer is simple: From the very beginning, some of Israel's neighbors refused to recognize Israel's very right to exist at *all*. It was that—the bone-deep opposition to a Jewish State itself, not later settlements in the West Bank—that led to the 1967 Six-Day War, and Israel's subsequent occupation of territory that Jordan had similarly occupied before.

Okay, but what about the settlements that Israel built after that period? Did the number and pace of Israeli settlement construction have any apparent effect on the prospects for peace?

Well, actually, the answer to that question may surprise a lot of people. That's because, if anything, increased settlement activity has actually coincided with some positive moves by Palestinian leadership toward peace. Counterintuitive as it may at first seem, it would appear that precisely on those occasions when Israel offered to significantly curtail—or even totally abandon—settlements, the Palestinian leadership's response was indifference or, worse, outright hostility and violence by Hamas and other terrorists.

For example, from 1967 to 1977, although Israeli settlement activity was relatively slow and spotty, with only a few communities being constructed, no peace negotiations took place. However, in 1977, as settlement activity increased significantly under the new leadership of Israeli Prime Minister Menachem Begin, Egyptian President Anwar Sadat made a historic trip to Jerusalem, and soon signed a peace treaty with Israel. In response, preexisting Israeli settlements in the Sinai were voluntarily razed by Israel.

In 1978, Israel froze settlement activity for ninety days as a goodwill gesture to induce other Arab nations to join the peace process at Camp David. They refused. Over the next several years, Jewish settlement construction continued to increase. In fact, between June of 1992 and June of 1996, according to the American-Israeli Cooperative Enterprise's Jewish Virtual Library,

Jewish population in Judea and Samaria increased a whopping 50 percent, and yet, the Palestinian leadership signed the Oslo Accords in September 1993, Jordan signed a peace agreement with Israel in 1994, and the Palestinian leadership again signed the Oslo II agreement in September of 1995.

Five years later, in 2000, Israel offered to dismantle dozens of settlements, but the Palestinian leadership would not agree to sign a peace treaty. Five years after that, in August 2005, Israel gave up all of its settlements in the Gaza Strip and several more in the northern part of Samaria, and received nothing but terror attacks in return. Three years later, in 2008, Israel offered to give up nearly all of the settlements in the West Bank—ceding nearly 94 percent of the West Bank—but once again, the Palestinian leadership rejected the offer. In 2010, responding to a request from President Obama to Israeli Prime Minister Bibi Netanyahu, all settlement construction was frozen for a period of ten months. The Palestinian leadership boycotted the talks for nine months, then initially agreed to talk, only to walk away as the freeze expired.

Looking at this history, it's hard to escape the conclusion that Israeli settlement construction seems to have frequently *not* been an obstacle, but actually an inducement for the Palestinian leadership to sit down at the bargaining table.

It would appear that one of the early beliefs of the Palestinians was that time was on their side. Concurrent with that belief was another, which apparently construed any impulse from the Israeli side to give up land or settlements as an expression of weakness. And so, when Israel began to accelerate the number and pace of settlements, the response from the other side was not so much anger as alarm. Allowing the Israelis to continue their settlement activity, unabated, became politically untenable. In effect, it forced the Palestinian leadership to confront a new reality emerging on the ground.

The question now was whether the settlements were a serious object of negotiations, or merely a flag to be waved. It seemed to me to be the latter.

I might not have been a bona fide White House negotiator yet, but my background in the law gave me the basis to carefully examine and evaluate the claims being made here, and my firsthand experience of actually living in one of those Israeli settlements for close to a year provided a lens through which the dangerously exaggerated image of these communities could be brought into what I felt was a clearer, more realistic, focus.

While the future of Israeli settlement construction is, of course, unknown, the media portrait of an out-of-control settlement program doesn't stand up to rigorous scrutiny. To be sure, the settlements, themselves, have grown enormously and continue to do so, just as the region itself has grown by leaps and bounds. But the idea that there is a constantly multiplying number of them in the West Bank is simply not factual.

According to statistics based on the Israeli Interior Ministry Population Registry, approximately 71 percent of all the Jews in the West Bank live in just five areas, or settlement "blocs"—all but one of which are close to the 1949 Armistice Line, which is often inaccurately referred to as the 1967 border. Polls through the years have shown that the majority of Israelis, both on the political left and the right, want these blocs to become part of Israel whenever final borders are drawn, something that both liberal and conservative Israeli prime ministers have pledged to do. Most of these settlement blocs are essentially suburbs of either Jerusalem or Tel Aviv.

While the Israeli population has continued to grow in the West Bank, it's not true that new settlement blocs are multiplying like rabbits. For example, it made international news when the Israeli Security Cabinet gave its unanimous approval to begin construction of a new settlement near the existing city of Shiloh on March 30, 2017.

As media outlets from New York to Cairo observed, the decision to build a new Israeli settlement had been on the drawing boards for more than twenty years before finally being approved. At the same time, however, the government forced the evacuation of Amona, a settlement that the Israeli Supreme Court ruled had been illegally constructed on what was ultimately determined to be private Palestinian land. The approximately two thousand people in that development were relocated to a state-approved area, called Amichai, for which construction commenced in July 2017.

I provide these examples to demonstrate that Israeli settlement activity is scarcely being conducted at a breakneck pace, and also to point out that, when settlements are deemed illegal, Israel itself admits it and corrects the matter. As for crowding out the Palestinians there, the numbers tell the story: As this book is being written, the Israeli Central Bureau of Statistics estimates that the Jewish population in the 128 West Bank settlements is approximately 475,481, which is a mere fraction of Israel's overall population of 9.3 million. The Palestinian population in the West Bank, by contrast, is approximately three million.

Also conveniently ignored in all this focus on Israeli settlements in the West Bank are the settlements that Palestinians, themselves, are building there as well. In many cases, they are building illegally because obtaining permits from Israel can be exceedingly difficult. Indeed, as I write this book, the permitting of Palestinian homes is a political hot potato, and there is an ongoing discussion about the extent and types of Palestinian structures that should be allowed under Israeli law. I realize this must be exceedingly frustrating to Palestinians in the area. Yet other Palestinians don't want to seek permits from Israel in the first place, since they do not want to accept that Israel is in charge there.

Both these arguments from the Palestinian side are worth hearing and discussing. In my opinion, these concerns should be the subject of serious negotiation. But why is the discussion in the media and diplomatic circles constantly about Jews building in Judea and Samaria? Why is there never a discussion among the critics of the substantial "Palestinian settlement movement" as well?

The answer, of course, is that it would spoil the narrative that the "fault" here is all on one side—the Israeli side.

The complaint that the Jewish population and its settlements have become so significant and pervasive in the West Bank that no future Palestinian State is possible in the disputed territory would seem to put stretch marks on credulity. Even organizations critical of Israel's settlements have admitted that these areas comprise less than 2 percent of the West Bank—or approximately 39 square miles. To be scrupulously fair, there is likely another 110 square miles or so of currently unbuilt areas that fall within the boundaries of the settlements that now exist. But adding in all of those areas as well still only comes to about 150 square miles in an area which is, in total, some 2,262 square miles.

Here's something else about Israeli settlements that badly needs saying. Over its existence as a nation, Israel has both established settlements in the Sinai Peninsula, and subsequently voluntarily removed them in 1982 as part of a peace agreement with Egypt. Israelis had likewise established communities in the Gaza Strip—an approximately 141-square-mile stretch of land along the Mediterranean Sea which borders Egypt on the southwest and Israel on the east and north. However, these settlements were voluntarily dismantled as well when Israel withdrew from that territory in 2005. The evacuation of the Israeli population from Gaza and the Israeli towns and neighborhoods there was an incredibly traumatic event for Israel, and haunts many to this day.

The point of these examples is to demonstrate that, just because Israel has constructed settlements does not mean—and historically has not meant—that those settlements are necessarily permanent. Like everything else in the long history of the Israeli-Palestinian conflict, Israel's settlements are merely one example in a long list of contested issues.

While I personally support the existence of these Israeli cities, towns, and neighborhoods in Judea and Samaria, what I think, and what the United States, the United Nations, and the European Union think, doesn't matter. Ultimately, whatever happens to these areas will be up to the government of Israel. By claiming that these settlements are illegal because they are built on land that supposedly belongs to a sovereign Palestinian State—a State that doesn't exist—you distort history, you distort the reality on the ground, and you drive peace further away.

Speaking of Gaza, Israel's exit from that area was supposed to reveal what Palestinian leadership would do, if given a chance to throw off the yoke of its supposed oppressor. Unfortunately, it did. Hamas terrorists have used the Strip as a staging area for years for continual rocket and mortar attacks against Israeli men, women, and children. Each time, Israel's military eventually manage to suppress the attacks, which leads to periods of relative calm, but the same UN crowd that had demanded the withdrawal to begin with now condemn Israel for defending itself too vigorously when once again Hamas and Palestinian Islamic Jihad attack Israel. Some even have the temerity to accuse Israel of bringing the terrorists' attacks on themselves.

Their rationale? Israel, they claimed, had supposedly withdrawn from Gaza too swiftly. If only they had handled the handoff more slowly and carefully, the argument went, everything would have turned out okay. The Israelis had only themselves to blame that it turned out otherwise. File that under the ever-growing and already voluminous "no good deed goes unpunished" archive maintained against Israel by its opponents and enemies.

Not content with that international slap in the face to America's staunchest ally in the region, Secretary of State John Kerry would go on to rebuke Israel less than a week later in what was, quite possibly, the harshest language any official of the United States government has ever used against an ally. In a seventy-minute speech in the Dean Acheson auditorium in the State Department's Harry S. Truman building—named for the president who first recognized the Jewish state in May 1948—Kerry took his talking points directly from that previous UN resolution, repeatedly and sharply condemning Israel, particularly its settlement policy, as the principal obstacle to peace in the Middle East. With a mere twenty-three days left in his term of office, Kerry could apparently no longer retain his diplomatic cool. He claimed Israel was fast undermining any remaining hope for a "two-state solution" to the decades-long dispute with the Palestinians by building settlements in the West Bank and East Jerusalem.

Israeli Prime Minister Bibi Netanyahu was having none of it, and I could scarcely blame him. "The entire Middle East is going up in flames, entire countries are toppling, terrorism is raging and for an entire hour the Secretary of State attacks the only democracy in the Middle East," Prime Minister Netanyahu said. "Maybe Kerry did not notice that Israel is the only place in the Middle East where Christmas can be celebrated in peace and security. Sadly, none of this interests the Secretary."

In Congress, criticism of Kerry's speech was equally swift and bipartisan. The late Republican Senator John McCain called Kerry's speech a "pointless" tirade. On the other side of the aisle, Democratic Senator Chuck Schumer said that Kerry had "emboldened extremists on both sides"—as indeed, he had—and Kerry certainly had to know it. That, in fact, seemed to be the whole point of his speech. It was an opportunity for America's chief foreign policy spokesman to dramatically break with Israel before the entire world, undermining its political leadership, while emboldening Israel's enemies and critics more than ever before, and giving those enemies and critics America's energetic consent to redouble their efforts to push boycotts, sanctions, and other anti-Israel legal challenges.

While Kerry did note that Palestinian violence and the unwillingness to recognize Israel's existence was a contributing factor in the inability to create a peace agreement, it appeared to me that he had spent far more time and passion on excoriating the Israelis about the settlements. Now, whatever your position on settlements happens to be, in the final analysis, they are physical structures: houses and businesses, hospitals and schools. These communities may well incense John Kerry and offend his sensibilities, but they are not bombs. They are not missiles. Their existence may bruise Palestinian egos, but they do no physical harm, much less kill anyone.

The same can't be said for Hamas's rocket and mortar attacks and other tools of the terrorist trade. The essence of Kerry's argument seemed to be that Israeli settlements were a provocation so extreme that, in their construction and consequences, they were a species of slow-motion terrorism. That was not merely overheated rhetoric, it was dangerously disingenuous. It was a poisonous proclamation aimed at directly harming our greatest ally in the region and giving solace and support to Israel's most dedicated foes. With "friends" like these, Israelis must have thought, who needs enemies?

According to the narrative espoused by Kerry, peace in the Middle East had been made impossible by hardliners like Netanyahu who refused to accept a Palestinian State and continued to build settlements at a briskly belligerent pace. Here, again, was a compelling and dramatic story, to be sure, but there was just one problem with it: it wasn't true.

The truth is, a fair reading of the history of the Israeli-Palestinian conflict shows that the State of Israel is, by and large, willing to live and let live with their Palestinian neighbors. Palestinian leadership, on the other hand, in both Gaza and to some degree in Ramallah, has long been committed to what might well be characterized as a "live and let die" position: Palestinians get a state, Israelis get a shroud.

The second truth concerns the supposedly intransigent Netanyahu, famously portrayed by opponents as the man who has done more than anyone in the last quarter-century to prevent a Palestinian State from becoming a reality, and yet has the distinction of being the only member of his party, Israel's Likud party, to accept, in theory, a two-state solution under certain very specific conditions.

The third truth is that Netanyahu was the only prime minister in Israel's history to agree to a total settlement freeze of ten months to prove Israel's commitment to peace talks, at significant political cost to himself.

Not surprisingly, none of that found a place in Secretary Kerry's speech. Instead, he went on to say that "some seem to believe that the US friendship (with Israel) means the US must accept any policy regardless of our own interests, our own positions, our own words, our own principles—even after urging again and again that the policy must change. Friends need to tell each other the hard truths, and friendships require mutual respect."

But where was this mutual respect with regards to Israel about which Kerry seemed to speak so movingly?

He seemed to regard Israel not as a friend or equal, with its own autonomy, but as some sort of vassal state that should do whatever America told it to do—or else. To be sure, Israel gets plenty of aid from the United States, but then, the United States gets plenty of benefits from Israel, too. They're an important ally, and they should be treated no differently than our other allies, many of whom we also help support financially or militarily. All of these nations get to make their own sovereign decisions, just as we do. And as for speaking "hard truths," where were the hard truths for the Palestinian side? Or, for that matter, America itself? How much money had America given, through the United Nations, to the Palestinian leadership over the years? And what, if anything, had that done to improve the plight of the Palestinian people or contribute to a more productive dialogue between the Palestinian leadership and Israel? How many times was the United States prepared to look away as Hamas tried to murder its way to a political "agreement" with Israel?

Toward the end of his seventy-minute harangue, Kerry finally acknowledged the elephant in the room: a new administration was about to take charge, one that, he warned darkly, seemed poised to "abandon" the lofty goals and principles that had guided the United States in its negotiations for decades. Left unsaid, of course, was that these negotiations, for all the importance he attached to them, and for all their good intentions, had gone nowhere and produced nothing.

David Friedman, a longtime friend of mine and a lawyer I had worked with on some occasions during my time at The Trump Organization and more recently as

Israel advisors to then-candidate Donald Trump and the Trump campaign, was to be nominated as the ambassador to Israel. David was no fan of Kerry's beloved "two-state solution," and had actually helped fund some of those Israeli settlements that the outgoing Secretary of State was so convinced were fatally derailing the "peace process," a process that had, to his obvious and deep dismay, not produced peace.

As angry and frustrated as Kerry obviously was as he neared the end of his watch, David was excited and eager to jump into his new role, just as I was into mine. Working together, Jared, David, and I would soon form a new triumvirate of sorts, coordinating our efforts to accomplish the marching orders President-elect Trump had given us. Those orders basically boiled down to the following: "Learn all you can from everyone you can—and then develop a plan that makes sense." I knew that many before us—intelligent people, dedicated people—had tried and failed. I respected their efforts. I didn't think we were smarter than all those other people, but we were absolutely committed to the idea that, one way or another, this problem, like any other problem, could be solved if both sides were willing to work together toward peace. If nothing else, we were eager to have our chance to try.

On vacation in Mar-A-Lago, the President-elect was ready for action as well. He posted one of his characteristically blunt Twitter messages, responding to both the UN Security Council vote and Kerry's speech: "We cannot continue to let Israel be treated with such total disdain and disrespect," he wrote that Wednesday morning. "Stay strong Israel, January 20th is fast approaching!"

Would we prevail where President Obama and Secretary Kerry had failed? I had no crystal ball to glimpse the future, but I sensed a long overdue change in the air. Maybe that was nothing more than wishful thinking on my part, combined with a dauntless naivete. But one thing was absolutely certain: As America's next president had succinctly phrased it, January 20th was fast approaching, indeed.

CHAPTER 3

Everyone Has a Plan

THE "TRANSITION PERIOD"

There is an old Yiddish saying, "*Mann Tracht, un Gott Lacht*," which means, "Man Plans and G-d laughs." It's an adage that neatly and compactly reminds us that, despite our most careful and dedicated attempts to plan the future, the road of life is neither neat nor predictable. Indeed, life is a labyrinthine affair. It routinely flaunts and frustrates, in its rambling and rebellious way, our desperate desire for pattern and certainty. And yet, we all continue to make our plans.

We do so, if for no other reason, because we fear that, in the words of that immortal philosopher, Yogi Berra, "If you don't know where you are going, you'll end up someplace else."

As the incoming Trump administration's point man on the Israeli-Palestinian file, I certainly didn't want to end up "someplace else." And so I was already deeply immersed in research on the matter and conferring with Jared on various ideas as they occurred either to him or to me. As someone who had grown up as an observant Jew, I was, of course, knowledgeable about the history of the Israeli-Palestinian conflict, but that did not mean that I was intimately aware of each and every prior point in each of those negotiations over the years. However, the lawyer in me demanded that I become conversant with each significant aspect of that massive file, and I was fast filling in any holes in that history as I simultaneously contemplated how our team might make some history of our own.

I reviewed several proposals, and heard from others about their plans, from every source and point of view imaginable. Each one of them supposedly held the recipe—or at least a crucial ingredient—for that secret sauce known as peace in the Middle East. In fact, my immediate problem seemed to be not a lack of plans but a superfluity of them. Everyone, and I do mean *everyone*, from ambassadors to auto mechanics, seemed to have an idea of how to solve what seemed to be an insoluble problem. I quickly realized that everybody loves to engage in such planning because it's an obligation-free exercise.

In so many ways, a plan is just another word for advice—something which is all too easy to offer, but which leaves the recipient with the ultimate burden of actually putting it into action. But which plan or plans should we consider? The main points of older peace plans were, of course, well-known, and some of the ideas contained in them had appeared, in different forms, several times over. While some of those ideas, both old and new, appeared to have undoubted merit, others were plainly non-starters that one side or the other would obviously dismiss out of hand. The pessimists I talked to during the presidential transition period from election day through early January darkly assured me that nothing could be done that hadn't already been proposed or attempted, while the sunny optimists seemed to believe that if Plan A hadn't worked, well, the alphabet had twenty-five more letters.

The main problem with that last bit of advice was simply a lack of time. I was scarcely the only person conscious of that notorious thief. Even though we hadn't yet taken our own oaths of office, Jared had a similar concern that we could easily get bogged down in procedure and process, and not actually achieve any forward movement. One of his favorite phrases along these lines was, "The sands of the hourglass keep going down." It was his way of inculcating a sense of urgency about this whole enterprise, of communicating to me and others that we had but a limited amount of time to accomplish this task. Whether that would turn out to be just four years, or eight, no one could know for sure. But we were here now, and neither of us regarded time as something we could waste. If I was going to get this job done, I would not only have to build this plane while I was flying it, I would also have to take flying lessons in my spare time.

The conductor Leonard Bernstein once observed that to achieve anything great, you needed two things: a plan, and not quite enough time. If assembling a plan under the proverbial gun was the surest path to greatness, I thought, somewhat ruefully, then I was well on my way! Maybe these next few years would yield something worthwhile after all. Still, I couldn't quite overcome the sense that our team was coming exceedingly late into a conversation that had been going on for a very long time, and we had some major catching up to do. If we had any hope of seriously contributing to that conversation, much less steering it toward a constructive conclusion, we would have to be mindful of history, yet at the same time, not be its prisoner.

At the outset, a few things seemed clear. Even at this juncture, I could see that the lack of a peace agreement between the Israelis and the Palestinian leadership was not for want of peace *plans*. Indeed, across the decades, there had been any number of them—proposals that contained some of the most sublime and aspirational statements about peace and the pursuit of peace which had likely ever been committed to paper—documents that had, nonetheless, not succeeded in producing a mutually agreeable settlement.

As I reviewed these plans, a familiar pattern began to emerge. For all their impressive and high-flown moral rhetoric, or perhaps because of it, they all seemed to share a blind faith in the transformative power of terms such as "fairness" and "justice"—as though there already existed a consensus on what those terms meant to both sides. The simple fact of the matter was that, in so many ways, "fairness" or "justice" were troublingly—even maddeningly—in the eye of the beholder.

Whatever the issue—boundaries, the disposition of settlements, or what was referred to as "the right of return" for Palestinian refugees—what was considered to be a "fair" compromise on these issues in Israel's view were decidedly "unfair" to the Palestinian leadership and vice versa.

These aspirational aphorisms sounded wonderful. Who doesn't support concepts like "justice" and "fairness"? But what, exactly did they *mean*? Worse yet, the same phrases apparently conjured up fundamentally different, even competing, images in the minds of the two parties involved in this dispute. Such concepts, without a specific context and agreed upon definition, were unhelpful at best and actively harmful at worst.

In the plans I had read, or had been described to me, I saw variations on the same slick slogans and pithy phrases. That almost all of these statements seemed primarily focused on process—on *how* something should be done rather than *what* should be done—was concerning as well. It was as if the authors of these peace plans were all saying, "Whatever the actual parameters of this or that plan finally turn out to be, the process should be a fair one."

This was a laudatory sentiment, to be sure, and one with which everyone could agree, in principle. On closer examination, however, I thought that that these statements were little more than elaborate expressions of goodwill. They were actually tendentious tautologies that ultimately led into an intellectual cul-de-sac.

For example, we can all agree, in the abstract, that we want "a just solution to the Palestinian refugee crisis." But among other things, that well-intentioned and admirable aim skipped over—or seemed to assume—that there was already a consensus on the issue. And that simply wasn't true. There were deep disagreements on both the number and nature of the refugees, much less what constituted a "just solution" to that problem. Any negotiation should be "fair" and the results "just"—but in the real world, what would a "fair" or "just" result actually look like? Similarly, and no less elusive intellectually, who would make that judgment, and by what criteria?

The whole thing reminded me a great deal of a cartoon I had seen years ago, which showed two scientists in white lab coats staring intently at a blackboard. The board was filled, from top to bottom, with a series of highly arcane equations worthy of Albert Einstein, except for a small, four-word statement in brackets placed squarely in the middle of it all, which read: "Then a miracle occurs." At the bottom of the cartoon, one scientist says to the other, "I think you need to be a little more specific in step two." In much the same way, these peace plans likewise seemed to assume a miracle would occur, despite the huge differences that separated the two parties. To say that the "devil was in the details" of these proposals didn't begin to describe what I saw as the almost unlimited places any number of devils could hide.

Just as troubling, if not more so, was the excessive—one might almost say obsessive—belief, that the "right" process, whatever that was, would, somehow, produce the "right" result. Judging from the lack of success thus far, that belief seemed seriously misplaced. Finally, overarching all of this was an absolute obedience to the notion that, no matter the number and intensity of inter-state and intra-state clashes across the entirety of the Middle East for the past seventy years, the only one that really seemed to matter to the wider world was the Israeli-Palestinian conflict.

It was an article of faith in Washington—and certainly among our European allies—that nothing whatsoever could be done to end the chronic violence in the region without first unraveling the Gordian knot that was the Israeli-Palestinian conflict. But was it, perhaps, possible to cut that knot, as Alexander the Great had done long ago, rather than attempt to unravel it? Or maybe the seemingly impossibly intricate knot would unravel itself if we could find its ends and pull on them at the same time?

It seemed to both Jared and I that a stubborn bias for a particular type of solution to only one, admittedly complicated, issue—the Israeli-Palestinian conflict—had blinded the diplomatic cognoscenti to other ways of approaching what was clearly a much larger and pervasive problem of violence in the region in general.

Was there not at least some merit in exploring alternate approaches for easing the Israeli-Palestinian conflict that took a different path? Might it not be possible that the decibel level on the Israeli-Palestinian conflict could, in effect, be lowered by pursuing talks with a nascent Arab coalition consisting of Saudi-Arabia, Jordan, the United Arab Emirates, Bahrain, Oman, Qatar, and Egypt? Might it not be possible to reduce tensions generally and quell multiple sources of conflicts with an alternative strategy? Wouldn't it be wise to look, simultaneously, at both a specific plan to address the Israeli-Palestinian conflict, while also making a parallel effort to engage Arab nations in establishing closer cultural and economic ties with Israel? These and many other thoughts were among our considerations as we came, ever closer, to actually beginning our work at the White House.

The Israeli-Palestinian conflict, while certainly a real and genuine concern, was scarcely the only place where conflict had occurred, or was occurring, in the Middle East. Indeed, since the end of World War II—within the same timeframe that Israel had emerged as its own sovereign entity—dozens of other conflicts have raged across the region. None of them had anything in the slightest to do with the presence of a Jewish state, boundary lines, settlements, refugees, their right of return, or the political disposition of Jerusalem.

For seven decades, civil wars and conflicts between states have been the rule, rather than the exception, in this part of the world. Large or small, ethnic or sectarian, these clashes have both defined and devastated the various societies contained in the Middle East—violence that has tragically sapped the potential of so many countries and their respective peoples, leaving them underdeveloped, poorly educated, and often lacking in basic healthcare. From Syria to Iraq, Yemen to Libya, the Middle East has been the scene of countless battles where millions of soldiers and tens of thousands of innocent civilians have lost their lives. Few countries in the region have escaped being at least a part—if not a major participant in—one deadly squabble or another.

Certainly, the longest and also perhaps costliest of all the wars in the region was that between Iraq and Iran in the 1980s. It ravaged the economies of both nations and cost the lives of at least one million people, although many believe the death toll was twice that number. Iraq's president, Saddam Hussein, in an attempt to escape from the tens of billions in loan debt he owed to Kuwait and Saudi Arabia because of that war, invaded Kuwait in the summer of 1990 and intended to do the same to Saudi Arabia. Then-President George H.W. Bush assembled an international coalition known as Operation Desert Shield to successfully rescue the Kuwaitis and push Hussein out. Since then, American soldiers have been on guard in the Middle East without interruption.

A bit of context here may be helpful. A September 2008 report by the Department of Defense placed the number of US military personnel in the Middle East at approximately 76,000, spread across several nations—Bahrain, Kuwait, Qatar, Saudi Arabia, Turkey, and the United Arab Emirates. In total, that represented nearly 16 percent of the jaw-dropping 484,000 US military personnel stationed abroad. In contrast, by the time I left the White House in 2019, that number had dropped dramatically to approximately 10,000, or roughly 4 percent of all overseas military personnel.

No matter what US troop levels have been in the Middle East over the years, it's worth noting something important. Many people often talk about the tremendous military and financial support that the United States gives Israel; that is certainly true. But those are just the "tools" if you will; Israel does all the work by itself. American troops have not and do not put their lives on the line to defend the State of Israel as they so often have, and continue to do, in the rest of the world. For example, although the conflict between North and South Korea ended on July 27, 1953, there are still nearly 30,000 American military personnel in South Korea to ensure the peace.

By contrast, the presence of military personnel and the rationale for their presence in the Middle East, yesterday and today, has basically been about keeping a watchful eye on the rest of Israel's neighbors, some of whom have had a nasty habit of terrorizing and killing one another. In recent times, the vast majority of that terrorism and killing is directly traceable to Iran or its proxies. And, while we're taking note of things, it's both sad and not a little sickening to realize that while practically every incident in the Israeli-Palestinian conflict is breathlessly reported to a waiting world, other, far more horrific situations seem to have become so routine they go largely unremarked upon.

For example, it's been estimated that there have been nearly half a million deaths in the ongoing Syrian civil war since 2011. It is further estimated by the United Nations Refugee Agency that as a result of the war in Syria, there are 6.7 million internally displaced civilians—people forced from their homes, but still residing in temporary camps within its borders—and another 6.6 million identified as refugees. Iran is in the thick of this bloody conflict as well. Talk about a crisis in need of a plan of action.

Unfortunately, no one in Washington or in Europe seemed to have given much thought to *that* plan beyond the usual diplomatic platitudes. Formulating a proposal that would truly address the much larger problem of violence in the region—and Iran's central role in practically all of it—was not the subject of serious contemplation, as far as I could tell. For America and its allies, it was far easier to simply continue the pretense that the Israeli-Palestinian conflict was a kind of political Pandora's box, from whence all the troubles in the region originated. That way, no one had to acknowledge the inconvenient truth—that things were more complicated than that; history had moved on; power, itself, was a relative concept; and another power center, Iran, had, for some time now, eclipsed any other conflict, any other threat, to become the chief menace to peace in the entire Middle East.

It is scarcely an accident that Iran's infamous Fordow nuclear facility, where enriched uranium has been secretly produced for years, lies just outside the Shiite holy city of Qom. That's the site where the twelfth Imam, Muhammad al-Mahdi, who is believed to have been born in 869 and never to have died, is supposed to reappear one day and establish Islam as the ruling faith across the planet.

This belief is not something on the fringe of Iranian society. A 2019 report by the US Department of State indicated that more than 99 percent of Iran's population is Muslim, with 90 to 95 percent identifying as Shiite. Of that group, many Shiites believe in the twelfth Imam. This end-times leader is expected to appear when the world is in a state of chaos and war. To many of these believers, no doubt, it makes perfect sense that anything which could be done to hasten that day of general calamity might well entice the twelfth Imam to reappear, ushering in a worldwide caliphate.

In its proximity to Qom, Fordow seems to deliberately mingle nuclear-age weaponry with middle-age apocalyptic belief. The military-style facility is set deep within a mountain, where its activities cannot be monitored by satellite or investigated by the International Atomic Energy Agency (IAEA), an independent monitoring group established in 1957 to promote the peaceful use of nuclear energy and inhibit its use for military purposes.

Western intelligence officials first discovered Fordow existed in 2008 from satellite imagery that picked up suspicious activity around the site. The world's response to this super-secret nuclear enrichment program was, in a word, craven. Instead of directly confronting Iran and completely isolating it, the Obama administration, together with China, Germany, Russia, France, and the United Kingdom, tried to bribe the Iranian leadership in return for a promise of good behavior in the future.

This, from a regime which had its beginning in the storming of the American embassy in Tehran in 1979 and the taking of fifty-two US diplomats and citizens in the American compound as hostages. In doing so, they had flagrantly violated the two most inviolable rules of internal law: embassies are sacrosanct and diplomats cannot be arrested, much less held as hostages. Iran did both and for well over a year during the Carter administration. The world watched as America was humiliated.

I was a teenager at the time, but I distinctly remember how CBS Television anchor Walter Cronkite, "the most trusted man in America," would end his nightly broadcasts by announcing the steadily accumulating days that our diplomats were being held at gunpoint in their own embassy. Only on January 20, 1981, mere minutes after Ronald Reagan took the oath of office as the next president, did the crisis finally end—444 long days after it had begun—with the formal release of our diplomats into US custody. Jimmy Carter had lost in a landslide, in no small measure due to his handling of the matter, while Ayatollah Ruhollah Khomeini, Iran's new leader, basked in the prestige of having humbled the world's greatest superpower.

Some thirty-four years later, having not absorbed the lesson that Iran was, at its core, fundamentally untrustworthy, America and four other nations came bearing gifts to the rogue regime in the summer of 2015. Chief among these was a 159-page agreement known as the Joint Comprehensive Plan of Action (JCPOA), a document that allegedly was going to put a stop to Iran's ambitions to produce nuclear weapons. But there was so much less to this agreement than met the eye.

Among the many key failings of the JCPOA was the lack of a requirement on Iran's part to submit to so-called "anytime, anywhere" IAEA inspections of their facilities, where nuclear activities were strongly suspected to have occurred. This was a potentially fatal flaw. Iran had already shown itself to be a serial cheater on any number of its other international obligations, among them its nuclear activities. Under the provisions of the agreement, Iran had an astounding twenty-four days, once it had been given notice of a visit, to allow inspectors into a site, obviously more than enough time to conceal or transfer any evidence of covert nuclear activities.

The IAEA had previously concluded that Iran had been actively designing a nuclear weapon years before the JCPOA was signed. The hard truth was, the signatories to this agreement really had no idea of the extent of Iran's nuclear program, which made establishing a baseline for future inspections ridiculous on their face. To make matters worse, there were so-called "sunset" provisions in the JCPOA that meant that even if Iran abided by the restrictions set forth in the agreement, it was free to expand its uranium-enrichment and plutonium reprocessing within ten to fifteen years. As one critic put it, this merely "rented" Iranian arms control promises for a limited period, after which the regime could scale up the number of advanced centrifuges and swiftly achieve enough weapons-grade uranium for a nuclear weapon in a matter of weeks, or even days.

In diplomatic parlance, this was known as "kicking the can down the road," but this agreement gave can kicking, itself, a bad name. In exchange for these "restrictions," Iran received immediate sanctions relief and approximately $100 billion that was not spent on social programs. In the immediate aftermath of the deal, Iran increased its military budget enormously over the following four years and doubled down on sponsoring terrorist organizations like Hamas and Hezbollah, seeking to destabilize Yemen, Iraq, Lebanon, and Bahrain, and also increased its support for the Assad dictatorship in Syria, which has resulted in the murder and maiming of hundreds of thousands of soldiers and civilians alike.

Through the implementation of Resolution 2231, the UN Security Council further aided Iran's ability to perfect its ballistic-missile program by weakening language that specifically enjoined them from participating in any such activities. Instead, the UN merely "called upon"—that is, politely begged—Iran not to test any ballistic missiles that were "designed to be nuclear capable." The almost complete lack of any real restrictions on Iran's ability to enrich nuclear fuel, combined with generous sunset provisions and the weak language surrounding their ballistic-missile tests understandably alarmed not only Israel, but many of Iran's Arab neighbors as well.

Surveying the new threat created by America and its fellow signatories, former Saudi intelligence Minister Turki al-Faisal certainly spoke for many of his neighbors in the Middle East and elsewhere, when he said the JCPOA was the first step down a very slippery slope, "If Iran has the ability to enrich uranium to whatever level, it's not just Saudi Arabia that's going to ask for that...The whole world will be an open door to go that route without any inhibition."

Here, again, was a most unwelcome "gift that kept on giving" from the outgoing Obama administration, one that left successive administrations with the equivalent of a ticking time bomb on our hands—and we were next in line. At many points during his campaign, Trump had made it clear that he thought the JCPOA was a terrible deal that made the entire Middle East more unstable, something which was already apparent to the mind and eye, but which would become even more evident as I began meeting with key leaders in the region.

My immediate task was to create a plan that would provide a reasonable path to peace between the Israelis and the Palestinian leadership after seventy years of previously failed attempts to craft one. At the same time we were pursuing that, however, the old "inside-out" strategy that had been used many times before, we were also looking at an "outside-in" plan as well, one that would include using some of the region's other Arab neighbors who might be willing to put their shoulders to the wheel for peace between the Israelis and the Palestinian leadership. It would be a two-track, parallel approach that could work separately, or in concert with each other. But the current political environment in the Middle East was, as always, uncertain.

After the previous year's disastrous JCPOA agreement, combined with the Obama administration's historically harsh rebuke of Israel at the United Nations and Secretary of State Kerry's caustic coda on Israeli settlements only days before, accomplishing either of those goals had been made infinitely more difficult. With all the chaos and confusion created by the Obama administration, together with the constant threats emanating from Tehran, where exactly should I start to formulate a plan?

America's thirty-fourth president Dwight D. Eisenhower, who, among other things was the architect of the D-Day invasion during World War II, once observed, "I find plans are worthless, but planning is everything."

In making the distinction between plans and planning, Eisenhower was pointing out that designing a specific plan, any plan, was far less important than the planning process itself—that is, the knowledge and insights that you gain by exploring options and contingencies. The fact of the matter was, *no* plan was so good, so perfect, that it could survive unscathed or unchallenged. Nothing ever happens exactly the way you envision it. The real key, I thought, would be how nimble, how creative and how adaptive we could be when something came up out of left field—as, indeed, it already had. We couldn't pretend that the JCPOA hadn't happened last year, that Iran wasn't dangerously on the ascendant, and that the entire region was increasingly worried about the prospect of an unchallenged terror threat emanating from Tehran. Nor could we ignore that the Obama administration had perversely reversed American policy on Israeli settlements mere days before we were to take office.

We could make our case that the Obama administration was wrong, but we couldn't undo the damage done to our ally, Israel, or the instant credibility it had given to those who had long portrayed Israel as the chief villain in the Israeli-Palestinian conflict. Our plan would have to deal with those realities, at a minimum, plus any other preexisting differences across seven decades that some of the best and the brightest minds had been unable to resolve.

So much of what I had seen with regard to previous plans seemed, so far, to be excessively focused on the process and logistics of negotiation, itself—who would be in the room, what the table in the room would look like, and how many chairs would be around it. We could easily spend the next six months just trying to design a setting for negotiations before any actual negotiations even began.

On the other hand, it seemed a waste of time to invite all the relevant participants to come together, like something out of an Agatha Christie murder mystery, and try to solve the conflict by debating issues that had already been debated dozens of times in the past. Similarly, it seemed to me the very definition of insanity to follow the previous administration's negotiation formula: "Nothing is decided until everything is decided"—that is, holding everything in abeyance until every "i" had been dotted and every "t" crossed in a final, comprehensive agreement.

This was, indeed, a prime example of those verbal tautologies so dear to the Obama administration. It was as if to say, "We have to have consensus—to have—consensus." But if you had consensus on everything, up to and including those elusive definitions of what was "fair" and "just"—there would be no need for negotiation in the first place. Then again, maybe not. That's because, in an infinitely evolving scheme like that, the parts themselves kept moving and morphing into another concern, and another, and another. It was diplomatic jabberwocky, an endlessly circular process seemingly designed to never, ever, result in a conclusion. But maybe that had been the point of the entire exercise: just keep your head down, mark time, and wait to hand the whole thing off to the next administration.

And we were the next administration.

My own instinct was to largely jettison elaborate designs about process and focus more tightly on results. It seemed far more preferable to us to design a single, comprehensive agreement, covering all the "asks" and concerns of both sides, with an actual map showing what actual boundaries would be. With that comprehensive plan in hand, we would then proceed to have the two sides address each issue, negotiating differences and arriving at an agreement, step by step, point by point, checking boxes and noting—and rewarding—progress as we went through it. If both sides were actually willing to make peace, that seemed like a common-sense way to proceed.

I knew that I still had a great deal to learn about the file, as well as the people—the political leaders themselves in Israel and on the Palestinian side—who had dealt with this issue far longer than I, and for whom it was a daily reality. I also had to hear and learn from the leaders in the rest of the region. But at this point, I did have some initial ideas and observations. At the very least, I was beginning to make two distinct files containing, respectively, the various ideas and concepts that had definitely captured my interest, as well as those that seemed, at least for the time being, more of a stretch, but worthy of further study.

During this critical transition period, as I was mulling various possible plans and avidly seeking input, one individual I encountered who offered to help was Ronald Lauder, the president of the World Jewish Congress. Ronald has an enviable resume and an even more enviable reputation. He is someone of diamond-bright intelligence, with degrees from the Wharton School of the University of Pennsylvania and the University of Paris, among others. Like Trump, he's a billionaire and wealthy enough to speak his own mind without an undue fear of others' censure. I like him, and more importantly, admire him for his lifetime devotion to Jewish causes around the world, most especially for his devotion to Israel. Although we have significant differences on how we see the ultimate solution to the conflict and the timing of achieving a solution, I know Ronald's offer to help was genuine and came from a good place.

Aside from listening to his own views on the Israeli-Palestinian conflict and his assessments of the various approaches to peace, perhaps the most useful and practical thing Ronald did was introduce me to two of his longtime consultants on all things Middle Eastern. One was an Israeli-American similarly situated along the right of the political spectrum as I was, and his "opposite," an exceptionally personable and polite, yet passionate, advocate for the Palestinian cause. I would like nothing more than to thank both of them, by name, publicly in these pages, but particularly for my Palestinian friend, the prospect of "outing" him could cause very real problems for his extended family, several of whom still live in the region.

Still, I honor the contributions both of these men have made to my understanding of the Israeli-Palestinian conflict, and count both of them as true friends to this day. Between the two of these outspoken, but thoughtful individuals, both of whom had close ties to the leadership on their respective "sides," I felt that I had something exceedingly valuable—my own private focus group on the Israeli-Palestinian conflict in microcosm. After that introductory meeting, the three of us would frequently meet over late-night drinks at the nearby Watergate Hotel, which was a short walk from my apartment. There, we would have quite spirited and frank exchanges about some of the thorniest issues confronting both sides. Over time, those sessions, as well as the meetings at my office in the White House, became both a way to understand their respective practical concerns, but just as important, to get a real appreciation of the emotional aspects that accompanied them. Our "cocktail hour conflict conferences"—together with countless meetings that I had with ordinary Palestinians, Israelis, and other Arabs from the region in hotel lobbies and conferences around the world—also gave me a rehearsal of sorts for my interactions with Palestinian and Israeli leadership, as I constantly probed and assessed possible points of agreement in what otherwise appeared to be the paralyzed peace process we had inherited. Their input helped flesh out the still-tentative points of an eventual plan. As I envisioned it, the plan would ideally borrow the best of what had been proposed previously, while recognizing that there were some new realities in the region. Whether that nascent plan would ever see the light of day, I couldn't say.

Across the years, there had been so many people like our small team, hoping that their turn at bat would result in a diplomatic home run. I was filled with that hope as well. I had no illusions it would be easy, but I at least consoled myself with the thought that I was doing my due diligence now and could only hope that the effort would pay off in the end. In addition, my two new friends—one Israeli, the other Palestinian—were helping me practice for the real "main event" that was yet to come. I was a newcomer to this arena, but I was gaining a greater appreciation for the task and how to tackle it, step by step, every day. At any rate, I wasn't about to let the next president of the United States down. My daily prayer was to gain the wisdom I needed to craft a plan that would win the day and bring peace to the Israeli and Palestinian people. Of course, I knew a lot of other people had felt the same way. Like me, they, too, had once hoped and dreamed and planned.

"Everybody has a plan," the great heavyweight boxer Mike Tyson once observed, "until they get punched in the mouth."

I hoped I wasn't going to be one of them.

CHAPTER 4

The Hour of Action

JANUARY 20, 2017

Naomi and I and our kids finally got our family vacation in Washington, D.C. after all.

After diligently looking at and discarding several alternatives, I had finally chosen and moved into a one-bedroom apartment exactly one day before the inauguration. The apartment was in Foggy Bottom, a neighborhood that takes its picturesque name from the morning mist that rises off the Potomac River. Nearby were the Kennedy Center, the State Department, and the southern tip of Rock Creek Park, a true place of refuge in the heart of the nation's capital and more than twice the size of the far more well-known Central Park in New York City.

Perhaps most important, however, my apartment was also within easy walking distance from the White House if I were to find myself running late on a Friday for Shabbos, a crucial consideration for me. In Orthodox Judaism, driving a car, making a purchase at a store, or even turning on a light switch after sundown on that day is strictly prohibited. The apartment was also only a short walk from Kesher Israel, a Modern Orthodox synagogue in nearby Georgetown, which would become my spiritual home during my time in Washington.

Although our family would all crowd into that small apartment over many weekends in the time to come, for inauguration weekend, Naomi and I decided to stay at the Trump International Hotel Washington, D.C. on Pennsylvania Avenue. I felt I already knew it well. It was, in fact, one of the last property developments I had overseen in my now-former capacity as chief legal counsel for The Trump Organization. A grand and ornate building constructed as the city's central post office in the closing years of the nineteenth century, its distinctive clock tower was one of the tallest structures in the entire district. Trump had seen the possibilities in it, and in reinventing the property, he and Ivanka Trump gave this old building a new look and a new lease on life as a lavish hotel. It had officially opened only a few months before, in the fall of 2016. As it turned out, it was only the first of many historic institutions in Washington upon which Trump would, metaphorically speaking, place his distinctive stamp.

My children had known Donald Trump throughout their lives, and I had made a point of bringing them to New York City when he announced his candidacy in 2015. Now, here we were in Washington, watching him once again, only this time, he was taking the oath of office as president of the United States. It was exciting for them, and for Naomi and me, and I was happy we could experience the moment as a family.

On that Friday at noon, as the swearing-in ceremony began, it was gray and overcast, and a light, chilly rain was falling. We were seated together in the audience, close enough that we could see and hear America's new president give his inaugural address.

Like Trump, himself, the speech was no airy concoction of gauzy rhetoric, but a straightforward expression of the themes he had so often touched on during the campaign. Just like one of his personal heroes, President Ronald Reagan, he felt that the political class in Washington had let the country down, and he was determined to turn things around, both here and abroad.

"The time for empty talk is over," the new president said. "Now arrives the hour of action."

That was certainly the Trump I knew well—a man in movement, a man driven to succeed, in whatever task that lay before him.

He also spoke about America's role in the wider world. "We will seek friendship and goodwill with the nations of the world—but we do so with the understanding that it is the right of all nations to put their own interests first. We do not seek to impose our way of life on anyone, but rather to let it shine as an example for everyone to follow. We will reinforce old alliances and form new ones."

I was a political neophyte, but I thought Trump correctly captured and characterized the desires and hopes of millions of Americans—honest, everyday people who craved change and were deeply dissatisfied with the status quo in Washington. To them, Washington was a place where appearance was often more important than accomplishment, and where eloquence held a higher value than plain-speaking. Trump had instinctively felt that profound sense of national anxiety—even despair—long before anyone else, and in his inaugural address, the nation's forty-fifth president promised that these "forgotten people" would be forgotten no longer.

Many of the president's critics complained that his inaugural address was an angry one, and claimed to hear sinister "dog whistles" that simply didn't register with me. Phrases like "America First" and "Make America Great Again," which Trump had popularized in his campaign, had, in fact, been slogans used by both Democratic and Republican politicians for at least a century. Democratic President Woodrow Wilson had used the term, "America First," as had Republican President Warren G. Harding. But because a lobby group opposed to America's entry into World War II had appropriated the phrase as their own, the media seized on that unsavory connection and ignored all the others.

Similarly, the oft-repeated "Make America Great Again" slogan of Trump's campaign was attacked as an effort to turn back the clock on race relations to the notorious Jim Crow era in the South. And yet former President Ronald Reagan had often used the same term without attracting any criticism. That didn't seem to matter. Hillary Clinton's husband—former President Bill Clinton—said the phrase reeked of racism, and many in the national media agreed. Campaigning for his wife in Orlando, Florida, the former president explained to an audience: "If you're a white Southerner, you know exactly what it means, don't you? It means I'll give you the economy you had 50 years ago" [back in the days of Jim Crow segregation]"and I'll move you back up the social totem pole and other people down."

There was only one problem with that pious political sermonette: Clinton, himself, had used the very same phrase in his own presidential announcement speech in 1991, and thereafter in other speeches. He would go on to use it again in 2008, in a campaign ad for his wife when she was running against Barack Obama for the Democratic nomination for president. "It's time for another comeback," he said, referring to his moniker as "The Comeback Kid" during the 1992 Democratic primary. "It's time to make America great again."

It seemed to me that the lesson in all this was, it's only "hate speech" if your Republican opponent says it. "Dog whistles" apparently only emanated from the right. But when demonstrators carrying BDS signs, representing the Boycott, Divestment, and Sanctions movement that sought to economically isolate Israel would show up at Clinton events, it produced only a collective, journalistic yawn. Indeed, the increasing hostility towards Israel generally in the Democratic Party concerned me on several levels—as a member of the incoming Trump administration, as a Jew, and as an American citizen.

The Democratic Party has been a welcoming political home for the Jewish community in America for a long time. It was a Democratic President, Harry S. Truman, after all, who had recognized Israel as a nation in 1948. But in more recent years, it seemed to me, that had begun to change. It wasn't because a majority of Jews suddenly woke up one morning and decided they were Republicans. Historically, the overwhelming majority of Jewish voters have self-identified as Democrats. This was not the desertion of a constituency within the party, but rather a divorce by the Democratic Party, itself, from a longtime and exceedingly loyal political partner.

In a larger sense, it seemed to me that there was a shared sentiment among a growing segment of the party which regarded faith traditions, themselves, as increasingly suspect. I was mindful that, as a candidate, Obama had famously spoken of those unfortunate Americans—apparently people like me and my family—who "cling to their religion" as essentially irrational, people incapable of discerning what was in their own best interests. The party that had once boasted of John F. Kennedy's Catholicism seemed increasingly bent on driving faith itself from the public square.

It would be another two years before "The Squad" first appeared in Congress—Democrats like New York's Alexandria Ocasio Cortez, Minnesota's Ilhan Omar and Michigan's Rashida Tlaib—but the increasingly outspoken—even militant—anger against Israel was already percolating through the party. This wasn't the usual difference of opinion on a specific Israeli policy position or opposition to a decision by the Knesset or even to a particular prime minister. Rather, this was a growing and general repudiation of the notion of Israel as a nation, of the very validity of a Jewish State itself. What had once been a looney, anti-Zionist fringe was now becoming increasingly mainstream.

The word *Zionism*, taken from the word *Zion*—an ancient synonym for Jerusalem and the Land of Israel—was a political movement envisioned and established by Theodor Herzl in 1897 for the re-establishment of Jews in their ancestral homeland. But now "Zionism," much like the word *settlement*, had assumed a pejorative character. It was used, increasingly, not as the description of the historical homeland for a distinct, yet long-scattered people that it so obviously was, but as an epithet, a term of abuse. In so many ways, it seemed to have become another means of saying increasingly bigoted things without using the word *Jew*. Like the word *settlement*, it quietly communicated a decidedly antagonistic and prejudicial point of view without seeming to be overtly anti-Semitic. In my mind, these were the real "dog whistles," but the so-called "progressives" in the Democratic Party had conveniently tuned them out.

The evidence for that was already reflected in the Obama administration's recent actions against Israel at the United Nations, and Secretary of State Kerry's rancorous denunciation of Israeli settlements a week later. But these actions had not occurred in a vacuum. As the Democratic Party's chief spokesman, President Obama's increasing antipathy towards Israel revealed itself in many ways, both on a personal level and a political level as well.

It was certainly no secret that President Obama, himself, was, to put it politely, no fan of Israel's prime minister. In a private exchange at the G20 Summit in Cannes in the fall of 2011, Obama and French president Nicolas Sarkozy were caught candidly discussing their mutual dislike of Israel's top leader.

"I cannot bear Netanyahu. He's a liar," Sarkozy told Obama. The president, who could have obviously dissented, or just said nothing at all, replied, "You're fed up with him but I have to deal with him more often than you." Neither of them apparently realized the microphones that had been attached for a press conference had already been switched on, allowing journalists waiting for a press conference to hear their private gripe session about Prime Minister Netanyahu. Apparently, neither man cared that their private criticisms about another world leader had become public. In any event, no apologies to Netanyahu were forthcoming from France or America.

But this overheard private exchange was just the tip of an exceedingly large iceberg. It not only reflected Obama's personal dislike of Netanyahu, but an apparent annoyance, even antagonism, toward Israel generally. The president had already publicly expressed his support for an independent Palestinian State that would have required Israel to give up all its land, back to the so-called pre-1967 borders. Netanyahu had, in my view, understandably resisted that effort, with the result that

Obama's special envoy, former Senate Majority Leader George Mitchell, had, after two years of effort, ended up resigning. It was clear that Obama saw Netanyahu as the chief impediment to peace in the Middle East.

Senator John McCain, famously a prisoner of the "Hanoi Hilton" during the Vietnam war a generation earlier, the Republican nominee for president during the 2008 campaign, and a leading voice on foreign policy, saw Netanyahu, Israel's precarious position, and the Middle East itself, a good bit differently.

Where Obama had disparaged Netanyahu, McCain praised him in a TV interview, adding that "Israel is under more pressure and probably in more danger than they've been since the '67 war and that kind of comment is not only not helpful, but indicative of some of the policies toward Israel that this administration has been part of." As for Sarkozy's comments, he said, dismissively that the "French have always been like that."

Inside the Obama administration, unsourced but deeply disparaging comments about Netanyahu had continued to appear in various newspapers and magazines with a regularity that was scarcely accidental. Perhaps one of the most outrageous examples appeared in an article by Jeffrey Goldberg, the editor-in-chief of *The Atlantic* in October 2014, in which the author quoted an anonymous source as saying, "The thing about Bibi is, he's a chickenshit...he has no guts."

This, from someone identified as "a senior Obama official" speaking about the leader of the only democracy in the Middle East, and America's greatest ally in the region. This, about a man who, as a mere eighteen-year-old, had left the safety of America and returned to his home to enlist in the Israel Defense Forces; a combat soldier who had served for five years in the Sayeret Matkal, an elite special forces unit of the IDF, where he was wounded in combat on multiple occasions and rose to become the team leader of that unit; who, after receiving his discharge, returned again to fight with that same elite unit in commando raids so extraordinarily sensitive in nature that they are still classified to this day.

Israeli Prime Minister Bibi Netanyahu may have been a lot of things, but there's one thing he most certainly was not, and has never been, and that's a coward.

And yet, to Obama and his coterie of advisers, Netanyahu exhibited a lack of "political courage" which boiled down to the Israeli leader's unwillingness to acquiesce to the Obama administration's desire for a "win" on the Israeli-Palestinian conflict. It was, they maintained, "cowardly" not to turn back time and pretend that the Six-Day War in 1967 never happened. It was "cowardly" not to give up all of Israel's buffering land and settlements, unilaterally, to the Palestinian leadership in Ramallah, and cross his fingers, hoping that the nation he led and the people living in it wouldn't be murdered afterward—something no other country in history had ever been asked to do.

Like Humpty Dumpty, whenever Obama administration officials used a word, it meant whatever they chose it to mean. And so they could scornfully and smugly assert that Netanyahu was "gutless" because he lacked the "courage" of *their* convictions. Of course, such courage was easy to come by when they would never have to suffer the consequences of such actions themselves.

It didn't take a professional diplomat to see that the "unbreakable bond" that had supposedly existed between America and Israel since 1948 had been strained to its breaking point over these past eight years. The rest of our allies knew it, and Israel's enemies certainly knew it as well—and were eagerly exploiting it. Members of the Democratic Party knew it, too, because the leader of that party had made it exceedingly clear that he considered Netanyahu and the country he led as unsustainably belligerent—and that, by contrast, he saw a sovereign Palestinian State as the last, best hope for peace in the Middle East.

In Obama's famous Cairo speech in June 2009, the president had drawn a parallel between the current "plight" of the Palestinian people and America's history of slavery. "For centuries," Obama explained, "black people in America suffered the lash of the whip as slaves and the humiliation of segregation. But it was not violence that won full and equal rights. It was a peaceful and determined insistence upon the ideals at the center of America's founding."

Leaving aside the highly questionable moral equivalency implied in Obama's remarks linking Black slaves and free Palestinians, the problem of slavery in America was "solved," according to the president, by what he implied was a peaceful coming together of people of good conscience. It was a powerful rhetorical image, powerfully delivered by a practiced speaker. It was also, deeply and demonstrably, false on its face.

Arguably, the bloodiest war of the entire nineteenth century was the American Civil War. *That* was what eliminated slavery—not a peace march nor a sit-in at a lunch counter. Indeed, had it not been for that previous four years of carnage, in which an estimated 750,000 people lost their lives—the modern-day equivalent of seven million US deaths—the much later, critical, non-violent work of people like the Reverend Dr. Martin Luther King, Jr. would obviously have never occurred. This was not merely a distressing distortion of American history on Obama's part, but a dangerous fantasy, presented as fact, and offered up as a prescription for peace. It was a belief that the chief problem in the Middle East was solvable if only Israel would stoop to hear the grievances of the Palestinian people. The clear implication here was that not automatically acquiescing to these grievances— refusing to strike the chains from an enslaved people, as it were—represented a moral failure on Israel's part.

So much for being "an honest broker" in the Israeli-Palestinian negotiations.

For all of the Obama administration's focus on solving the Israeli-Palestinian conflict, the overarching strain between America and Israel had, ironically, made solving that conflict all the more difficult, to say nothing of neglecting the rising threat of Iran. Just as a matter of political optics, it set a bad example when America and Israel seemed to be engaged in a bitter dispute of their own while ostensibly working in concert to pursue peace in the Middle East. For much of the past eight years, America and Israel had literally been fighting one another, in full public view, about the best way to achieve that peace. The whole thing would have been laughable if the consequences for failure weren't so dire.

The Obama administration's years of rebukes and slurs about Netanyahu were, it seemed to me, at least in part, a convenient cover that helped divert attention from that administration's inability or unwillingness to adequately address the far larger threat in the region, which was Iran. The hard truth was, solving the Israeli-Palestinian conflict would not bring peace to the Middle East, but merely to one small corner of it. What actually might bring peace to the region was a strategy to counteract the potentially disastrous reality of a nuclear-armed terrorist state that threatened both Israel and its neighbors. For eight long years, the previous administration had focused the world's attention on the Israeli-Palestinian conflict so that no one bothered to ask about the mullahs in Tehran. As the Obama team exited, stage left, they placed all the blame on Prime Minister Netanyahu, while escaping blame themselves for leaving Israel, and the Middle East in general, in far worse shape than they had found it. Not only had they failed to support a key ally in the region during a time of peril, they had done nothing to contain a far more dangerous demon that could cause almost unimaginable chaos if left unchallenged.

Sitting there on that inaugural day, I already knew we in the Trump administration were facing an uphill battle in the Middle East, one that would simultaneously require a long overdue mending of fences with Israel, but also a sincere and genuine outreach to the Palestinian leadership as well. As I had been considering how best to make that approach, my new Palestinian friend was advising me to "think outside the box" about the Israeli-Palestinian conflict, something I was already dedicated to doing. Certainly, the old "box" had not served Israel nor the Palestinian people very well at all.

While I hoped we could improve on the last eight disastrous years of the previous administration's misadventures, I was also mindful that if we had any chance of ending this seventy-year dispute, our team would have to find a way to build new bridges, and not merely revisit old battlefields. I also knew that the former administrations' "ostrich diplomacy"—pretending the problems don't exist, as typified by the JCPOA with Iran—would have to be addressed as well if anything resembling true Middle East peace were possible. And yet, that was a proverbial hornet's nest that none of the other signatories to that agreement wished to disturb. That Trump had amply and repeatedly signaled his disapproval of that agreement on the campaign trail now loomed as a foreign policy divide that seemed likely to seriously disrupt the previous status quo.

To hear his critics tell it, both here and abroad, Trump was dangerously isolationist and wanted to retreat, behind a wall, from all of America's practical and moral obligations around the world. He was, as the saying goes, the proverbial bull in the china shop, only worse, because he had brought his own china cabinet with him to the White House.

Because I came from a non-political background, I looked at this criticism from an entirely different perspective—the perspective of an average American citizen. It seemed to me that Trump was being willfully misunderstood in so many ways. At any rate, it didn't seem to occur to these critics that Donald Trump's job title was president of the United States, not the president of Europe, not the president of the United Nations. He saw his task as that of looking out for the people of the United States, of watching out for their interests; in short, of protecting America and Americans. That seemed sensible to me.

Many of America's allies in Europe had greeted the Trump administration's arrival in Washington with reactions that ranged from skepticism to barely disguised alarm. Typical of the latter response was French President François Hollande, Sarkozy's successor, who observed somewhat ominously that Trump's victory in November opened "a period of uncertainty." Speaking in a televised address to his nation, he said that with Trump as the next US president, there was "a greater need for a united Europe able to wield influence on the international stage and promote its values and interests whenever they are challenged."

From Germany, Chancellor Angela Merkel said, "The US is an old and venerable democracy. Someone elected to be president by the American people in free and fair elections has importance far beyond the USA. For us Germans, other than with the European Union, we have no deeper connection than with the United States of America."

Even a diplomatic novice like me could see that the chancellor was carefully praising the democratic process, but was conspicuously silent on the result of that process itself.

These statements and others like them were congratulations of a sort, albeit delivered through clenched teeth. It was a preview of what our administration could expect from many of our allies as we began our work, and the view wasn't exactly exhilarating. More encouraging by far were some of the congratulatory statements from Arab leaders, who seemed to sense a new breeze was blowing from Washington.

Egyptian President Abdel Fattah al-Sisi had been the first Arab leader to congratulate the then-president elect, saying he looked forward to "bolstering ties between Egypt and the US."

Kuwaiti Emir Sheikh Sabah Al-Ahmad Al-Jaber Al-Sabah also sent greetings, wishing Trump success while praising the "special" relationship between the US and Kuwait. Qatari Emir Sheikh Tamim bin Hamad Al Thani and United Arab Emirates President Khalifa bin Zayed Al Nahyan also conveyed their congratulations, voicing hope for stepped-up bilateral relations. Saudi Arabia's King Salman Bin Abdulaziz joined in as well, expressing his hope that Trump would "contribute to greater security and stability in the Middle East."

Even Palestinian President Mahmoud Abbas congratulated Trump, expressing the hope that "peace will be achieved" during his term. And, not surprisingly, Israel's Prime Minister Bibi Netanyahu gushed that he hoped to reach "new heights" in relations with Trump, whom he described as "a true friend of Israel" and with whom he looked forward to working "to advance security, stability and peace in our region."

I would soon be meeting the authors of some of these messages, rather than just reading their words. While that prospect was exciting, it also made me doubly mindful that I couldn't stint on the preparations I had been making during the transition for actually living up to the title of Special Representative for International Negotiations. The Obama administration was, quite literally, leaving town that day—indeed, the vast majority had already cleared out their offices earlier that week—and so, amidst all the pomp and ceremony of that inaugural day, as our family walked along with the crowd moving down Pennsylvania Avenue, I checked my watch and realized I was due for my official onboarding appointment at the Transition Office, a couple of blocks from the White House. I would see my family later that afternoon back at the hotel for Shabbat.

There were several of us being processed that Friday. After filling out some preliminary paperwork at the Transition Office, we were all hustled into a van and then driven a short distance to complete our onboarding. As we approached the White House gates, there was a large group of protesters who were clearly not feeling the love for the next occupant of the Oval Office. A more unhappy group of people I don't believe I've ever seen. Actually, unhappy doesn't begin to describe it. The look of hostility on their faces, contrasted with what had been a joyous mood among a crowd of Trump supporters only moments before, is something I don't think I'll ever forget. These were people who had, no doubt, looked forward to this day as well—but with one, critical difference—and their bitterness and rage were obvious, even as seen through the tinted windows of our vehicle. They were so close I could look into their eyes. It seemed to me that some of them wanted to start rocking the van. They were so incredibly angry, and they obviously knew we had some connection to the incoming administration. Fortunately, we managed to get through the gates without incident.

After we parked, we were quickly led into the Eisenhower Executive Office Building, a beautiful old structure in the French Second Empire style that stands just opposite the White House, next to the West Wing. It was my first hour on the White House grounds, and I must admit, I was pleasantly surprised at how efficient the process was. There were tons of career staff there, handing out our iPhones, laptops, passwords, and pass cards. From there, we were led through a rather labyrinthine set of passages and up a narrow set of stairs, where we finally emerged into a nondescript hallway. "Is this the White House?" someone asked. It might have been me. This incredibly unassuming, really unimpressive place looked nothing like the stately surroundings I had come to expect from the TV series Naomi and I had watched a few months earlier.

My initial, less-than-favorable impression of the surroundings improved, however, as we were ushered into the Roosevelt Room, an elegantly appointed space where paintings of both Theodore Roosevelt and Franklin Roosevelt hung opposite one another. We sat around the large conference table in the center of the room and received a lengthy briefing and more material relating to our duties and responsibilities. After that, it was back to the EEOB, where I was assigned an office on the main floor of the building. I loved the view, because it overlooked the West Wing and the White House. I proudly hung a mezuzah I had brought with me from Teaneck on the door frame to my office, and spent the next hour or so catching up on paperwork and just generally trying to get organized for my official first day on the job on Monday.

Efficient as the onboarding process was, the afternoon had gone quickly and I now realized I had to get back to the hotel in time for the Sabbath—and also to try to shower and get ready to go to synagogue—but I found that I was stuck in place. That was a new thing to me, the notion that the White House complex could be locked down for some danger. As it turns out, it was the protesters we had encountered on our way into the White House earlier in the day.

Still, I had to leave, so I went to the Secret Service guard and I explained my situation. He said, "Okay, we really are on lockdown, but what I can let you do is go from post to post, and see if they'll actually let you off the complex." He was extremely polite and professional—as I would soon find them all to be—and he directed me to the next checkpoint. I proceeded in that way, slowly but surely, and each Secret Service officer would let me through, one checkpoint at a time, although there were no guarantees I'd make it through the next one. Thanks to them, I eventually made it to the front gate and they let me out. Luckily, the hotel was only a short walk away, so I made it back, although just in time, and then went to synagogue. I think the whole family thought it was funny that I almost spent Shabbat at the White House.

Naomi was originally supposed to leave Washington on Sunday to take the kids to Disney World, but because I had been offline since Friday evening, I had missed the notification that I and other senior staff were going to be sworn in on Sunday morning. Fortunately, Naomi was able to change the flight plans, and I'm so glad she did. It would have been such a huge disappointment if they had missed it. Having my family there to witness this life-changing moment meant the world to me. The president gave some very moving remarks, and then the vice president administered the oath of office to me and about two dozen other assistants to the president.

Although I had already spent a great deal of time contemplating the task before me, there was something about standing there in the East Room of the White House, reciting the oath and realizing in that moment the responsibility that was being thrust upon me. For a brief time afterward, we all had the opportunity to wander around and take family pictures, and just drink in the beauty and history and prestige of the most important building in the world. It was an unforgettable experience.

After that emotional high, I drove Naomi and the kids to the airport and said goodbye. Naomi and I had talked about her bringing the family back to Washington for my first Shabbat in Washington so I wouldn't be alone. But I decided that, as much as I did not want to spend that first Shabbat by myself, I really wanted our kids to enjoy their vacation at Disney. They had already given up so much because of my commitment to this new job, this new life. And so they stayed in Disney for Shabbat and I spent my first Shabbat alone in my tiny—but seemingly quite empty—apartment. It was winter, so it was not a very long Shabbat. A day or so later, on their return from vacation, they landed at Reagan National and I got to see them, briefly. Then, all too soon, Naomi packed the kids into the van and headed back to New Jersey. I was off on my own again—until the next Shabbat. And so began the cycle of our unusual, crazy, exciting, and thrilling life. Whatever the future held for us, I knew one thing for sure. It was definitely not going to be boring.

CHAPTER 5

An Honest Broker

JANUARY–FEBRUARY 2017

> *"The only time progress has ever been made in the Middle East is when the Arab nations have known that there is no daylight between us and Israel. So the idea of being an 'honest broker' is not...the answer. It is being the smart broker, it is being the smart partner."*

It would be hard to find a more fulsome and energetic expression of America's stalwart support for Israel than what is contained in those two sentences. But the words are not those of President Donald Trump, as you might suppose—the man Prime Minister Bibi Netanyahu once called "the best friend Israel has ever had." Those are, instead, the words of a US Senator in the March 20, 2007 edition of *The Forward* magazine. That Democrat from Delaware would go on to become the forty-sixth president of the United States—Joe Biden.

A decade before Donald Trump won the White House, Biden's rock-solid commitment to Israel was actually commonplace on both sides of the political aisle, from liberal Democrats to conservative Republicans. Such views, in turn, reflected a host of national polls that routinely revealed that the vast majority of Americans held highly favorable views of the only democracy in the Middle East. Those were the days when Democrats and Republicans were unified on the proposition that a robust US-Israel relationship was both a moral imperative and a military necessity.

By 2017, those days were gone. Memories of the Six-Day War in 1967, when Israel's very survival hung in the balance, had begun to fade. For most Americans under the age of fifty, that was all ancient history, something they had perhaps read about but only vaguely remembered. Nor did it help matters that, for the past eight years, the Obama administration had portrayed Israel as more adversary than ally in its tenacious pursuit of a sovereign Palestinian State. True, the Obama administration had signed a Memorandum of Understanding (MOU) the previous September, which continued a long-standing commitment in military aid to Israel over the next decade, but that word, *aid*, was a misnomer.

In fact, in return for that money, Israel provided America with vital "eyes and ears" in terms of surveillance and intelligence gathering in the region, and a general military readiness that America had long depended upon and could not effectively—or more economically—obtain in any other way. But in practically every other regard in its relations with Israel, a new narrative had taken root, not only in the Obama administration, but on the political left generally. It was a narrative that cast the Palestinian people as the powerless, oppressed victims of unbridled Jewish aggression. In this storyline, the fledgling nation of Israel that had twice faced extermination by some of its strongest Arab neighbors was, itself, now an unquestioned military powerhouse in the Middle East. The underdog had become a top dog, attracting a level of hyperbolic criticism that, mysteriously, remains unique on the world stage.

At the United Nations, of course, the view that Israel was the principal source of evil, not only in the Middle East, but around the globe, was an old, old meme. It seemed to be a strange admixture of jealousy over Israel's stunning economic and military prowess in such a short time, combined with a generous dollop of standard-issue anti-Semitism. How else to explain UN support for the Palestinian position that the recognition of Israel's very "right to exist" should be subject to negotiation? Is France required to negotiate with other nations for its right to exist? What about Germany or the United States?

During her time as President Trump's UN Ambassador, Nikki Haley repeatedly criticized the UN for its fixation on anti-Israeli resolutions, observing that the UN Human Rights Council had passed more resolutions condemning Israel than the rest of the world combined. The staggering bias against Israel at the United Nations is indeed so legendary and long-standing that the late Abba Eban, who for many years served as Israel's ambassador to the

United States, once quipped, "If Algeria introduced a resolution declaring that the earth was flat and that Israel had flattened it, it would pass by a vote of 164 to 13 with 26 abstentions."

By the time our team arrived at the White House, the idea of America being a "smart" broker where Israel's interests were involved had become a political non-starter, certainly among a growing number of Democrats on Capitol Hill. Worse, the notion of what constituted an "honest" broker had become so linguistically circumscribed that the word *honesty* itself had become largely robbed of any meaning. In its place was an enormously elaborate "peace process" that seemed designed to obscure rather than illuminate, to avoid rather than analyze. In this way, American diplomatic efforts surrounding the Israeli-Palestinian conflict had become a primarily performative act rather than a pragmatic one. What had initially begun as a well-intentioned desire on the part of the United States to be seen as an "honest broker"—that is, a fair judge in negotiations between Israel and the Palestinian leadership—had by now devolved into something altogether different and, ultimately, quite dysfunctional.

Particularly over the previous eight years, the role of the United States in this "peace process" had been reduced to that of an almost infinitely temporizing goalkeeper, maintaining an artificial, even illusory, balance of "blame" between the Israelis and the Palestinian leadership. For example, on the one hand, Hamas rockets maimed and killed innocent Israeli men, women, and children, and from time to time the prior administration condemned those attacks, since the attacks were wrong. On the other hand, Israel defended itself—no, make that "retaliated"—by striking at the missile targets that had targeted them; and the prior administration noted that was "wrong," too. Since both of these actions were "harmful," both sides were "equally" guilty. The goal of the "honest" broker had thus been achieved, which was to decry "the violence" on "both" sides. Worse yet, the narrative that Israel was actually "more" at fault than the terrorists began to gain traction with a growing segment of the political left.

The "thinking" here—and I use the term advisedly—was that because Israel was so big and strong, it should just shrug off such attacks, rather than respond to them. You know, like the United States or any sane country does after it is attacked. At any rate, whatever Israel did in response to such attacks, the intelligentsia, both here and abroad, agreed that it certainly shouldn't "overrespond" to them. But, of course, whatever Israel's response ended up being, it was, invariably, never, ever, the right one. It wasn't "proportional," Israel's critics complained—as though there were some sort of established algorithm for correctly calculating the appropriate price for a dead son or daughter.

As far as I was concerned, such Tweedledee and Tweedledumber sophistry made America's original pledge—to treat both sides fairly and equitably—little more than the lame punch line to a joke. All that survived now among the majority of the Beltway's diplomatic establishment was an obsessive, even relentless, devotion to the notion that such "fairness" was a worthwhile end in itself. Come to think of it, some of those who came before us weren't really pursuing "fairness" either, but "symmetry"—and these were not the same thing. In the law, a "fair" process was one where all parties to an action would be equally subject to the same set of rules. But that "fair" process could end up producing an unequal or asymmetrical result. A "symmetrical" process, on the other hand, would, by definition, produce an equal result, but that result might very well be unfair to one of the parties. Imagine, if you will, a criminal proceeding where the jury verdict in a trial would be characterized as "fair" if both the perpetrator and the victim received equal prison sentences. This would be a "symmetrical" result, to be sure, but it would be legally outrageous and morally repugnant.

The shameful result of all this striving for symmetry was that, in order not to disturb this delicate diplomatic balancing act, which would immediately open us to charges of favoritism, it no longer seemed possible to publicly declare the difference between fact and fiction, or even right and wrong. In short, it was essentially American policy to consider the "narratives" of Israel and the Palestinian leadership as equally valid, equally compelling, and equally deserving of serious attention. This absurd impartiality expressed itself in the seemingly sensible and familiar phrase, "There are two sides to every story." And yet, we all know there are not always two sides to every story. There aren't two sides to child abuse. Or the Holocaust. Fiction is not the equal of fact. Wrong is not right.

Sometimes the truth is obvious. It stares back at you from the mirror.

If Donald Trump's ultimate concern had been not offending anyone, he would never have run for president, and neither I, nor anyone else, would ever have arrived at the White House. I was certainly conscious of wanting to proceed carefully, thoughtfully, deliberately, even humbly, and of listening first and talking second. It was my intention to engage everyone openly and honestly, to begin with dialogue, not debate. That said, I was determined not to be sucked into the pointless punctilios of which so many diplomatic exchanges seemed to chiefly consist, vague statements that said nothing and accomplished nothing.

During the initial weeks and months of the first year, I was simply trying to wrap my head around the history of the Israeli-Palestinian conflict, identify what all the issues were, consider the solutions that had previously been proposed, and assess how realistic those peace solutions, if any, could be in today's political climate.

Because Jared, David, and I were all from the business world, I would describe our process as akin to that of crafting a "term sheet"—a summary of where we were and where we thought we could go in addressing the many disagreements between the Palestinian leadership and the Israelis. For my part, I was very fortunate to work with what I regarded as a very good group of people at the National Security Council and the State Department. They rolled up their sleeves and educated me about everything. With their help and guidance, I did a deep dive into this extraordinarily thick file. Naturally, they did it through their "lens," their perspective, which was not infrequently at odds with my own. Nevertheless, it was obvious to me that they tried very hard to keep their personal feelings and political leanings to themselves. They were, at all times, scrupulously accurate and truthful, and provided me with the history of the various peace efforts, how previous teams had gone about putting those efforts together, and, of course, how they had ultimately failed.

The permanent staff at State and the NSC were convinced that the human dimension in all of this was vitally important and they were strong advocates for things like people-to-people exchanges and trust-building exercises. Jared disagreed, both because he was not a personal fan of trust-building exercises, and also because he saw that these approaches had been tried without any apparent positive results, many times before.

On the one hand, I totally understood Jared's position. Building trust between a couple of people, or two groups of people, is a great thing, but it hadn't necessarily done anything to solve the very tough issues and the political conflicts between Israel and the Palestinian leadership. But today, with the 20/20 hindsight that three years of working on this problem has given me, I think there's something to be said for that personal contact. In my view, part of the problem between the Israeli side and the Palestinian side is that, with each passing year, there is more distrust, more coldness, between the two sides. Over time, this ultimately results in an inability on both sides to really understand the other. It certainly makes the job of establishing connections between them, which was a big part of my job, much harder to do. The question here, ultimately, is one of time and resources. How many members of the White House, State Department, and the NSC, for example, do you devote to these sorts of exercises—especially when doing them hasn't seemed to advance prospects for peace previously?

And yet, in my own case, anytime I was involved in human-to-human connection, I felt that I had made a contribution, however small, to a greater understanding of the problem we faced. Every connection I made with a Palestinian, every connection I made between an Israeli and a Palestinian, and I'll even go a step further and say, every connection I made between ourselves in the White House and the Arab countries, and Israelis and the Arab countries, only enhanced the possibilities of peace. And if peace between the Israelis and the Palestinians is ever established, it needs to be more than just a situation where fewer people are being harmed in conflicts of one kind or another. It needs to be a warm peace, something that is active and productive and fruitful for both sides.

Building that trust and those connections now, during a time when there is no peace, should still be a priority, and America should help foster that, however it can.

Large as it was, it didn't take all that long to gain an appreciation for the Israeli-Palestinian file that had been assembled over the past several administrations. After multiple meetings with different members of the permanent staff, I could see that there were many people there who had spent an extraordinary amount of time examining the history of this conflict, and every one of them had an opinion about it. These were the "experts," if you will. And yet, it soon became obvious to me that there really were no "experts" on this conflict. I don't mean to be disparaging here of either the knowledge or intelligence of these dedicated staffers—their commitment and contributions were invaluable to the team and to me. But the plain fact was, their knowledge base—their "expertise," if you will—consisted entirely of what had transpired in the past, none of which had worked. To put it bluntly, these were people who were exceptionally well-versed in how we had failed, albeit in different ways, to bring this conflict to a successful resolution.

In a strange way, this was reminiscent of the efforts by the Royal Air Force during World War II to carefully document the damage to aircraft returning from missions over Germany, with an eye on beefing up their airplanes' structural integrity. What they overlooked, in all their careful calculations, was that the airplanes that came back were the airplanes that, well, *came back*. The damage these analysts really needed to document was from the planes that hadn't made it, that had been shot down. Similarly, if we were going to succeed in creating a peace plan that would work, it would do no good to become an expert on "solutions" that hadn't solved anything. Indeed, this was the definition of insanity: repeating the same, failed formulas and expecting a different result. The team and I agreed it was a waste of everyone's valuable time to endlessly rehearse the past. What we needed now were new ways of thinking, not simply scenarios that involved putting old wine into a new bottle.

I was beginning to see a familiar, yet distressing, pattern. Almost every time I would ask one of our "experts" a question that related to the current reality on the ground politically, whether among the Palestinians, other Arab countries, or the Israelis, they didn't have much in the way of helpful answers. They had opinions, of course. Strong ones. But they didn't actually have any expert answers on how to fix the problem as it existed now. For example, it's quite easy to say that the solution to the Israeli-Palestinian conflict is what is known as the "two-state solution," with two nations, Israel and Palestine, existing side by side. As a concept, it's easy to articulate as a kind of bumper sticker phrase. But translating the bumper sticker into a fully articulated reality was something else again.

How would this "two-state solution" scenario work in practice? Would Israel have security under such a scenario? What would that security look like? Would a Palestinian State have full autonomy over its own security? What would *that* look like? But perhaps more to the point, would a Palestinian State allow Israel the right to enter their sovereign territory to, say, prevent terrorism? And if they didn't, would Israel simply cross its fingers and trust that a Palestinian State would protect Israeli citizens from terrorism? If you're intellectually honest in the slightest, you realize that working out a security arrangement that would logically satisfy both a Palestinian State and Israel would be an exceptionally complicated affair, which would, itself, depend on an extraordinary level of goodwill and trust that simply didn't exist. Indeed, if such goodwill and trust existed, there would, arguably, be no security problem to begin with! This was, yet again, another one of these "then a miracle occurs" scenarios that are no doubt proposed by well-meaning and earnest people. But as a serious plan of action, they are politically and practically untenable.

Another such example is the division between Gaza, which is ruled by Hamas, and the West Bank, which is ruled by the Palestinian Authority. These are two very different societies, governed by two very different kinds of leadership. The leadership between the two sides, between Gaza and the West Bank, is not just divided, it's a bitter rivalry. How do you solve that? Here again, the so-called "experts" don't like to talk about that conflict because it's not between Israel and the Palestinians. From a political point of view, the divide between the

Gaza Strip and the West Bank upends the simple story line that there is one villain—Israel—against which a united Palestinian people are fighting.

But the truth is a lot more complicated. The experts don't want to talk about that deep divide in political leadership. Instead, they want to focus on helping improve Palestinians' lives in Gaza, and they certainly need that help. Please understand, it's impossible not to feel for the horrible conditions of the people living in the Gaza Strip. But the practical effect of sending financial aid and building materials to Gaza is that much of it ends up being siphoned away from the people who need it most, and plowed into terrorist activities of various kinds, from missiles and tunnels to fortified bunkers for Hamas. Again, if you're intellectually honest, you have to ask yourself, what's the point of trying to "help" the Palestinians in Gaza if that "help" comes screaming back as "harm" in the form of Hamas missile attacks on Israel? Attacks to which Israel will have to respond and be harshly criticized for. And so the whole, cynical cycle continues. Millions of US taxpayer dollars—along with millions more from other nations—are spent, year after year, in the name of helping the distressed Palestinians in Gaza, only to have it diverted to fund terrorist attacks on Israel, whom we then hector and chivy not to "overreact."

Funding for the Palestinians in both Gaza and the West Bank is collected and funneled through the Ad Hoc Liaison Committee (AHLC), a body set up in 1993 and composed of fifteen members. That group normally meets twice a year, either in New York City or Brussels. The members of that group include the United States, the European Union, the United Nations, International Monetary Fund, World Bank, Russia, Norway, Japan, Saudi Arabia, Canada, Palestinian Authority, Israel, Jordan, Egypt, and Tunisia. The AHLC receives reports from the United Nations Special Coordinator for the Middle East Peace Process, the Quartet—a foursome of nations and supranational entities involved in mediating the Israeli-Palestinian conflict, that consists of the United States, the United Nations, Russia, and the European Union—as well as the World Bank, an international financial institution that provides loans and grants to the governments of low- and middle-income countries for the purpose of pursuing capital projects. The World Bank acts as the AHLC Secretariat.

Aside from the chronic misuse of the funds in Gaza, the team and I were also concerned that the aid we were giving to the Palestinian Authority, in effect, gave that group increased capacity to pay Palestinians convicted of politically motivated killings, something we felt was deeply immoral and which is correctly characterized by some as a "pay for slay" policy. As for Gaza, our stance was that we were no longer going to spend US taxpayer money to support building structures in "The Strip" that were just going to be destroyed. That's because Hamas would use those structures from which to launch attacks on Israel, and Israel would inevitably defend itself by targeting those sites in return. It was a ridiculous cycle of construction and destruction, all financed on the taxpayer's backs, and practically none of it was actually going to materially improve the lives of Palestinians living in Gaza. The team agreed that it was ultimately useless to pretend that we were helping the Palestinians in Gaza for the simple reason that we weren't really helping them; we needed to stop. While many of the other members of the AHLC would agree with me privately, they would not do so publicly. Both at the AHLC and within our own government there was a "go along, get along" attitude. It was familiar, it was "safe." It is fair to say that my honest, blunt speeches at the AHLC conferences were rather unpopular with the other member countries of the AHLC, at least that's what was telegraphed publicly.

There's a widely quoted admonition from the Hippocratic Oath that physicians swear to upon entering their profession that says, "First, do no harm." One of the most interesting interpretations I've ever heard on that principle came from an individual who had spent many years in the US government, in many senior roles. On one occasion, in private, he told me, "The rule that you have to follow, Jason, is 'First, do no harm.'" He went on to explain that I was quite right, and that the problems I had identified had no solutions at the moment. "You're not wrong in how you see the answers. But the reality is, you'll never be able to fix this now. Therefore, just do what you need to do to keep things simply moving along.

Maybe one day there will be a solution, and then again, maybe not, but if you are careful not to make a fuss, not upset the applecart, the status quo, everything will be as alright as it could be."

I explained to him that while I understood what he was saying, I simply couldn't accept his "advice." I didn't leave my family in another state and take a huge pay cut to be in Washington and do nothing. Nor did anyone else on our team. Nor, for that matter, did President Trump. I admitted that while we might not ultimately succeed, we were, nevertheless, going to give it our best shot. And perhaps just as important, we were going to do it in an honest and open way. I told him that we were going to propose solutions that we thought could work, but it would be up to the two sides, themselves, and other countries in the region, to agree. We weren't going to continue former administrations' "ostrich diplomacy"— putting our heads in the sand and pretending the problems didn't exist, that everything was okay. Because it wasn't.

I've given that conversation a good deal of thought since then. I know that the person who gave me that advice meant it kindly. But I thought he was dead wrong at the time. And my opinion hasn't changed since. In fact, if anything, I'm even more convinced now that our approach was the right one. As far as I'm concerned, those who think the best way to deal with a problem is by tiptoeing around it shouldn't be at the White House. The blunt truth is, the applecart that is the Middle East is going to get upset from time to time whether we're prepared deal with it or not. The real question is, are we willing to engage with those problems in an open and honest way?

Down through the decades, there had been so much said and written about the so-called "peace process" with respect to the Israeli-Palestinian conflict—some of it worthwhile, but so much of it worthless—that the original goal of that process had, somewhere along the line, been mislaid. After listening to all the experts around me for the first several weeks, I was beginning to realize that we were speaking two different languages. Their language was one almost exclusively concerned with process, while mine was almost completely about results. I was beginning to see that this conflict had gone on for so long, under so many administrations, that a kind of cottage industry had grown up around it, an industry that no longer had as its goal the solution to a problem, but an altogether separate allegiance to the "peace process" itself. Time, and time again, the ever more intriguing approaches to the process of peace had made actually achieving peace somehow less urgent than preserving the proper political "optics." This, then, was the diplomatic version of a perpetual motion machine, one that, ironically, no longer depended on actually solving the problem for which it was originally designed.

What our team was attempting to create was the polar opposite of a "peace process." That's not a criticism of those who tried a process before. Maybe that was the right approach in the past, but we didn't think it was the right approach now. We did not believe that there was some magic process that could make the Israelis and Palestinians love one another. Nor were we so arrogant that we thought we could, somehow, "force" a deal. We were all too aware that *real* peace—not merely a temporary truce in terror—could not be imposed from the outside, but would have to come from the participants in the conflict, themselves.

In the weeks and months ahead, there would be all sorts of articles written about what Jared Kushner, David Friedman, and I were supposedly doing behind closed doors. All of it was pure speculation—and some of it was outright fabrication—for the very simple reason that, aside from President Trump, only the three of us were involved in this work, and we weren't talking out of school. Unlike so many other teams in the White House, there were no palace intrigues to whisper about, no intramural jockeying for one another's jobs, or stealing credit for another's accomplishment. We knew and liked one another, and respected the separate talents that each brought to his respective responsibilities. We were each exceedingly comfortable with the tasks we had to perform, and we were busy performing them. The media, as usual, were following the people who fed them the juiciest scraps of information, and except for the relatively bland readouts that recapped a meeting with a foreign leader or other official, we had no "news" to share, and powerful disincentives not to signal our next moves. What we did have, however, was a common belief that whatever the experiences of our predecessors, or our own deficiencies, peace was still possible and within our grasp. We knew that material conditions in the Middle East had changed, and with that change, we sensed a new opportunity in the air, a new truth, a new transition from an old way of thinking to a new one. Or so we hoped.

I had entered a strange new, upside-down world, where many assured me that process was paramount. But I thought differently. In the end, it's not the process, but the results, that give legitimacy to any pursuit. A pathway to peace that hadn't produced peace was not a path worth following any longer. For years, there had been an almost complete abandonment of the sort of reality checks that were routine in my former world, the business world. In any business "process" worthy of the name, you periodically assessed whether the intermediate "deliverables" were contributing to the overall project goal. If they weren't, you reconsidered the process and the people responsible for it. But when it came to the Israeli-Palestinian "peace process," no such "reality checks" were ever really made. Indeed, the dirty little secret was, they *couldn't* be made, not without declaring to the world that the process was a bankrupt one. It was a world where the gap between rhetoric and reality made the Grand Canyon look like a pothole. The result is that we had been going nowhere for years, but at least we were doing it perfectly!

Our approach would not be dominated by those whose knowledge base was long past its "sell-by" date, nor by the UN's international "norms" that were anything but normal. Nor would we continue to be manipulated by a thuggish regime in Tehran whose transparent lies were accorded a legitimacy that ultimately undermined and poisoned the far more comprehensive peace we were also simultaneously pursuing in the region. We were going to throw out the old diplomatic "rule book" precisely because the old "rules" no longer resonated with present-day reality. After all, high-sounding words only mattered if they were matched by equally high-impact actions.

It was time to stop pretending. It was time to face facts. It was time to speak hard truths. With negotiations between Israelis and the Palestinian leadership at their nadir, it was also time to discard the disingenuous notion of an "honest" broker for a "smart" broker—one who would unashamedly acknowledge Israel, a critical ally in the region—rather than striking an artificial pose of indifference to its fate. Whether we would ultimately succeed in our efforts was still clouded in mystery, but to me, our direction and destination could not have been clearer.

CHAPTER 6

Destination: *Jerusalem*

MARCH 13, 2017

It had been one of those relatively rare weekends during my early tenure at the White House when I spent Shabbat in Teaneck, rather than having Naomi and the family come to visit me in Washington. When I left the nearby Newark airport Sunday afternoon to make my first overseas trip as the Trump administration's Special Envoy to the Middle East, it had been overcast and freezing. As I arrived Monday morning at Tel Aviv's Ben Gurion International Airport some ten hours later, the morning sun had broken through a thin fringe of clouds along the Mediterranean coast, and the temperature was already in the low sixties. I wouldn't need my heavy trench coat here.

The name "Tel Aviv" comes from the title of a book by Theodor Herzl, the father of political Zionism, called *Altneuland*, or *The Old New Land*, a name chosen in 1910 that embraced Herzl's idea of a renaissance in this ancient homeland of the Jews. The word *tel* comes from

the ancient "tel" of Jaffa to the south, a manmade prom-
ontory overlooking that ancient port city, said to have
been built by one of the sons of Noah after the flood,
and the word *Aviv* is Hebrew for "spring," symbolizing
renewal. Today, Tel Aviv is second only to Jerusalem as
the most populous city in Israel, with close to half a million inhabitants. Much like its California counterpart,
Silicon Valley, it is renowned as a center for cutting-edge
technology and super-charged entrepreneurs.

It was no more than a forty-five-minute trip from Tel
Aviv to Jerusalem, where I quickly checked into the King
David Hotel, a legendary landmark of pink limestone
named in honor of Israel's most legendary ruler, located
in the heart of Jerusalem. The view from the King David
is, I think, unmatched in all the world, overlooking as it
does Mount Zion and the Old City, home to the Temple
Mount and the Western Wall, as well as the Church of the
Holy Sepulchre, the Dome of the Rock, and the Al-Aqsa
Mosque. Since it first opened its doors in 1931, it has
played host to practically every foreign head of state and
or diplomat visiting Israel. Donald Trump would soon be
a guest here as well in May. In honor of the occasion,
the hotel management would graciously make all of its
233 rooms available to the president and the extensive
entourage that accompanied him. But more about that
visit a little later.

After receiving a short, classified briefing from the
US Jerusalem Consul General Donald Blome, it was on
to a meeting with Reuven Rivlin at Beit HaNassi. It was

the official residence of Israel's president, in Talbiya, a beautiful old neighborhood in West Jerusalem set amid elegant homes in the Renaissance and Moorish style, replete with flowering gardens and sheltering trees. The president's residence is a veritable museum of Jewish history, filled to overflowing with ancient books, maps, and archaeological displays. In 2009, when Pope Benedict XVI had visited the residence, then-President Shimon Peres inaugurated the custom that all visiting world leaders would plant an olive tree in the Beit HaNassi peace garden, a ritual that was already beginning to turn the grounds into somewhat of a nascent olive grove.

Israel's head of state has the power to appoint senior state officials in many special and important positions. He accredits Israel's envoys to foreign countries, accepts the credentials of foreign diplomats who work in Israel, and receives government visitors, such as myself, from overseas. He signs every law enacted by the Knesset, Israel's legislature, as well as treaties and other agreements with foreign countries that have been previously ratified by that body. He's in constant contact with the government through regular meetings with the prime minister and other officials. It's a big job and an important one. That said, it's far less powerful than that of an American president or Israel's prime minister. Elected to serve a seven-year term by a majority vote of the Knesset, in a secret ballot, Rivlin was now in the third year of his term of office.

A major, longtime figure on Israel's political scene who was now in his late seventies, Rivlin had been born in Jerusalem almost a decade before his country's modern rebirth in 1948, during the Mandate era, and his family traced their roots in the city back to 1809. His father, Yosef Rivlin, who had once been a candidate for president in 1957, had created the first Hebrew edition of the Qur'an. Rivlin himself was fluent in Arabic and had been elected as Israel's tenth president with both strong Arab support and those on the far right who supported his vision of making the West Bank a part of Israel proper. He was a man of uncompromising and complex views— especially as they regarded Israel's security—and he set high standards for his country and his fellow Israelis.

He had been one of Ariel Sharon's harshest critics when that former Israeli prime minister had pursued the Tokhnit HaHitnatkut, the Israeli disengagement from Gaza in 2005. Under that policy, Israel had unilaterally dismantled all twenty-one of its settlements in the Gaza Strip, in an ultimately unsuccessful attempt to foster peace, forcefully evicting 8,000 Jewish settlers from the area. And yet, he was also the man who would condemn, rightly so—in the strongest possible language—the fire-bombing of a Palestinian home by suspected Jewish extremists that resulted in the death of a Palestinian toddler, saying that they had "chosen the path of terror," and charging that Israel was too lax in confronting such acts. Rivlin had not infrequently crossed swords with the current prime minister, as well, on matters ranging from the procedural to the substantive. Although a Likud Party member, he was no rubber stamp for its leaders or their policies.

President Rivlin had long decried Israel's increasingly tense and strained relationship with the Obama administration, and had pledged to make mending that relationship a priority of his presidency. While his attempts to improve relations between Israel and America had not borne fruit during the previous administration, President Rivlin told me he was encouraged by what he hoped would now be a fresh start between our two countries. While he wished me luck in what he called my "complex mission"—the restarting of what had been long-stalled negotiations between Israel and the Palestinian leadership—he had seen folks like me come and go many times. He emphasized that the "most fundamental issue" of all was security for Israel. Though ours was a brief meeting, President Rivlin's concerns about Israel's security would prove to be a recurrent theme throughout my visit. That issue, more than any other, would be an unstinting focus on the Israeli side. Any plan that didn't adequately address that overriding concern would obviously be a non-starter. Still, it was an encouraging first visit, and the relief in Rivlin's face that a new administration from Washington, with a fresh approach to the long-standing conflict between Israeli and the Palestinian leadership, was apparent. With this introductory meeting behind me, it was on to the prime minister's office, only a few minutes away.

1 P.M. PRIME MINISTER NETANYAHU'S OFFICE

If it weren't for the robust security surrounding it, the office of Israel's prime minister would likely not attract much attention. It's an exceptionally plain, eight-story low-rise building on Kaplan Street, named for Eliezer Kaplan, one of the signatories of the Israeli Declaration of Independence, and the country's first minister of finance. The prime minister's office inside was similarly plain and unadorned, a working space, not a ceremonial one. In the months ahead, as I visited with so many other leaders in the region, I would often mentally contrast the opulent exteriors and interiors I would encounter elsewhere with the almost spartan character of this place. Somehow, it seemed to fit the man, himself—serious and ready for action.

I had previously met Prime Minister Bibi Netanyahu less than a month before, when he had visited the White House to meet with President Trump in mid-February. The memory of that previous encounter was still fresh in my mind. I especially remembered the look he gave me as we shook hands in the receiving line—it was something just shy of a stare. It was, no doubt, part practiced political technique, part personal temperament, but he seemed to focus on me with those intense green eyes of his in a way that was a bit unnerving. In that moment, he seemed to be taking my measure, both personally and politically. I remember recounting the circumstances of that meeting with Naomi and remarking that, in some strange way that I couldn't quite explain, he seemed to already know me. Or then, again, maybe like me, he had been briefed about this new face in an already old discussion going back for decades—the latest in a long line of newly minted White House officials, eager to solve the previously unsolvable.

Over the past several weeks, in preparation for this initial sit-down with Netanyahu—and another the next day with President Mahmoud Abbas—I had been on the receiving end of my own briefings about the history and nuance of the various peace proposals of the past, together with what sometimes seemed like a suffocating supply of "information" about Netanyahu—a lot of it, invariably, negative. To hear his critics tell it, Bibi Netanyahu was guilty of everything except the French Revolution and global warming, and he might well be indicted any day on that latter charge. And yet, if he were as bad as all that, I had to wonder: If Netanyahu really was the culmination of all those derogatory descriptions, how he had managed to fool so many voters in Israel so many times? Maybe he was a master of mass hypnosis as well.

In the weeks and months ahead, I would find that Netanyahu was, indeed, an exceptionally serious man. But I happily failed to confirm all those negative stereotypes I had heard. To be sure, he was resolute, even relentless, in his pursuit of what he felt was the right course for his country. But, like Trump, he made exceptions when it came to things personal, especially if they were of a religious nature.

One day, for example, I was in the prime minister's office for a long meeting. It was the anniversary of the day of my mother's death, something we call Yahrzeit day. On that day you say a prayer called "Kaddish." You say it three times a day—morning, afternoon, and the evening before. So, that afternoon prayer was falling around the time of the prime minister's meeting. I said, "I have to go to a synagogue"—and you can't exactly leave the prime minister's office and find a synagogue on the corner—you have to go in and out with all the attendant security and all that. So, instead, we gathered a Minyan, a quorum of ten people, and said Kaddish there. But the most surprising thing of all is that the Prime Minister joined the quorum. It was so very remarkable to see him just stop everything and pray the afternoon service with us, just so that I could say Kaddish and continue the meeting. I'll always remember that day and his kindness to me.

In the end, of course, it was less important to me whether Netanyahu or Abbas were likeable, or whether I liked them. Far more important was what I might learn from them, and how I might use that knowledge and insight to craft a plan that would satisfy the needs and desires of both sides. Today's meeting would begin that process.

"Hello, Jason," said Prime Minister Netanyahu, as though we were old friends, cameras flashing in a photo-op to record our handshake. "I hope we can do some good things together."

"I think we are going to do great things together," I replied, trying to look and sound equally, if not more, upbeat and cheerful. Between his hopes and mine, I thought, maybe that elusive thing called peace might just be possible after all.

The four-hour discussion that followed behind the closed doors of Netanyahu's office was what is known in diplomatic parlance as a "four eyes" meeting, meaning that it was just the two of us talking over the issues that were paramount, at least to Netanyahu and Israel.

This first overseas meeting was part of an elaborate diplomatic dance that had already begun with Netanyahu's visit to the White House in February. The previous week, on Friday, President Trump had officially phoned President Abbas and invited him to the White House—a meeting that would take place in early May. After Netanyahu's visit, the beloved "symmetries" of diplomatic protocol demanded no less! Similarly, my meeting with Netanyahu today had to have, for optics' sake, an identical meeting with Abbas tomorrow. In the weeks and months ahead, I would sometimes think that what I was engaged in, as I shuttled back and forth between Washington and the Middle East, was not so much a "negotiation" as it was an excessively tedious and prolonged ping-pong match.

Despite all the media reports about my arrival here, I was not, at this point anyway, focused on unthawing a "peace process" between the Israelis and the Palestinian leadership—a process that had more or less been frozen for years during the Obama administration. Instead, I was very much on a "listening tour"—trying quite earnestly to gain a better understanding of how the alleged "settlement issue" as well as other issues—might best be addressed going forward.

Netanyahu knew that I was one of a very small group of people entrusted by President Trump with carrying out his wishes, and I think that is one of the key reasons I gained his trust from an early stage. That trust was essential to any chance of formulating any sort of a potential solution. I was especially mindful that he viewed the previous administration's efforts to try to push him into negotiations without regard to conditions on the ground in Israel as imperious and spiteful.

When Netanyahu talked about Israel's need for security, it wasn't theory from a briefing book. He had literally bled for his country as a member of the elite commando unit, Sayeret Matkal. So had his older brother, Yonatan—"Yoni"—who had died as the commander of that same unit during Operation Entebbe in 1976, while rescuing 102 of 106 hostages held at Entebbe Airport in Uganda. His fame was such in Israel that after his death, Operation Entebbe was renamed "Operation Yonatan" in his honor. Netanyahu had moved back to Israel from the United States in 1978 to found the Yonatan Netanyahu Anti-Terror Institute. His baby brother, Iddo Netanyahu, had also served in Sayeret Matkal.

Like any independent leader of any country in the world, I knew if I or any member of the team came in and tried to tell Bibi Netanyahu *what* to do, he would very quickly tell us *where* to go. I wasn't going to make that mistake. My approach, therefore, was to listen very carefully, especially in the beginning. The team ended up taking ideas from everyone; some were generated by Netanyahu, some generated by others, and some generated by prior people who had worked on the file. My approach was to present these ideas not as dictates from Washington, but as something to be considered. As these talks progressed, if I thought the Israelis were being unreasonable about a certain point, I would press back, asking, essentially, "Why? What's wrong with this?" If the response to that question appeared to us to be legitimate, we'd show them alternatives. However, if they came back with answers that weren't good or especially convincing, we'd press back. In a way, that process helped to build trust. Over the next several months, there were a lot of these soul-searching, heart-searching conversations, at least on the Israeli side, although far less so with the Palestinian leadership. They were far more interested in making demands than they were engaging in dialogue.

The alleged "settlement issue" was certainly an early focus for us at the start of just about every diplomatic meeting I had with all countries interested in the Israeli-Palestinian conflict, and there were so many of those meetings. It was always in the top three items people would raise, often the first item. I was well aware that, in both political and practical terms, there had long been a strong pro-settlement constituency within Israel, one that, as prime minister, Netanyahu simply couldn't afford to ignore even if he wanted to, and he didn't want to. As he looked at the issue from a strategic perspective, Netanyahu believed Israeli settlements had actually been an inducement for the Palestinian leadership to, at least, come to the negotiating table, if not actually sign a deal. The settlements were also essential to his own domestic political viability and they were likewise leverage, politically and practically, with the Palestinian leadership. It was a political dynamic that Netanyahu had used, certainly—some said abused—but it was not as if he had invented the idea of settlements himself. For all the consternation their construction had caused the Palestinians, they were an authentic and organic expression of Israelis' understandable defiance in the face of their enemies that long predated Netanyahu's appearance on the political scene.

Even if Netanyahu had not been pro-settlement, it was not as if the settlements would, somehow, simply disappear into the ether if he were not prime minister. In politics, as in life, context is everything. Although the media, particularly in America and Europe, had made much of Netanyahu's recent announcement that an entirely new settlement would be built in the West Bank—the first in more than two decades—what was widely portrayed as a tone deaf and belligerently provocative act had actually come after a decision by Israel's Supreme Court that declared the settlement outpost of Amona illegal, and subsequently ordered its evacuation. In Israel, the images of hundreds of Israeli soldiers and local police forcefully evicting approximately two thousand people from their homes had filled television screens. For many of Netanyahu's core supporters, the "new" settlement he had announced with such fanfare seemed more like a belated appeasement for the loss of Amona than it did a bold advance in settlement construction.

The evacuation of Amona was, in many ways, the least of Netanyahu's problems. By the time I had arrived in Israel, media reports of the past weekend's telephone call between President Trump and President Abbas were percolating through the press. The call, initiated by President Trump, was the first personal contact between the two men—and the brew that resulted had a bitter taste for the entire Israeli right. A columnist for the liberal newspaper, *Haaretz*, the oldest continuously published newspaper in Israel, seemed to sum it up quite nicely in an ominous prediction that America's new president "could turn out to be the Israeli right wing's worst nightmare." How wrong they turned out to be. It sometimes seems to me that the principal exercise some people get is in jumping to conclusions—and false conclusions at that.

There was endless speculation that Trump, like so many presidents before him, was getting "cold feet" on moving the US embassy from Tel Aviv to Jerusalem, a promise that he had made more than once during the campaign the previous year. And why wouldn't he? As all the "experts" helpfully pointed out, such a move was outrageous on its face and would set the entire Muslim world on fire. The fact that Trump hadn't announced the move on Day 1 of his presidency seemed to attest to his change of heart on the matter. Similarly, in February, when Prime Minister Netanyahu visited the White House, many in the media had a collective case of the vapors after hearing the President's response about a "two-state solution" when he said, "I'm looking at two-state and one-state (solutions) and I like the one that both parties like....I can live with either one."

This, the "experts" said, was simply unconscionable. It seemed to casually disregard what all the "experts" had agreed was the "right side" of history. A two-state solution was the only morally right answer. The universe bent toward justice, and it was Israel's duty to bend with it—or else. Surely, even this New York neophyte had, by now, realized the considerable consternation he had caused among many in Europe and the Arab world. It was unthinkable that this new US leader would upend the old verities of a peace process and the two-state solution it embodied. Candidates for president often said improvident, even ridiculous things in the heat of a campaign—but they never, ever carried through on them. Similarly, a new administration, particularly one as untutored as Trump and his team, were bound to make a few early mistakes. But their "friends" in Europe, who were wiser about such things, would set them straight. And of course, the establishment media were there as well to both catalog and correct any mistakes they might make along the way. Besides, it had already been widely reported that the new CIA chief, Mike Pompeo, had met with President Abbas and other top officials in Ramallah, and the Palestinian leadership had supposedly opened Pompeo's eyes to a stark reality: disaster on an unimaginable scale would result if the Israeli-Palestinian peace process were to fail. It was a two-state solution or the apocalypse. So, no pressure here.

There were also rampant rumors that on his phone call with Abbas, President Trump had walked back his earlier equivocation and was now decidedly committed to a "two-state solution." Furthermore, several media reports openly speculated that, Trump being the deal maker that he was, would be less interested in Netanyahu's political future than his own bragging rights. If settlements were the obstacle to a Nobel Peace Prize, then the settlements would have to go. While this made for a compelling narrative, anyone who had known Donald Trump for as long as I had realized instinctively that that wasn't how he thought. To put it bluntly, if the only way we could achieve a deal between a longtime and cherished ally like Israel and the Palestinian leadership was to double-cross that ally, Trump wouldn't do it. He wouldn't have put his own son-in-law, and two people close to him—David Friedman and me—in charge of the file if that were his intention. When he had tweeted out his encouragement to Israel that "help was on the way" after the UN vote that condemned Israel's settlements, he meant it. That wasn't to say he wouldn't push and probe both Netanyahu and Abbas to gauge how committed they might be to this or that bargaining position. But he was in no doubt about what he wanted to achieve, which was, above all else, an Israeli people, secure from harm. A peace agreement was, after all, only a piece of paper. It was a promise—and promises could be broken.

Unlike so many before him, Donald Trump didn't want a "peace deal" for the sake of making a deal. He had a far bigger ambition. In the plan he and our team envisioned, "peace" wouldn't be the principal goal, but merely the byproduct of a deeper and more durable agreement between two peoples, two partners. And if one of those partners—the Palestinian leadership—refused to negotiate, as indeed they had so many times before, there were other possible partners out there as well. To be sure, the conventional wisdom was that a successful conclusion to the Israeli-Palestinian conflict was the necessary predicate for any other putative partnerships between Israel and other countries in the region. But that advice was beginning to prove more conventional than wise. Netanyahu had been discreetly making just such outreaches with several Sunni states for some time now. Our team sensed that the ground was beginning to shift in this regard. A satisfactory resolution to what was known as Israel's "occupation" was still the first thing mentioned in practically any diplomatic meeting between our team and other countries in the Middle East. But raising the issue was beginning to seem more procedural than substantive, more perfunctory than passionate. It was, to put it mildly, an odd turn of affairs. In a region that was often plagued by intramural strife of one sort or the other, the "Palestinian cause" had long been one of the exceedingly rare things that all Arab countries could always agree on. The sympathy for Palestinian Statehood was steadfast, the opposition against Israel a grievance shared. But, increasingly, that quest had seemed to become, with each passing year, more and more remote, even quixotic. Focusing on the Palestinian cause meant not focusing on the internal and external problems with which these other Arab states increasingly also had to contend. They were still compassionate about the plight of individual Palestinians, but compassion fatigue, or at least a sort of fatalism, had begun to take hold where the larger Palestinian cause was concerned.

Ironically, the decades-long prominence of the "peace process" that had depended so much on public relations and slogans, rather than sustained and serious negotiations, had become little more than a tired slogan itself. Much like a fading bumper sticker from an old election campaign, it advertised a previous political allegiance that no longer had a compelling hold on the passions of a former era. What had, at first, been authentic commitment to a cause, had turned, over time, to weariness, and the weariness to apathy and even annoyance. After so many years, so much attention, and so much money spent, nothing had changed or seemed at all likely to change. At the same time, a new adversary, Iran, was on the march, but the Palestinian leadership's old campaign against Israel kept eating up all the oxygen in the room. In a curious, but altogether and completely understandable way, the "problem" many of these Sunni countries had now was how to pivot politically from the myopic focus on the Israeli-Palestinian conflict to a far more concerning menace. They may not have exactly been looking for a way out of the former conflict, but they certainly wanted a way forward, and that meant forging some sort of arrangement with Israel against the common foe they faced together.

This sea change in attitudes was an opening for our team, but we didn't consider it a binary thing. It certainly didn't mean that we were going to abandon our work on solving the Israeli-Palestinian conflict, which we were fully committed to. But it did give us another tactical tool that we sensed might prove helpful. It didn't make sense to us that the conflict between the Israelis and the Palestinian leadership should be considered in isolation as it had so far. If we could move on two simultaneous and parallel political tracks to craft a satisfactory agreement between Israel and the Palestinian leadership *and* pursue agreements between Israel and its key Arab neighbors at the same time (with or without the Palestinians), that would be a proverbial game-changer.

Could dozens of different things go wrong? Of course. But then it wasn't as if there were some halcyon period in the region that had somehow been lost or mislaid. We already knew what the past was like, and it wasn't idyllic and peaceful. This so-called "outside-in" strategy of attempting to enlist Arab leaders to sit down together with Israel's then-Prime Minister, Yitzhak Shamir, had been tried before by President George H.W. Bush's Secretary of State, James Baker. President George W. Bush had made a similar attempt to convene an Arab summit in 2007. One of my predecessors, President Obama's first special envoy, George Mitchell, had similarly tried to persuade other key Arab nations to be partners for peace. Unfortunately, none of these efforts bore fruit. Nevertheless, we still believed that the idea was a good one, but that the timing had not been right before.

Since those previous attempts, we thought, some key changes had occurred. Chief among these was the threat posed by Iran. As a consequence, Israel and the Sunni Arab nations had become closer under the age-old dictum: "The enemy of my enemy is my friend." Prime Minister Netanyahu had already been pursuing a de facto "outside-in" strategy, albeit largely under the radar. His hope coincided with ours, that Iran's hegemonic ambitions had altered the political calculus in the region. As well, many of these Arab countries wanted to focus more on their own countries' futures beyond oil. Like us, he had concluded some time ago that the "inside-out" strategy of solely pursuing a separate agreement with the Palestinian leadership had hit a dead end. He was hopeful that if enough Arab countries could be enlisted in a common effort to confront Iran, that coalition could also be helpful in solving Israel's long-standing conflict with the Palestinians as well. And if the Palestinians didn't want to participate, that was their choice. Maybe they no longer had the power and sway over the Arabs they used to have.

On our side, we were already beginning to reach out to several key leaders in the region, among them President Abdel Fattah al-Sisi of Egypt, Saudi Arabia's King Salman, and the Crown Prince, Mohammed bin Salman, Sheikh Mohammed bin Zayed al-Nahyan, the crown prince of Abu Dhabi in the United Arab Emirates, King Abdullah II of Jordan, and the Emir of Qatar, among others. The hope here was that if we could obtain some indication, particularly of a public nature, that they were supportive, that could encourage both the Israelis and the Palestinian leadership to agree to a plan that they might otherwise not be able to do just by themselves. It was a major investment in time, particularly for our team, but we felt the potential payoff was well worth the effort.

As I left the prime minister's office, I felt a sense of promise. I could feel a new sense of direction in the Middle East. Part of it was, frankly, negative—a common fear of a rogue Iran—but another part of it was simply the positive presence of Donald Trump on the scene. Certainly, his reputation as a superb negotiator, as someone able to accomplish big things that others couldn't, had preceded him. Doors were opening that hadn't been opened before. Attitudes were changing.

When President Trump said he was going to do something, people believed it. And it gave them hope. I was also extremely impressed with Netanyahu and was optimistic that he was ready to commit to a real negotiation.

I knew I did not have the experience of the dozens of diplomats who had worked this region before me, but perhaps that very lack of experience was, somehow, an advantage. Like Trump, I might lack political polish, and I certainly didn't have slick, prepackaged answers or certainty of my opinions. What I did have was a genuine desire to listen and understand the issues. I didn't think that just because I represented the United States that I could run roughshod over people and enforce my will.

I pledged to Netanyahu that we in the Trump administration would do our part, which we regarded as providing recommendations and proposals for the consideration of both sides. I think he also knew that we could be counted upon not to leak or otherwise talk out of school. While we wanted to help, I told him, the burden would still be on Israel and the Palestinian leadership to do the heavy lifting. We were here to counsel, not coerce. I certainly wanted to see a peaceful resolution to this seemingly intractable problem, but I also knew that my wanting it wouldn't make it happen if the two parties to this conflict didn't want it more.

Today had been a good beginning, I thought. I was determined not to let this beginning become an end.

CHAPTER 7

A Rendezvous in Ramallah

MARCH 14, 2017

I had left the King David Hotel that morning for a windshield tour of East Jerusalem and the Ramallah-area West Bank "tension points" with Consul General Don Blome and US Army Lieutenant General Frederick S. "Rudy" Rudesheim, who was then serving as the US Security Coordinator for Israel and the Palestinian Authority in Jerusalem. Along the way, we went through Qalandia, a military checkpoint through which several thousand Palestinians had to pass each day to access work in Israel. This checkpoint, which has now been replaced by a modern, comfortable, and far more efficient one, then consisted of three narrow metal cage-like walkways through which Palestinians needed to pass before reaching one of five checking stations, where they then had to go through metal detectors and manually present their permits to soldiers. What I observed that day was concerning to me. The whole process was needlessly and excessively slow, cumbersome, and irritating, to say the least. At the same time, I certainly understood the reason for it, and the critical need for Israel to be safe and secure. Israel was aware of the problem and was already planning to address it before my tour, but I certainly encouraged them to make it a priority, and they did. I'm happy to report that what at that time took Palestinians approximately an hour to navigate, today takes only a few minutes. In my opinion, it was a long-overdue and welcome improvement.

Qalandia is also the name of a nearby Palestinian refugee camp, established by UNRWA, the United Nations Relief and Works Agency. Established in 1949 by the UN General Assembly, UNRWA provides relief to those it labels "Palestinian refugees" resulting from what Israelis call the War of Independence and which Arabs call the "Nakba" or "The Disaster," and for the Palestinians, it was indeed that. On November 29, 1947, the United Nations had voted to divide what was then called "Mandatory Palestine" into separate Jewish and Arab sovereign states, with Jerusalem being designated as a shared "international" city.

I hasten to add here that the term "Mandatory Palestine" is not the same thing as the "State of Palestine" that Palestinians seek and some countries recognize. America is not among them. The Palestinian leadership often uses this as propaganda to suggest that there was a State of Palestine all along, but this is not the case. Mandatory Palestine was an area in southern Syria, in which nearly two dozen different ethnic peoples lived.

But none of them were identified or identified themselves as "Palestinians."

While the Jewish leadership accepted the partition plan, Arab leaders of those who lived in Mandatory Palestine, as well as a coalition of the Arab states, unanimously opposed it. What the Arab world originally envisioned as an easy victory over an upstart nation turned, instead, into a bitter and humiliating defeat. The 1947–1949 war ended with the territory of Mandatory Palestine divided among the new State of Israel, the Hashemite Kingdom of Jordan, which annexed territory on the West Bank of the Jordan River, and Egypt, which established something called the "All Palestine Protectorate" in the Gaza Strip. This would mark the beginning of a refugee crisis for the Arabs who lived in the area that only became worse after a second such war in 1967, in which Israel again prevailed against Egypt, Syria, and Jordan. It seemed almost unbelievable that "refugees" from events that occurred a half-century ago in 1967, much less those from seventy years ago, still exist in what seemed to be a permanently impermanent environment.

Although precise numbers are hard to come by, most historians agree that somewhere between 250,000 to 300,000 Arabs fled or were expelled during the war in Mandatory Palestine between 1947 and 1948. The Arab exodus in 1967 is estimated at between 280,000 to 325,000 out of the territories captured by Israel during, and in the aftermath of, the Six-Day War. Of these, however, an estimated 145,000 were earlier refugees from the 1948 War.

By December 1967, approximately 245,000 had fled from the West Bank and Gaza Strip into Jordan, while approximately 11,000 had fled from the Gaza Strip into Egypt. It's estimated that 116,000 Arabs and Syrians fled from the Golan Heights further into Syria. That's certainly a large number of people. And yet, in 1945, almost one million Jews lived outside of what is now Israel in the greater Arab world of that period. Today, there are only about 4,500 Jews in Arab countries who live outside of Israel, the vast majority of whom reside in Morocco. It wasn't the lure of Zionism that caused them to leave. It was, instead, plain, old-fashioned anti-Semitism of the type almost exclusively associated with Russia and Europe. The majority of the Jewish population fled, rather than stay and let themselves be murdered. In doing so, most were required to relinquish their citizenship, after which their property was routinely plundered by local authorities. But *this* Jewish refugee crisis has all but disappeared from the pages of history. What *does* survive is a curious devotion to maintaining, and even expanding, the group of individuals identified as "Palestinian refugees."

UNRWA was founded in 1949 for "Palestine refugees," not "Palestinian" refugees—an important distinction, since the name "Palestinian" came into use later. UNRWA has a mission that is unique in history: to identify not only the original "Palestine refugees" from 1948, but to perpetually extend that same refugee status to their children and their children's children, into perpetuity. Originally, "Palestine refugees" were "people whose normal place of residence was Palestine between June 1946 and May 1948, who lost both their homes and means of livelihood as a result of the 1948 Arab-Israeli conflict."

UNRWA estimates that this original group of refugees numbered 750,000, which would seem, itself, a substantial exaggeration, but let's accept that estimate at face value. Unless that original group of 750,000 were mostly infants or toddlers, most would obviously have already died in what has now been more than seventy years. But thanks to UNRWA's ever-expanding definition of what constitutes a "Palestine refugee," that number has actually grown—a lot. As of 2019, 5.6 million Palestinians were registered with UNRWA as refugees. That's because UNRWA has continued the refugee status of any refugee who subsequently became a citizen elsewhere.

But wait, that's not all. In addition, it granted refugee status to "descendants of Palestine refugee males, including legally adopted children." UNRWA has also added to its ever-expanding Palestine refugee population those from the 1967 Six-Day War. To top it all off, UNRWA considers many in the Gaza Strip and in the West Bank as "refugees" too. There is also talk of adding any descendant of a refugee female to that figure as well in the name of gender equality. Grossly inflated as these current figures obviously are, some at UNRWA have calculated that even the jaw-dropping 5.6 million number only represents about half of all who might ultimately be eligible for "Palestine refugee" status. That's 11.2 million people—a figure that is completely untethered from reality. To put that in context, the entire population of Israel is, at present, just 9.2 million. Obviously, if all these "Palestine refugees" were actually allowed a "right to return," Israel, in its current form, would simply cease to exist. The whole idea of an infinitely expanding "refugee" population, infinitely expanding into the future, is absolutely absurd. Nowhere else in the entire world are there people who were displaced by World War II-era conflicts, who are still considered "refugees"—much less their children, grandchildren, or even great grandchildren. That UNRWA continues to foster such a fiction with respect to "Palestine refugees" is not merely delusional but dangerous. It raises false hopes among millions of Palestinians for a future "right of return" that is a chimera—and a deeply cynical one at that.

This is scarcely some academic abstraction for me. My own mother and father were refugees from Hungary, who escaped to America with little more than the clothes on their back. I grew up hearing their stories as a child, and those stories are now a cherished part of our family lore. But those stories are only that—stories. They are an oral history, not a real estate contract. We cannot go, key in hand, and once again unlock the doors to those long-lost homes as though we had returned from some extended trip. They are not some never-ending, living legacy that I or my children seriously believe the Hungarian government of today has an obligation to return to us. And even if we did, that door—and millions of doors just like it all over the world over—closed long,

long ago. There are no permanent UN Relief Agencies set up to make *Jewish* refugees whole again, whether they hail from the Middle East or Hungary, or indeed, anyplace else.

War is a terrible and destructive thing in which property and lives are lost and destroyed. The Jewish people know this better than anyone. These wars wreak havoc on all our carefully laid plans, with the result that nothing is ever quite the same again. Homes are abandoned or destroyed—and the people who once inhabited them are often hurled, like leaves in the wind—to another place, another adopted home. Such was the case for my parents. Such is the case for tens of millions of others around the world. Such has been the case throughout the history of man's journey on this planet. So many of us are refugees, or the sons and grandsons and the daughters and granddaughters of refugees. Should all of these people and their descendants forever identify as refugees, martyrs to some distant moment in time? Qalandia was one of those places. But there were many others here just like it. All of them seemed to be stuck in a time warp, where lives were lived in an everlasting limbo, where nothing had changed or even *could* change.

Only a short time later, in what was a complete contrast to the somewhat bleak Qalandia checkpoint, I had a wonderful meeting with some young Palestinian entrepreneurs in Al Masyoun, an upscale neighborhood in Ramallah, which boasted modern condos and upscale stores and restaurants that would not have been out of place in any mid-sized American or European city. It was encouraging to hear that many of them had benefited directly from American aid programs to jumpstart their businesses. I thought to myself that Donald Trump would have responded well to this group of budding business tycoons. Their dreams for a better, brighter future for themselves, and for a future Palestinian State, were an inspiring contrast to what I had seen earlier that morning.

Ramallah, a Palestinian city in the central West Bank, about six miles from Jerusalem, is an Arabic word that literally means "G-d's Height"—and at an average elevation of nearly 2,900 feet above sea level—it is certainly aptly named. It is from this airy perch that President Mahmoud Abbas's "Muqata"—an Arabic word for headquarters—is located. Like others of its kind, this Muqata had been one of the Tegart Forts, so named after their designer, a British police officer and engineer, Sir Charles Tegart. They were impressive, high-walled, and easily defended militarized police outposts, constructed as a defensive measure to house top administrative staff throughout the British Mandatory period. After the British left, the buildings remained. This one had functioned as the administrative hub of the Palestinian National Authority since 1996, when Abbas's flamboyant predecessor, Yasser Arafat, was its president. When Arafat died in November 2004, the Palestinian leadership wanted him to be buried in the Dome of the Rock compound on the Temple Mount in Israel, but then-Israeli Prime Minister Ariel Sharon had refused the request. Today, as if to remind visitors of his continued spiritual presence, a large tomb, designed by Palestinian architects and clad in Jerusalem stone, majestically presides over the entrance to the Muqata. A message on the mausoleum optimistically states that the final resting place of Arafat shall be in Jerusalem if it comes under Palestinian control.

President Abbas might have been Yasser Arafat's one-time disciple and successor, but he was a world away from that diminutive man with the outsized ego and his distinctive, revolutionary air: the scruffy beard and wrinkled military fatigues, all topped off by a fishnet pattern keffiyeh, arranged to resemble the outlines of what was presumably an historic Palestine, which of course, was propaganda, not history.

A man who had infamously appeared before the UN General Assembly in November 1974, wearing a pistol which he reluctantly removed mere moments before mounting the rostrum, declared, "Today, I have come bearing an olive branch and a freedom-fighter's gun. Do not let the olive branch fall from my hand. I repeat: do not let the olive branch fall from my hand." That the UN General Assembly interrupted his "olive branch and gun" speech with nine standing ovations tells you a lot about the moral discernment of that body as well. Suffice it to say, despite the Nobel Peace Prize he shared in 1994 with Israeli Prime Ministers Shimon Peres and Yitzhak Rabin, I considered Yasser Arafat an unabashed thug and killer, responsible for the cold-blooded murder of so many Israelis.

But here, standing before me now, was definitely no terrorist, but what many in international diplomatic circles would view as the very model of a statesman—a genial figure in a tailored, dark blue suit and gold-rimmed glasses that framed warm, chestnut-colored eyes. His neatly trimmed white moustache and equally white hair gave him an almost grandfatherly air.

I wasn't quite sure what sort of reception I would receive from President Abbas. But then, he probably had similar apprehensions about this Orthodox Jew and ardent supporter of Israel, who was now the new envoy from Washington. I think we were both pleasantly surprised with one another.

Beyond his outward appearance, my second surprise about Abbas was not what I *saw*, but rather what I *didn't*. According to many reports, President Abbas was a heavy smoker—at least two packs a day—and yet there were no cigarettes on the table between us, although I did observe a sparkling crystal ashtray, but without a trace of ash in it. As it turns out, Abbas was trying his best to be polite in my presence and refrained for more than an hour before finally succumbing to his habit, drawing an electronic cigarette from his pocket, which he began puffing on contentedly.

As with Prime Minister Netanyahu, I was conscious of proceeding slowly in this initial meeting, rather than launching into debate. I wanted to engage in dialogue when the opportunity presented itself. But mostly, I was listening intently and trying to gauge what issues were most important to President Abbas. As with Netanyahu, there were the vocationally cheerful expressions from both of us about future prospects for peace. President Abbas, who had received a phone call from President Trump only a few days before, inviting him to the White House for a personal one-on-one meeting, was in seemingly high spirits. He was evidently buoyed by that conversation. And he obviously had grasped the political significance of Trump's victory and what it could mean to restarting a genuine dialogue between himself and Prime Minister Netanyahu.

After eight years of a Democratic administration that had, according to Abbas, failed to deliver on repeated promises of a peace deal, he was optimistic that a Republican president, especially *this* Republican president, could deliver the goods. Under President Trump's leadership, Abbas said, he was encouraged that a peace deal of historic dimensions could be possible, one that would give the Palestinian people what they had long sought, while in theory giving Israel the safety and security that they insisted on. He was very much looking forward to discussing the parameters of that peace plan directly with the president. For my part, I told him that President Trump and our team were committed to working honestly and openly with both parties to produce an agreement that might finally put an end to this long-running conflict.

It felt to me that we were planting the seeds of something important here, carefully nurturing a vision that might produce a result that both the Israelis and the Palestinians could, quite literally, live with. I knew of course that I was barely scratching the surface in this meeting and that a lot of hard work and serious, hard compromises by both parties would have to be made. Dreams, as always, come easily and without effort. Reality, on the other hand, is a stern and unforgiving taskmaster. In the weeks and months ahead, I would come to know President Abbas quite well, as I would his chief aide, Saeb Erekat, the Secretary General of the PLO executive committee. Like me, Erekat was a fellow lawyer, and I was to discover that he had an almost eerie, encyclopedic knowledge of the various peace negotiations over the years, combined with a memory for obscure facts and details that would put a herd of elephants to shame.

For President Abbas, like his Israeli counterpart, Bibi Netanyahu, the Israeli-Palestinian conflict was not a political theory, but an integral part of a life lived. He had been born in Safed, a beautiful mountain community which has the distinction of being the highest city, not only in Galilee, but in all of Israel. Abbas was an impressionable thirteen-year-old when he fled from Safed with his family to Syria during the 1948 Arab-Israeli war. Despite the fact that his life had been turned upside down, he went on to earn a law degree from the University of Damascus before eventually becoming involved with Fatah, a group Arafat had cofounded. That group had taken a page out of Ho Chi Minh's North

Vietnamese playbook using an old technique, that of guerilla warfare, hitched to a nationalist crusade, that sought a new, sovereign Palestinian State. Famous as "Mr. Palestine," the ubiquitous face and voice of the Palestinian people, the essential problem with Arafat, it seemed to me, was that he was never able to move beyond his terrorist roots to actually do something constructive, to actually lay the practical foundations of a functioning Palestinian State. Was his successor any different? I hoped so, but I wasn't sure.

I knew that within Fatahs' ranks, Abbas had been more of a facilitator than a fighter. He had been the PLO's point man in developing contacts with Israeli peace groups who were sympathetic to the Palestinian cause. I also knew about his deeply troubling dissertation on Zionism and Nazism, for which he was awarded a doctorate in history from the Institute of Oriental Studies in Moscow in 1982. He would later try to smooth over some of the most disturbing assertions contained in it with western journalists in what ultimately became a published book on the subject, *The Other Side: The Secret Relationship Between Nazism and Zionism*, but Abbas had never retracted a single syllable of its overall conclusion. It remained, unaltered, on President Abbas' website—albeit in Arabic, not in English. Here's a small taste of it:

> Zionism adopted the Nazi selection principle, when it went to save Jews from the slaughter. It made itself the ultimate arbiter regarding Jewish

life, deciding who deserves to live and who deserves to die.

The Zionist movement did not make any effort to convince Western countries to take in the Jewish refugees escaping the horrors of the Holocaust. It even placed obstacles in the way of efforts made by Christian groups or by non-Zionist Jews or a number of countries that saw fit to find a solution to this humanitarian problem.

All of this wasn't enough – the Zionist movement led a broad campaign of incitement against the Jews living under Nazi rule to arouse the government's hatred of them, to fuel vengeance against them and to expand the mass extermination.

Although the arguments contained in Abbas' book are couched in a seemingly clinical academese, it bears a nauseating familiarity with the infamous *Protocols of the Elders of Zion*, a fabricated anti-Semitic text that purports to describe a nefarious Jewish plan for global domination. The latter was a favorite textbook, pushed on German schoolchildren after the Nazis came to power in the early 1930s. Had Abbas's book existed at the time, I have no doubt it would have been a standard part of the curriculum.

Side by side with Abbas's truly disgusting private view of the movement that had created Israel was the knowledge that he had also been instrumental in shaping the Palestinian side in negotiations both at the Madrid Peace

Conference in 1991 and in the far more secretive meetings between the Palestinian leadership and the Israelis in Norway that resulted in the Oslo Accords, an important (though ultimately considered a failure by both sides) interim step in the peace process, as well as the Camp David talks in 2000. He made sure he was on the record as being opposed to the violence as expressed in the various "intifadas" of his more militant fellow-travelers such as Hamas, arguing that they were an impediment to the peace process. Indeed, he had been, for a time, a favorite of both the United States and Israel, and preferred over Arafat as a more reliable negotiating partner in the peace process. Installed as the Palestinian prime minister, he had publicly denounced terrorism and talked of forming a single, Palestinian armed force that would bring an overdue and steady hand in securing and stabilizing the sovereign state he hoped to bring into existence. But it was not to be. He soon resigned from office, complaining that he had been undermined by everyone—the Israelis, the Americans, and Arafat as well. As it turned out, however, his was only a temporary farewell. Arafat would mysteriously sicken not long afterwards and ultimately die in a French hospital. Abbas seemed to be the only logical heir apparent. He was soon back, and soon more powerful than he had ever been before.

Now eighty-two, but still looking vigorous despite health challenges from time to time, President Abbas—like Prime Minister Netanyahu—had extraordinary intramural political challenges that had nothing to do with his rival or their long-running rivalry with one another. After first being democratically elected after Arafat's death to a four-year term, Abbas had canceled the next election on a flimsy pretext and was now on his fourteenth year as a leader who ruled by diktat, by turns ignoring or silencing his critics and continuing to lead through the logic of his own self-declared legitimacy. Although he still had a certain political currency in the West Bank, where he could easily silence any nascent opposition, he was openly reviled in the Hamas-led Gaza Strip. They portrayed him as a weak, temporizing old man who wanted his own creature comforts more than he wanted a proud, Palestinian State. His inability to bring that terrorist group to heel was a constant source of aggravation and anxiety for him. As much as he had fought with Israel over the years, that other, intramural power struggle between himself and Hamas seemed, all too frequently, more intense, more *personal*. He *was* like Arafat in that way, I thought; he might be carried out of office, but he would not be voted out. As long as he could keep a firm grip on the levers of power within the Palestinian Authority, he would be sitting here in this office, just as he was today, proud and defiant to the end.

As I sat listening to the Palestinian president in the office of his Muqata, I heard what I hoped was Abbas's genuine interest in, and commitment to, peace. I had sensed a similar impulse in Netanyahu the day before. I was aware that both men had been here so many times before. They had heard one another's arguments until each of them had literally memorized the other's talking points. Both were understandably wary and not a little weary. Both felt they had endured unendurable slights from the other side. And yet, neither man had made a single personal or disparaging remark about the other, at least not in my presence. True, they fundamentally disagreed on practically every issue, but there was nothing that either man said that smacked of personal animus against the other. This, in itself, seemed to me a good sign. There was very little faith that the other leader would actually make the hard choices required to make peace between them, but there yet remained a whisper of willingness to engage in the attempt.

For me, one of the most important takeaways in these initial meetings with Netanyahu and Abbas was that both seemed actually happy to see me. That wasn't due to my sparkling personality, of course, or my skill as a diplomat. It was really all about President Trump. For Prime Minister Netanyahu, it was an obvious relief to finally have a partner again, rather than an opponent. In Trump, Netanyahu saw a leader and a team who really understood Israel's story and its challenges. For President Abbas, it was that Friday phone call from Trump, himself, and hearing the president say he was committed to providing both sides with a fair and acceptable solution.

That all of this was still a gigantic gamble for everyone involved was unspoken but nevertheless obvious and true.

President Abbas had already experienced the satisfaction of watching the Israelis being humiliated by the former Obama administration at the United Nations late last year. But that was a temporary and a purely political victory only, though the Palestinians did not see it that way. A United Nations vote condemning Israel—or a thousand of them—wouldn't make nearly a half-million Jewish settlers suddenly vanish from the West Bank or give him East Jerusalem as a capital of the sovereign State of Palestine.

For Prime Minister Netanyahu, the stakes were high as well. He had famously clashed with two previous Democratic Party presidents, Clinton and Obama. If he couldn't conclude a deal favorable to Israel from a Republican president—one he had already extravagantly praised as a "friend"—it might cause other headaches for him.

And there was danger as well for our team, and for Trump, himself, if this effort failed. The president's surprise victory had unleashed a fury on the Democratic side that only seemed to build by the hour. There were already rumblings about the Trump campaign's supposed collusion with Russia and other similarly lurid and ridiculous rumors. Earlier that month, Attorney General Jeff Sessions, who had served as a top national security adviser to the campaign, officially recused himself from any campaign-related investigations. It was less than two months since the inauguration, and it already seemed as if the entire Trump White House was under a gigantic electron-scanning microscope.

I was becoming ever more conscious that our team was working in an entirely new atmosphere, both at home and abroad. Gone were the days when Democrats and Republicans commonly agreed that they should, and would, work together to support and promote a solid relationship between ourselves and Israel. It was as if the old, familiar agreement about politics ending at the water's edge was no longer valid if disregarding it served an expedient partisan purpose back home. Criticizing Israel had become a political shorthand for criticizing President Trump. Consequently, a diplomatic stumble in what had been one of the most closely watched and widely reported conflicts in the world would be used to portray Jared, David, and me as a latter-day version of the Three Stooges, and Trump, himself, as both feckless and reckless. Not that there was anything resembling the usual respect for the president or for our team and its efforts to begin with. Indeed, with a few notable exceptions, the national media's disdain for the entire administration was so commonplace that it no longer registered as bias.

The greater issue here was not just about political optics and personal reputations. We were all engaged in an effort that could calm, or incalculably inflame, conditions in the Middle East. This at a time when a foe common to all of us—Iran—was silently waiting and watching and mulling over its next moves.

Almost all the foreign policy experts were united in the opinion that the conflict between Israel and the Palestinians had to be solved before any other diplomatic opening between Israel and its other Arab neighbors could even be contemplated. That was their view and they were certainly entitled to it. But if putting the Israeli-Palestinian conflict front and center was the key to Middle East peace, why hadn't it already worked?

Of course, just because the "experts" had been wrong didn't necessarily mean that we were right. Indeed, I lived with the constant concern that we would fail, too. The concern wasn't about my reputation, or that of the team's or even that of the president. It was the concern that, if we failed, it might leave the Middle East a more dangerous place than when we arrived, and delay the day when the larger goal of confronting and containing the growing terror threat from Tehran could be achieved.

As Jared was so fond of observing, "The sands of the hourglass keep going down." Would they run out before our team had a chance to complete our work? Although these last two days had given me reason for optimism, I knew this political honeymoon wouldn't last forever. All too soon, we would have to begin speaking those hard truths upon which the future of negotiations between the Israelis and the Palestinians ultimately rested. We could be aspirational and constructively ambiguous, as previous administrations had been, but sooner or later the large differences in the political perspectives of Mahmoud Abbas and Bibi Netanyahu—and what was ultimately practical—would have to be dealt with.

CHAPTER 8

An Appointment at the Dead Sea

MARCH 23, 2017

With my initial positive talks with Israeli Prime Minister Netanyahu and Palestinian President Abbas behind me, a demanding schedule of meetings commenced. I was frequently on the road. Today, I was at the annual Arab League Summit in the Dead Sea region of Jordan, in the unofficial capacity of an observer. King Abdullah II, the summit's charming host, was scheduled to meet with President Trump the following week in Washington. Sophisticated, yet unpretentious, Abdullah II is the template for what a king should be. Like his late father, he has long been considered a voice of moderation and realism in a region that badly needed both. King Abdullah's devotion to the Palestinian cause was both deep and clear to me. Although I did not see eye to eye with him on this issue, I nevertheless was able to have a respectful dialogue with him.

The King of Jordan is also the proud owner of what has to be one of the most impressive collections of classic automobiles in the world—something my son, Noah, envied as only a then-teenager with a new driver's license could. "They all have to be driven, you know—to keep them in shape," the king once said after our family toured his museum of motor vehicles. It was a casual remark, but I could see that it had clearly sent Noah's hopes of getting behind the steering wheel of one of these mobile pieces of artwork soaring into the stratosphere. I assumed the king was joking, but in case he wasn't, I said, "I can see the headlines now: 'Trump Envoy for Peace's Son Crashes Car, Peace Over'"—a comment that made the king smile, but my son scowl. The king taught my kids an important lesson that day, one that I think encapsulates the essence of his character. "In the end, this is a hunk of metal. Most important is life, most important is respect," he said. Alas for Noah, he never did get the chance to demonstrate his driving skills with the Jordanian monarch's exquisite automobiles, but getting to know King Abdullah II was, and remains, one of the more pleasant and rewarding experiences I and my family had during my time as a White House envoy.

Aside from his steadfast advocacy for the Palestinian cause, King Abdullah had for some time been part of a US-led military coalition against the Islamic State Group, which controlled territory in neighboring Iraq and Syria. Those militants had made a series of recent attacks that posed both an internal and an external threat to his kingdom, and he was considered an exceedingly important—if not vital—partner in the fight against these extremists, a fight that was all too likely to increase in pace and intensity in the near future. That continuing struggle against ISIS was certainly a timely reminder—as if any were needed—that the long-running conflict between the Israelis and the Palestinian leadership was scarcely the only source of tension and violence in the region. Ironically, Israel has been a key ally of its Arab neighbors in working to defeat ISIS as well, particularly when it came to Israel's vast intelligence capabilities and its equally well-known capacity for successful covert operations.

In addition to King Abdullah, among those in attendance at the summit were the foreign ministers of Saudi Arabia, Qatar, the United Arab Emirates, Tunisia, Morocco, Jordan, and Algeria. This summit would give me an opportunity to have a follow-up meeting with President Abbas, and also his ever-present top aide, Saeb Erekat. The summit also provided a good opportunity for me, as President Trump's envoy, to have discreet, private discussions with these same Arab representatives as well. The hope was that I could informally engage them in dialogue, not only on the Israeli-Palestinian conflict, but also on a larger, regional rapprochement with Israel that we were envisioning. For Abbas, of course, the summit was his chance to confer directly with Egyptian President Abdel Fattah al-Sisi and King Abdullah II, and to plead his case for what he saw as his demands to resolve the Palestinians' long-running conflict with Israel. Although no one could know it then, this would mark the last time such a trilateral group meeting would occur during the Trump presidency.

What came out of this summit was, not surprisingly, a flashing yellow sign that the road ahead was going to be tough, despite the glimmer of hope created by my recent meetings with Abbas and Netanyahu. Side by side and consistent with my meetings at the Arab League Summit was the knowledge that previous peace negotiations had failed, and that the same yawning gaps on settlements, security, right of return, and the like had not been narrowed since the two sides met nearly a decade ago. The main difference now, at least so far, was an expressed interest on both sides to work with President Trump and our team to renew their attempts to bridge the chasm between them. Of course, issue-based differences in perspectives or judgments were one thing, and I certainly expected a different "take" on the Israeli-Palestinian conflict from this group than my own. But this was not merely a difference in perspective. It appeared to be—as so many times in the past—the same old stubborn refusal to face facts, especially as they were now, on the ground.

The Arab Peace Plan presented at this summit was essentially the same peace plan that the members had backed more than a decade before, in 2002. That deal had offered official recognition of Israel in exchange for Palestinian statehood, and a retreat by Israel back to its pre-Six-Day War borders, plus a recognition on Israel's part of East Jerusalem, including the Temple Mount/ Haram al Sharif, as Palestine's capital.

While I knew that any realistic peace proposal would require Israel to make some tough compromises on territory in order to give the Palestinians a viable state, this was deeply unserious. It seemed to ignore or gloss over many important facts. For starters, any withdrawal from land captured in a defensive war is practically without precedent. The desperate war of self-defense that Israel fought—and won—in 1967 was certainly a prime example of a defensive war and universally recognized as such by the world's democracies at that time.

Nevertheless, following the end of that war, Israel had given an important indication of the depth of its desire to negotiate a peaceful solution with its neighbors by deciding not to annex the West Bank or Gaza Strip. However, in August 1967, the Arab League, in their meeting at the Khartoum Summit famously issued their "Three no's"—No peace with Israel, No recognition of Israel, No negotiations with Israel. Israel's then-Foreign Minister Abba Eban said of the Arab response, "This is the first war in history which has ended with the victors suing for peace and the vanquished calling for unconditional surrender."

For the past fifty years, the United Nations Security Council Resolution 242 has been at the heart of the peace process between the Israelis and the Palestinian leadership. Important as that resolution is, it is perhaps the most misunderstood and misrepresented resolution in UN history.

The Palestinian leadership routinely depicts Resolution 242 as a document that calls for Israel's unilateral and complete withdrawal from all of the territories as a precondition for the start of negotiations. But that's not what Resolution 242 says. Rather, it calls upon Israel to withdraw "from territories" occupied in what was then the recently concluded 1967 War, not from "all" territories, or even from "the" territories. As then-US Ambassador Arthur Goldberg would explain, these omissions regarding territorial matters "were not accidental...the resolution speaks of withdrawal from occupied territories without defining the extent of the withdrawal."

The absence of these tiny words is hugely consequential. The obvious point here is that there never was a guiding definition from the United Nations about a precise amount of land, or some particular border that Israel was to withdraw from or recognize. In this instance, the UN recognized that any such withdrawal would naturally be within Israel's discretion to decide, and subject to conditions on the ground.

It's also vital to note here as well that Resolution 242 recognized the need—actually, the *right*—for Israel to have secure borders. At the time, it was apparent to the mind and eye that Israel's previous borders had been, for all intents and purposes, indefensible. As then-UK Ambassador Lord Caradon would observe, "It would have been wrong to demand that Israel return to its positions of June 4, 1967, because those positions were undesirable and artificial."

It's also worth mentioning that Resolution 242, as well as a later one, Resolution 338, adopted by the UN after the 1973 Yom Kippur War, had something to say about all sides in these conflicts, not just Israel. The UN Security Council placed several responsibilities and obligations on the Arab side as well. The UN didn't envision the Israeli withdrawal in isolation. It was to be simultaneously accompanied by a corresponding pledge from its neighbors to make peace with Israel and renounce further violence, something which had not been done. Here are some clauses from Resolution 242 that rarely, if ever, receive a public airing. These are clearly primarily aimed at the Arab states, which had initiated the hostilities in the first place, although they are expressed in the context of mutual responsibilities and obligations:

o "a just and lasting peace in which every State in the area can live in security;"

o "termination of all claims or states of belligerency;"

o "respect and acknowledgement of the sovereignty, territorial integrity and political independence of every State in the area;"

o respect and acknowledgement of "their right to live in peace within secure and recognized boundaries free from threats or acts of force;"

o "freedom of navigation through international waterways in the area;"

o "guaranteeing the territorial inviolability and political independence of every State in the area, through measures including the establishment of demilitarized zones."

The point here is that the UN Security Council never expected Israel to withdraw from any territory without the Arab countries making reciprocal moves as well. The resolution did not call on Israel to simply withdraw as a pre-condition to the *start* of negotiations, but as an integral *part* of them. Even so, by the time this book was being written, Israel has already withdrawn from a whopping 88 percent of the territory it had captured. Was Israel supposed to give the remaining 12 percent back as well, and then trust that peace would follow? Was it supposed to believe, against all experience, that Hamas—a brutal terrorist organization that had been the source of tens of thousands of rocket and mortar attacks killing countless Israelis—would suddenly renounce violence and start picking flowers?

If this "back to the future" proposal actually represented the Arab consensus on a "two-state solution," they were fifteen years too late to the party. True, at Camp David in 2000, then-Israeli Prime Minister Ehud Barak had offered Yasser Arafat a sovereign Palestinian State on the West Bank and Gaza as well as the division of Jerusalem, something which had never been offered by Israel before. But Yasser Arafat had refused to accept the deal. Arafat similarly refused an arguably even more generous deal the following year, the "Taba Plan," which took its name from the Egyptian town near the northern tip of the Gulf of Aqaba where the talks were held. That agreement included the creation of a Palestinian State on the West Bank and Gaza, a division of Jerusalem, and a compromise on the future of what was then 3.5 million "refugees." Again, Arafat walked away. That had been followed by the 2008 peace proposal from Israel which had offered Palestinian Statehood, the entirety of the West Bank, and all of the Muslim areas of Jerusalem designated as the capital of the new sovereign state. Plus, the cherry on top had been the offer to turn over all of Jerusalem's holy places, including the Western Wall, to an international governing board overseen by Jordan and Saudi Arabia. By that time, of course, Arafat was dead, but his successor, the now-current Palestinian Authority President, Mahmoud Abbas, had similarly walked away.

Since Prime Minister Netanyahu's election in 2009, there had been no serious Israeli-Palestinian leadership talks. And while Netanyahu had not formally rejected the principle of a two-state solution, he had certainly stopped talking about it, and it was well-known that most of his Cabinet members opposed the idea. For Israel, at this point, a two-state solution was no longer a given, as it had once been. As Netanyahu saw it, after so many olive branches from the Israeli side had been contemptuously rebuffed, it was time for the Palestinian side to make some serious concessions of their own.

As for Abbas, his position was that the people he represented had given up so much already that they had nothing left to give.

But apart from these well-known and opposing points of view, certainly one of the biggest stumbling blocks in all of this wasn't actually the much-celebrated conflict between Israel and the Palestinian Authority, but between the Palestinian Authority and Hamas, the terrorist group that ruled Gaza. A particularly ruthless and relentless foe, Hamas was devoted to the extermination of the Jewish State. They thought Abbas was a feeble old man and they had no respect for a leader who wouldn't lead a literal fight. As their all-too-frequent rocket and mortar attacks on Israel over the years plainly revealed, their goal was annihilation, not negotiation. As a practical matter, reaching a deal with Abbas was only half of the battle here, and the easier half at that. Any negotiating strategy that had the slightest chance of actually making it off the drawing board would involve, somehow, getting Hamas to renounce terror and make common cause with Abbas, so that a truly united Palestinian leadership, whether in the form of the Palestinian Liberation Organization or the Palestinian Authority, or even some newly created Palestinian body, could represent all Palestinians and their interests at the negotiating table.

It was in this decidedly chilly environment, then, that it seemed all the more remarkable that President Abbas—but more importantly, the other participants at the summit—believed they could now reach back and ask for the diplomatic version of what in golf is called a "mulligan," a "do-over" after a previous poor shot. But this plan was a mulligan multiplied. Could they really be serious about this?

Several times over, Israel had demonstrably offered a sovereign Palestinian State, including either much or all of the West Bank, with East Jerusalem as its capital—even an extraordinarily favorable consideration of the "right of return" of refugees—but the Palestinian leadership had not taken the offer, and Hamas continued to launch its rockets into Israeli towns and cities. How many times would Israel be asked to this diplomatic dance, with the same tired music playing in the background? How many bites of the proverbial apple did the Palestinian leadership get? Did they really believe that Prime Minister Netanyahu, or any Israeli prime minister, would agree, in 2017, to roll the clock back fifteen years? Would these gentlemen be willing to sell a barrel of oil at 2002 prices? Why not also demand to buy Amazon stock at the price it sold for when it was still just an online bookstore?

The world had moved on. Conditions had changed. Pretending they hadn't was a recipe for a rude awakening. Our team could assist in reviving peace efforts between the Israelis and the Palestinian leadership, but we didn't own a time machine. Unless this was merely an opening bluff, an attention-getter that would be quickly jettisoned for something more reasonable later on, this was clearly a nonstarter. It simply wasn't going to happen. Part of this was, no doubt, about political optics—a tactic by the Arab states to satisfy their respective peoples that they weren't "abandoning" the "Palestinian cause"—but another significant part of it seemed to stem from a calculation that Trump brought something new to the seemingly ceaseless cycle of negotiations. Many of these leaders were by now convinced that President Trump was in a unique position to squeeze historic concessions from Netanyahu, and that he would do so. However, the Israeli prime minister was similarly counting on the president to make the Arab countries do more than just talk a good game this time around, and actually take some active steps that they couldn't walk back later. Those two positions—and the outcomes they described—weren't necessarily mutually exclusive, but tone and timing could be as important here as the actual contents of a plan itself. The expectations on both the Israeli and Palestinian sides were sky-high. In an atmosphere where almost anything seemed possible to each side, would an expectation for political perfection be the enemy of the good?

I knew that Prime Minister Netanyahu was mindful that he needed to appear—and be—open to genuine, serious negotiations. He saw President Trump as someone who could completely alter the status quo, not only in the conflict between Israel and the Palestinian leadership, but in the entire Middle East. President Abbas appeared equally mindful that he had perhaps his last best chance to do something that his predecessor and mentor, Yasser Arafat, had been either unable or unwilling to accomplish: the creation of an independent Palestinian State. Both men were, in their way, born optimists, and each, consequently, thought he had a critical opportunity to win the day. If our team could craft the right plan, both could walk away with a victory worth claiming—but this wasn't it.

In the months ahead, I would continue to shuttle back and forth between Washington and meetings with Netanyahu in Jerusalem and Abbas in Ramallah several times, as well as meetings with others in the Middle East, from Bahrain to the United Arab Emirates, from Saudi Arabia to Qatar, and of course Jordan and Egypt. Our group was keenly aware that this period offered an historic chance to not only bring the Israeli-Palestinian leadership conflict to an end, but to open an era of unbridled prosperity for the Palestinian people themselves, something that was far beyond anything that had ever been contemplated in prior negotiations. But just as important, or perhaps even more so, it was a chance to recalibrate the geopolitical focus of the entire region. It was the opportunity for these states to seriously consider the possibility of a shared future that included Israel as a critical partner in their common progress.

Particularly in more recent years, the Middle East had been undergoing a profound transformation. The most forward-looking leaders were envisioning a transition away from an economy based exclusively on oil to one far more diversified and technologically advanced. And yet, for all its modernizing moves, this region continued to be stuck, in so many ways, in the same old paralyzing political paradigm, one that continued to revolve around a seemingly unresolvable conflict between the Palestinian leadership and Israel.

Mahmoud Abbas had seemed, at first, to offer a fresh start and a fresh perspective when he succeeded Yasser Arafat in 2004. Unlike his stridently militant predecessor, Abbas was moderate in mien and method. Professing to be a steadfast opponent of violence, he seemed to be the antithesis to Arafat's moody tantrums. But, in death, Arafat had assumed a political deification that still dictated Abbas' actions in the here and now. A dead man's decisions had, in effect, established political red lines that could not be crossed or erased by his successor. Among these were: all of Israel's settlements must be destroyed; all the land returned; all the accumulated refugees across seventy years, together with their children and grandchildren, would have a "right of return"; East Jerusalem would be the capital of Palestine—and those were just the preconditions for negotiations.

The result was that Abbas could not demand less than Arafat without seeming to be a traitor to the "Palestinian cause" to which he had pledged himself, something Hamas had been openly saying for years. At the same time, Abbas suffered by constant comparison to Arafat, for the simple reason that today's living reality would always place a distant second to his dead predecessor's dreams.

By 2017, Abbas's longtime Arab benefactors were still publicly supportive of the Palestinian president and the Authority he led—as the summit in Jordan was demonstrating—but behind the scenes, a different picture seemed to be emerging. Abbas and the "Palestinian cause" itself had become a diminished presence in a broader political discussion in the region. More and more, at least in private talks, Arab governments were mulling tentative ties to Israel. At the same time, they were beginning to seriously tire of being asked to fund what seemed, increasingly, a chronically corrupt, weak, and incompetent organization in Ramallah. What had once been seen as a shared symbol of pan-Arab aspiration was, more and more, viewed as a source of annoyance. An intransigence in negotiations with Israel that had once seemed heroically defiant was fast becoming an irritating inconvenience. Something had to change, and soon. Otherwise, we were all just the latest in a long line of people scratching meaningless words in the sand that the wind would wipe away.

The Middle East, I reflected, had been the scene of countless conflicts for as long as recorded history. It was also where the world's first peace treaty was drawn up in 1259 BC between Egyptian Pharaoh Ramses II (Ramses the Great) and Hattusilis III, King of the Hittites. Two copies of the treaty were made, one in hieroglyphics, the other in the Mesopotamian language of Akkadian. A clay replica of that agreement was now displayed in a place of prominence at the United Nations as an inspiration to its members. It was only after a last, brutal engagement known as the Battle of Kadesh that these two ancient foes would tire of fighting one another. The terms of the Kadesh Peace Treaty that followed were not agreed to until sixteen years later. Negotiations to end the Israeli-Palestinian conflict, meanwhile, were now in their seventh decade. That didn't seem to say much for the advancement of diplomacy over the last 3,276 years. Indeed, this was a land steeped in so much history and so many memories that it was easy to get lost in them. But history didn't have to be a circle made by people who were doomed to repeat their mistakes. While progress wasn't guaranteed, it was possible.

A half century ago, during a conference of Arab chiefs of state—much like this one in Khartoum—King Hussein of Jordan, Abdullah's late father, had addressed his Muslim brethren, saying, "We should face reality and our past mistakes in an honest, adult way. Boasting of glory does not make glory, and singing in the dark does not dispel fear."

King Hussein was right. And what he had said so long ago had renewed relevance today. If the assembled Arab leaders in this room had the courage to confront them and learn from them, the mistakes of the past could actually lead to a new understanding of the future and their part in it. History was a never-ending relay race from one generation to the next. Now it was their turn—and ours—to grasp that baton and run with it, to push history, itself, forward. It was time to disrupt the status quo and shake things up. It was time to start thinking about the future, rather than endlessly revisiting the past. It was time, in short, for President Trump himself to come to the Middle East.

Two months later, almost to the day from the date of this conference in Jordan, he would do just that. It would be his first international trip as president, lasting eight days and covering five different countries. Donald Trump would have the distinction of being the first president in US history to choose Saudi Arabia as the destination for his first trip abroad, and his visit would most certainly shake things up.

CHAPTER 9

Changing the Conversation

MAY 20, 2017

King Salman's extravagant welcome for President Trump and the First Lady, Melania, at the King Khalid International Airport in Riyadh was a stark contrast to the muted reception that had been accorded President Obama the previous year. Jets screamed low overhead, streaming red, white, and blue contrails. Countless American and Saudi flags lined the streets of the capital, as did billboards featuring President Trump's face.

After the chill that had previously descended on US-Saudi relations as a consequence of the Iran nuclear deal—an agreement that the Saudis and their Sunni neighbors had strenuously opposed—Trump's presence here was cause for the warmest of celebrations. As a candidate, Trump's deep opposition to the JCPOA that had been reached two years before in Vienna was well known and mirrored that of the Saudi government. The so-called P-5, the five states to whom the United Nations grants a permanent seat on the UN Security Council—

China, Russia, France, the United Kingdom, and the United States—had concluded a deal that supposedly insured that Iran's nuclear program would not be weaponized. Trump, Netanyahu, the Saudis, and indeed the rest of the Sunni Muslim countries in the Middle East thought that was a pipe dream, however. That Iran could not be trusted to keep its word about its nuclear ambitions, or anything else for that matter, was a skepticism shared. It's certainly worth noting that both the idea and the orchestration of this important trip to Saudi Arabia was Jared's brainchild. Although it was the work of many hands, including the State Department and the National Security Council staff, as well as my own, Jared certainly captained the ship.

The Trumps' subsequent welcome at the historic Murabba Palace was an equally opulent occasion to fete a new friend in the White House. The Murabba Palace is an impressive structure in the traditional Najdi style, with walls of adobe and wooden beams supporting the ceilings with geometric patterns in red, yellow, and black. It was a museum now, but it had once been the palace of Abdulaziz bin Abdul Rahman Al Saud, or Ibin Saud, the tribal leader and statesman who had founded Saudi Arabia and ruled it until his death in 1953. There, King Salman awarded President Trump the Collar of the Order of Abdulaziz Al Saud, his country's highest honor given to non-Muslim heads of state.

That same day, the president signed an historic arms deal with King Salman. It was a very public expression of a strengthened United States relationship with Saudi Arabia, as well as an unmistakable signal to Iran that its desire to dominate the Middle East would no longer go unchallenged, something then-Secretary of State Rex Tillerson, as well as his eventual successor, Mike Pompeo, would make exceedingly clear. In a statement to journalists that day, Tillerson noted that this package of defense equipment and services supported "the long-term security of Saudi Arabia and the entire Gulf region in particular in the face of malign Iranian influence and Iranian-related threats, which exists on Saudi Arabia's borders on all sides."

That deal was, indeed, so enormous that it sparked some natural concern from Jerusalem. Yuval Steinitz, Israel's energy minister, wanted assurances that despite this purchase of US military hardware by Saudi Arabia, his country's "qualitative military edge" would be maintained.

Tillerson assured Steinitz that the United States was fully committed to Israel's security and predicted that the deal with the Saudis would, in the long run, actually help foster a closer relationship between Israel and the Arab world in a shared effort to deter Iran. Although deep differences remain between Israel and its Arab neighbors, Tillerson said, "In many respects (these) threats (from Iran) are common to all of us."

The next day, President Trump delivered a keynote address at the Arab Islamic American Summit, a meeting that included fifty-five leaders of Muslim-majority nations inside the King Abdulaziz International Conference Center in Riyadh. It was a powerful speech, unprecedented in its directness and honesty. "We are not here to lecture," the president said. "We are not here to tell other people how to live, what to do, who to be, or how to worship. Instead, we are here to offer partnership—based on shared interests and values—to pursue a better future for us all."

In plain, blunt language, the president directly challenged the countries present to eradicate the terrorists in their midst. He said:

> Terrorism has spread across the world. But the path to peace begins right here, on this ancient soil, in this sacred land. America is prepared to stand with you—in pursuit of shared interests and common security. But the nations of the Middle East cannot wait for American power to crush this enemy for them.

> The nations of the Middle East will have to decide what kind of future they want for themselves, for their countries, and for their children. It is a choice between two futures—and it is a choice America CANNOT make for you. A better future is only possible if your nations drive out the terrorists and extremists. Drive. Them. Out. DRIVE THEM OUT of your places of worship. DRIVE THEM OUT of your communities. DRIVE THEM OUT of your holy land, and DRIVE THEM OUT OF THIS EARTH.

In hindsight, what Trump said then certainly seems even more prescient in light of the disastrous fall of Afghanistan under the Biden administration.

The president went on to observe that evolving threats and new facts in the Middle East would mean that new approaches would have to be found. "We discard those strategies that have not worked," he said, "and will apply new approaches informed by experience and judgment. We are adopting a Principled Realism, rooted in common values and shared interests. Our friends will never question our support, and our enemies will never doubt our determination."

The president specifically called out Iran as a menace to the region. No discussion of stamping out terrorism, he noted, would be complete without mentioning the government that gives terrorists safe harbor, financial backing, and the social standing needed to aid in recruiting more of their kind. "I am speaking, of course, of Iran."

The president said:

From Lebanon to Iraq to Yemen, Iran funds, arms, and trains terrorists, militias, and other extremist groups that spread destruction and chaos across the region. For decades, Iran has fueled the fires of sectarian conflict and terror. It is a government that speaks openly of mass murder, vowing the destruction of Israel, death to America, and ruin for many leaders and nations in this room. Among Iran's most tragic and destabilizing interventions have been in Syria. Bolstered by Iran, Assad has committed unspeakable crimes, and the United

States has taken firm action in response to the use of banned chemical weapons by the Assad Regime—launching 59 tomahawk missiles at the Syrian air base from where that murderous attack originated. Until the Iranian regime is willing to be a partner for peace, all nations of conscience must work together to isolate Iran, deny it funding for terrorism, and pray for the day when the Iranian people have the just and righteous government they deserve.

At the close of the summit, the leaders inaugurated the new Global Center for Combating Extremism in Riyadh, a center of excellence dedicated to fighting violent extremism and hosting a number of international counter-extremism experts. It was not lost on anyone that much of that fight would be directly aimed at Iran. While other presidents in other times had given lip service to these same issues, their rhetoric had not translated itself into specific policy goals and directives in their respective administrations. Certainly, in none of those previous speeches had a president been so direct in spelling out his expectations both politically and practically. This was not vague virtue signaling for the sake of satisfying their vanity or his. This was something different. It was a direct challenge to these Muslim-majority nations to join the United States as equal partners to confront a common foe. This was not a paean of praise for a "peace process" but a forthright challenge to produce results and actions.

President Trump was extremely encouraged, especially by many of the private comments he had heard during the summit in Riyadh—and he told Bibi Netanyahu so when he arrived the next day for private talks with the Israeli prime minister in Jerusalem.

As I had done a couple of months before, the Trumps stayed at the King David Hotel, but with a decidedly Trumpian difference. No other American president had come to Israel so early in his term of office. President Clinton had come in the second year of his first term, President Carter in his third year. Presidents Nixon, George W. Bush, and Obama had not visited Israel until their second terms. To honor the president who had honored Israel, the hotel management decided to make available all of their 233 rooms to the president, the first lady, and their extensive entourage, which included a massive Secret Service detail. The Trumps, fittingly, were provided with the especially large and lavish Presidential Suite. For this one day, the King David Hotel had been turned into Fort Trump. Hundreds of guests previously booked into the hotel were reassigned to another one. Haim Shkedi, the hotel's general manager, said the other guests seem to take it in stride. "After all, not every day do we host the President of the United States."

Trump also made history as the first sitting US president to visit the Western Wall in Jerusalem, the holiest site where Jews are allowed to pray. Trump rested his hand on the wall for a few moments and then placed a note inside of the wall, as did Melania. It is a time-honored tradition for worshippers to place slips of paper containing prayers to G-d in the cracks of the wall. That same day, the Trumps also visited the Church of the Holy Sepulchre, the site where Christians believe Jesus of Nazareth was crucified and buried and resurrected.

In a private meeting with the Israeli prime minister, Trump told Netanyahu that he sensed that the conditions were ripe for a deal between Israel and the Palestinian Authority. The problem, of course, was that the Arabs wanted Israel to conclude a peace with Abbas as a prelude to larger regional negotiations.

"King Salman feels very strongly and, I can tell you, would love to see peace with Israel and the Palestinians," Trump told Netanyahu. "There's a growing realization among your Arab neighbors that they have common cause with you in the threat posed by Iran, and it is indeed a threat, there's no question about that."

Netanyahu said he felt encouraged as well. "For the first time in my lifetime," he said, "I see a real hope for change. The Arab leaders who you met yesterday could help change the atmosphere, and they could help create the conditions for a realistic peace."

In many ways, this trip marked the beginnings of what was to ultimately become the Abraham Accords. Of course, we did not know if, or how, or what form, such agreements might ultimately take. But the seeds that we would plant and nourish, and that President Trump instinctively recognized and encouraged, were established at that time.

Despite that shared feeling of optimism, I think it was evident to all of us that negotiations with Abbas needed to proceed on a track of their own, and not as a pre-condition to establishing relationships with other Arab countries. Our team saw the old inside-out peace process as an industry in its own right, one with its own selfish set of imperatives that precluded any other diplomatic moves in the meantime. It was a diplomatic straitjacket and the prospect of returning to it without also pursuing alternate diplomatic initiatives seemed shortsighted. Despite the obviously changing zeitgeist in the Sunni Arab world, agreeing to negotiate with the Palestinian leadership first before engaging with any other Arab neighbor gave Abbas, a president without a country, a virtual veto over the entire Arab world vis-à-vis Israel. It was a veto that, until this moment in history, had seemed absolute. But maybe that was changing, we reasoned. And if it was, that could change everything.

However, what hadn't changed was Palestinian Authority President Mahmoud Abbas. When Trump met with him the next day in Bethlehem, it was clear that Abbas envisioned the new peace process as simply a replay of the old one. He wanted to rehash his debating points about illegal occupation, settlements, 1967 bound-aries, and Israel's lack of recognition of a Palestinian State. This was the second time that the president and Abbas had met. Abbas had accepted Trump's invitation to come to the White House earlier that same month, on May 3, and at that time, the president had raised

the issue of Palestinian Authority payments to families of prisoners and other terrorists who were killed
while attacking Israelis—a practice that had long been
described as a "pay to slay" policy by its critics both in
the United States and in Israel. I did not consider this
a minor matter. The *Washington Post* calculated that in
2017 alone, some 13,000 beneficiaries of these "prisoner
payments" received $160 million in compensation for
their crimes, and a further $183 million had been paid to
33,700 families of these "martyrs." That a large propor-
tion of those payments had come from the foreign aid
the United States had sent with the express purpose of
improving the living conditions and the lives of average
Palestinians was all the more galling.

The Palestinian Authority had long claimed that this
money was a welfare fund, but the World Bank, which
oversaw that money, had found that the program was
"clearly not targeted to the poorest households. While
some assistance should be directed to this population,
the level of resources devoted to the Fund for Martyrs
and the injured does not seem justified from a welfare
or fiscal perspective," a World Bank report had recently
concluded. What an understatement.

In raising the issue once again, Trump told Abbas,
"Peace can never take root in an environment where
violence is tolerated, funded and even rewarded. We
must be resolute in condemning such acts in a single
unified voice."

Abbas, clearly annoyed, responded that the problem
wasn't one of violence or the funding that went to "mar-

tyrs" or the families of terrorists imprisoned by Israel. The problem, Abbas said, "is with the occupation and settlements and the failure of Israel to recognize the State of Palestine in the same way we recognize it. The problem is not between us and Judaism. It is between us and occupation."

Abbas was well aware of Trump's recent visit to Riyadh and was no doubt hopeful that some of the key Arab rulers had caught his ear. As he saw it, the Palestinian Authority had no real leverage with Israel, but the prospect of a broader peace with these other Arab states could be an inducement to finally getting an advantageous deal with Netanyahu.

What didn't seem to occur to Abbas is that there was another way to look at the leverage argument, and Jared and our team were there ahead of him. The fact is, Arab states had already begun to realize it was in their long-term self-interests to forge a closer relationship with Israel on a whole raft of issues, ranging from the common threat posed by Iran to technology transfers and trade. Indeed, under the proverbial table, many of those nations had already been cooperating on just these fronts, albeit with the greatest of discretion. What our team had already seen quite clearly is that the absence of peace with the Palestinian leadership—long a barrier to moving forward on these other relationships in the Arab world—was no longer an insurmountable one. What had already begun to germinate in private, we hoped, could finally flower in public. From this perspective, the Arabs would, indeed, be bringing renewed pressure to solve the long-running conflict between the Palestinian leadership and Israel. However, this time, unlike previous negotiations, the pressure wouldn't be on Netanyahu and Israel, but on Abbas and the Palestinian leadership.

This was the fiftieth anniversary of the 1967 Six-Day War, but other anniversaries had come and gone before and the media weren't expecting much from our team of former "real estate guys"—as more than one media source styled us. What they didn't know, of course, is that we were already diligently at work on a plan for both the Palestinian Authority and Israel, as well as pages within the plan designed to forge separate agreements between Israel and other Arab countries. The ideas were designed to work in concert or separately. If, for example, negotiations between Netanyahu and Abbas stalled, that didn't mean our other plan couldn't continue to proceed along its own separate, but parallel, path. If, G-d willing, Netanyahu and Abbas could reach a deal, the separate accords we were pursuing between Israel and other potential Arab partners would be the proverbial icing on the cake. It would be a new Middle East political landscape. Both of those were, of course, still works in progress.

But there were other plans in progress as well. There were other promises that Donald Trump had made as a candidate on the campaign trail that now, as president, he was determined to redeem. While these particular promises—to recognize Jerusalem as the capital of Israel and to move the United States embassy from Tel Aviv to Jerusalem—were promises that I privately supported, I also knew they had the potential to wreak havoc on the diplomatic efforts in which our team was currently engaged.

These particular promises had seemed to much of the media, both in America and abroad, to have already been quietly discarded by the Trump administration as both politically and practically untenable, as indeed so many US presidents had decided before us. But the media and the confident foreign policy experts they had been quoting had mistaken the president's lack of public comment with a lack of action. They interpreted his silence as a sullen recognition that he had been wrong. They assumed that what he had so confidently promised in the heat of a contested campaign for the presidency could not withstand the cold realities and time-tested truths of America's foreign policy as it was practiced and perceived by the world at large. Finally, at last, they all seemed to say in unison, cooler, calmer heads had prevailed. It was the old Washington circular reasoning at work: absence of evidence was evidence of absence. Besides, all the experts had known the whole thing was impractical from the start. Now, it seemed, Trump himself had come to his senses. It was about time.

But I knew that Trump had meant what he said. So did Jared. So did America's new ambassador to Israel, David Friedman. The promise concerned an old and familiar spot on the map in the Middle East. It had once been a tiny town amid the Judaean hills, a place that was the home of one G-d, and three religions. Across the ages, it had been witness to patriarchs and prophets, kings and conquerors. Abraham, David, and Jesus had once walked its streets. Today, that small village had become a city of more than 800,000 people, comprising more than a half-million Jews, more than 300,000 Muslims, and about 16,000 Christians.

It was a holy city, existing simultaneously on Earth and in heaven.

It was Jerusalem.

And Donald Trump had promised to recognize it as the capital of Israel and move the American embassy there from Tel Aviv. Before this year was done, he was going to make good on that promise to recognize Jerusalem as the capital of Israel and about five months later he would make good on his promise to move the embassy there as well.

CHAPTER 10

This Year in Jerusalem

DECEMBER 6, 2017

Every year, for what has been more than two thousand years, in nations around the world where they were often marginalized, excluded, and even murdered for their faith, Jews have exclaimed, expectantly, at the conclusion of each Passover Seder, "Next year in Jerusalem!"

It's a Passover tradition—just like the matzah we eat, the four cups of wine we imbibe, and the songs we sing—that both reminds of us our ancestor's plight, and our yearning for a brighter future. No other people in the history of the world have expressed such a persistent and passionate hope and desire for a specific spot on this blue marble we all call home. There are more than 1.3 billion Catholics around the world, but after Sunday Mass, none of them cry, "Next year at Vatican City!" which is, technically, its own state within the city of Rome. Admittedly, the population of Israel is a fraction of that—just 9.2 million people—smaller than my own state of New Jersey, which boasts 9.4 million people. Come to think of it, I don't recall anyone ever shouting "Next year in Washington, D.C.!" either.

My point here is simply this: Jews both self-identify and have been known around the world for more than two millennia as a distinct people with a distinct ancestral home, located in a distinct and unchanging spot in the Middle East. All of which brings me to a simple question: If Jerusalem doesn't qualify as Israel's capital, what does?

And yet, incredible as it may have seemed, in all the years of Israel's existence as a modern nation, from its founding in 1948, the United States, Israel's closest ally, had never officially recognized Jerusalem as its capital.

Successive American presidents had said they would do so, but never had. Bill Clinton came into office saying he supported "the principle" of moving America's embassy to Jerusalem. But he didn't go through with it.

In October 1995, the US Congress passed a law called the Jerusalem Embassy Act, which described Jerusalem as the capital of Israel and said the city should not be divided. This wasn't one of those measures that squeaked through on a party-line vote. It passed in the House of Representatives overwhelmingly, 374–37, and in the Senate 93–5. It became law without presidential signature on November 8, 1995. The law required the US embassy to be moved to Jerusalem by May 1999. But that didn't happen. Instead, Clinton signed a waiver, postponing the move for reasons of "national security."

In 2000, in his last year as president, Clinton told Israeli reporters: "I have always *wanted* to move our embassy to *West* Jerusalem," making a distinction that seemed to ignore the indivisibility of Jerusalem that Congress had stipulated in 1995. "We have a designated site there," he continued. "I have not done so because I didn't want to do anything to undermine our ability to help to broker a secure and fair and lasting peace for Israelis and for Palestinians."

George W. Bush promised that "As soon as I take office, I will begin the process of moving the US Ambassador to the city Israel has chosen as its capital." But eight years later, he hadn't done so. Like Clinton before him, he signed waivers as technically required by law, postponing the move.

Then-Senator Barack Obama, speaking at the American Israel Public Affairs Committee (AIPAC) on June 4, 2008, in his first foreign policy speech after securing the Democratic nomination the day before said: "Let me be clear. Israel's security is sacrosanct. It is non-negotiable. The Palestinians need a state that is contiguous and cohesive, and that allows them to prosper—but any agreement with the Palestinian people must preserve Israel's identity as a Jewish State, with secure, recognized and defensible borders. Jerusalem will remain the capital of Israel, and it must remain undivided. I have no illusions that this will be easy."

But, when asked afterward by CNN whether he meant to say that Palestinians had no future claim on the city, Obama replied, "Well, obviously, it's going to be up to the parties to negotiate a range of these issues. And Jerusalem will be part of those negotiations."

In his last press conference as president, Obama had dropped all his previous pretense about moving the US embassy to Jerusalem, saying that to do so would have "explosive" consequences. Like Bush and Clinton before him, he signed waivers, again and again, citing national security concerns.

As a candidate for president, Donald Trump joined this long line of men who had made promises concerning Jerusalem and our embassy there. Would he, like them, fail to keep his promise as well? Many in Washington and elsewhere thought he had quietly done just that. But they were wrong.

In June 2017, the US Senate unanimously passed a resolution (90–0) that reaffirmed the 1995 Jerusalem Embassy Act and called upon the president to implement it. Today, after six months of careful internal review, President Donald Trump was recognizing Jerusalem as Israel's capital, as well as making plans to move the US embassy there from Tel Aviv.

Speaking, appropriately enough, from the beautiful old Diplomatic Reception Room of the White House, President Trump said, "Today, we finally acknowledge the obvious: that Jerusalem is Israel's capital. This is nothing more or less than a recognition of reality. It is also the right thing to do. It's something that has to be done."

The president was certainly right about that. It was a huge break with the past, but the past had been a formula for failure. If nothing else, today's announcement corrected a long-running historical hypocrisy: every other sovereign country in the entire world, except for

Israel, had a right to determine where to locate its capital. Today, President Trump was calling out his own country on this decades-long diplomatic charade.

In announcing this historic change, the president was nonetheless clear that he remained committed to brokering an agreement "that is a great deal for the Israelis and a great deal for the Palestinians." He emphasized that today's decision to recognize Jerusalem should not be construed as the United States taking a position on whether, or how, the city might ultimately be shared.

I thought the speech hammered home the point that, in a way, while everything had changed, nothing had changed. Jerusalem was the place where Israel's Knesset met, where their president and prime minister had their offices, where their supreme court met. It was where every foreign diplomat and leader came to speak with the political leaders of that nation. None of that was new. The president's speech hadn't changed the reality on the ground, but merely recognized it. Now *that* was absolutely new. The president of the United States of America had stood up and publicly announced it to the rest of the world. And yet, here again, nothing had changed about our desire to achieve an agreement between the Israelis and the Palestinians. America's abiding commitment to peace endured.

Here are the President's final words:

Let us rededicate ourselves to a path of mutual understanding and respect. Let us rethink old assumptions and open our hearts and minds to the possibilities. And finally, I ask the leaders of the region, political and religious, Israeli and Palestinian, Jewish and Christian and Muslim, to join us in the noble quest for lasting peace... G-d bless you, G-d bless Israel, G-d bless the Palestinians.

This ending was an incredibly important part of the speech. We understood the Palestinians would be angry; we understood that they would cut ties with us, at least for a period of time. But we wanted them to know that even as we were righting an historical wrong, at the same time, we weren't giving up on our hope of peace. We wanted the whole world to know that we were going to roll up our sleeves, so to speak, and do everything we could to achieve peace—and that included everyone. We weren't going to just bless ourselves; we were going to bless the two parties who were most interested in the city that is holy to so many. We didn't intend to play favorites, even though I'm sure that's how it was perceived on the Palestinian side. Perceptions are important, but so are facts. If stating the fact that Jerusalem is Israel's capital was harmful to the so-called "peace process," what did that say about that process? If that process could only be sustained by pretending something that wasn't so, where did it end? President Trump, to his credit, had decided that it ended here. Today. Now.

There were so many issues that depended on these sorts of pretenses. For example, only Muslims are allowed to pray on the Temple Mount, or Haram al-Sharif. One of the things I was recommending in the plan that our team was developing was that Jews actually be allowed to pray on the Temple Mount as well. After all, it is just as holy, just as sacred, to Jews as it is to Muslims. Jews are allowed to visit the Temple Mount in limited numbers, with very strict rules, but they are prohibited from praying there. That was wrong, too, and needed changing. It still does. That holy place should be open for prayer to everyone—Muslim, Jew, and Christian alike.

For optics' sake, as well as to accommodate a large media contingent, the only people in the room were President Trump and Vice President Mike Pence, standing just behind him. Later that month, the vice president would make a tour of the Middle East to emphasize our continuing commitment to peace in the region. Just outside of the cameras, along with Jared, David, and a few others, I was able to watch the president deliver this history-making speech, one that was incredibly moving to me and, I'm quite sure to those present, as well as millions more watching in Israel. Several of us gathered later in the president's private dining room off the Oval Office for a small reception there, as we watched reactions, here and abroad, to the speech. When I left the president's private dining room and walked back to my office, I remember calling Naomi with a lump still in my throat and tears in my eyes. Of all the many experiences I had while being in the White House, it was clearly one of the most meaningful.

This public speech, of course, had been the subject of weeks of private debate and consultation, prior to its delivery. We knew that the Israelis would be overjoyed at the news of the recognition of Jerusalem as Israel's capital and the commitment to move the US embassy to Jerusalem, and that the Palestinians would vehemently protest it. Some countries tried to convince us to choose a spot in West Jerusalem, rather than East Jerusalem, knowing that the status of East Jerusalem was highly contentious and would require negotiation. We did not buy into that argument. Jerusalem is a city that should not be divided, and the law we were following was clear about that.

As for East Jerusalem, interestingly enough, around the time President Trump actually moved the embassy, I asked perhaps one of the most knowledgeable members of the career staff in the State Department to locate the document that "recognized" East Jerusalem as Palestinian. I realized in all my time at the White House, I never saw any source for why people took the position that East Jerusalem belonged to the Palestinians. When I asked, my colleague shifted uncomfortably in his seat and replied that he would investigate the matter. Days passed without any document to satisfy my query or my increasingly piqued curiosity. Finally, I asked again, and the somewhat sheepish reply I received was both troubling in its way, but in retrospect, not all that surprising. As it turned out, there was no such document. "It's just something everybody says," the embarrassed staffer told me. "It's just come to be accepted." In a lot of ways, that described pretty much the entire file, itself. There were myths and realities, co-existing side by side, and no one dared any longer to make a distinction between the two. That is, until now. Until Donald Trump. Indeed, I would go on to make what was a landmark speech at the United Nations Security Council, one which openly and honestly made the point that when it came to East Jerusalem being the capital of a Palestinian state, an "aspiration was not a right." To say it ruffled feathers is an understatement. But they needed to be ruffled, and I was glad I did it.

We were assured by all sorts of serious people at State, elsewhere in our own government, and in conversations with our allies in Europe and with several Arab countries that the recognition of Jerusalem as the capital of Israel and the move of the US embassy to Jerusalem was a colossal error. Announcing the recognition of Jerusalem as Israel's capital and committing to move the US embassy, they said, was the worst idea since Adam and Eve noshed on an apple. It was listed in the diplomatic dictionary under D for disaster—you could look it up. The whole Middle East would go up in flames, blood would run in the streets. Oh, and forget about any idea of a peace process; this would probably start a war. Doing this would reserve you a ringside seat to Armageddon. Didn't we realize there was a *reason* that all those presidents kept signing national security waivers, every six months, to delay just such a possibility? What were we thinking? Were we even thinking at all? Or so they all seemed to say.

Jared, and I—and other White House colleagues—were all receiving phone calls telling us we shouldn't do this, or we couldn't do it, or that we had better not do it. But the pressure on us was nothing compared to the pressure on the president. As you might imagine, many of the European capitals, certainly many of the Arab capitals, were beside themselves. It was a full court press to stop this train before it reached the station.

All the intelligence assessments, all the collective wisdom of all the collected career staffs in Washington, Europe, and the Middle East were agreed that, while this was something that had been American policy and American law for more than two decades, as determined by overwhelming bipartisan votes in both chambers of Congress, we should just sign another waiver and go to lunch.

Many of the calls I received pointed out that recognizing Jerusalem as Israel's capital and moving the embassy to Jerusalem would kill the Israeli-Palestinian peace process. But my view was, there was no peace process to speak of now, and delaying the recognition and the embassy move for the past twenty-two years had not helped the peace process before. We assumed the Palestinian leadership would definitely walk away for a while. We couldn't know that they would end up walking away for the rest of Trump's term of office, but in my mind, that was not an adequate argument for not following US law and righting this historical wrong.

One of the other big arguments against the recognition of Jerusalem as the capital of Israel and the embassy move was that it would isolate the United States of America from the rest of the world. This was not an argument that President Trump, or anyone else on the team, regarded seriously. This was a US law, promulgated and passed by Congress on a bipartisan basis. If the rest of the world didn't like that, so be it. We weren't going to let fear of what some other country thought of America and of US law dissuade us from doing what we felt was right, nor were we inclined to give them a vote on which of those laws we should ignore to keep them happy.

None of my calls were pleasant ones, and they had a fatiguing familiarity to them as well. Somebody must have distributed a Xerox talking point card with the exact same points. Again and again, there was dark talk of blood in the streets, anti-American riots, US embassies under siege, and the like. Moreover, they argued, the recognition of Jerusalem as Israel's capital and the US embassy move blatantly favored Israel and was thus, impermissibly biased; the law that required it was twenty years old and no one had followed the law in the past. My refrain to all of that was familiar as well, which was, "This president is different. He follows through on things."

Once Trump made the announcement, we had another round of criticism, this time in public. In their way, all of them were a tribute to the idea that, while truth is generally a good thing, too much of it can be a moral hazard. UN Secretary Antonio Guterres worried that recognizing Jerusalem as Israel's capital would "jeopardize the prospect of peace for Israelis and Palestinians,"

French President Emmanuel Macron called the decision "regrettable," and British Prime Minister Theresa May called it "unhelpful in terms of prospects for peace in the region." Even Pope Francis expressed his "deep concern" for America's recognition of Jerusalem as Israel's capital.

There were former Obama administration officials who also offered their "expert" opinion on the recognition of Jerusalem. Chief among these was John Brennan, Obama's former CIA director, who called the move a "reckless" one that would "damage US interests in the Middle East for years to come," and would "make the region more volatile." As it turns out, Brennan's seemingly sage prediction about the effect of the Jerusalem announcement didn't pan out. Then again, I'm not aware of any of his many derogatory statements about Trump or our administration that did. But at least he was in good company. Iran's supreme leader, Ayatollah Ali Khamenei, said at a conference in Tehran that week that Trump's recognition of Jerusalem reflected the "incompetence and failure" of the American government.

I wasn't surprised that, at this juncture, Abbas took this opportunity to break off talking with us. In hindsight, if we hadn't made the announcement about Jerusalem, it would almost certainly have been something else. He was never really willing to engage in any kind of constructive discussions, nor was his chief aide, Saeb Erekat.

I had hoped, of course, that this was only an inflection point and not an ending. That hope, I suppose, was informed by my business background and by my own very methodical, very logical nature. I can certainly be emotional, but when it comes to business transactions and negotiations—that is, getting things done—I let the logical side of my brain dictate my actions.

Emotionally, I may want to be upset, to stamp my feet, or brood. But at some point, you have to realize that your real mission in any negotiation is to get whatever it is you're seeking. In the case of the Palestinians, for Abbas, this was some kind of sovereign state. It didn't seem logical to me that Abbas would just wait for another three years—and potentially another seven years, if we had a second term—and just refuse to talk. Of course, he would be upset. Of course, he would go away for a period of time. But in six months, a year, tops, I felt he eventually would be back.

At the time, everyone—particularly in the Middle East—used this rather odd metaphor about Abbas being up a tree. They would say, "Abbas needs to climb down from the tree. What are you going to give Abbas to climb down from the tree? Will you give him a ladder—some new incentive—so that he can climb down from the tree?"

I thought that was a remarkable question, and not in a positive way. It seemed to me that if Abbas felt he was up in a tree, he should want to climb down from it for his own set of reasons, not because I provided him with some incentives to do so. Either he wanted a better life for the Palestinians or he didn't. I wasn't in the ladder business. He had the lumber, he had the nails. I told these folks I would be happy to hold the ladder while Abbas climbed down but I wasn't going to give him one. The ladder they were talking about was really the desire for peace. If Abbas didn't have that desire, that drive to accomplish something great for his people, I couldn't give him that desire. He would have to find it within himself.

We sent a very strong statement to all the intermediaries who said they spoke for Abbas, and also to the press, that we were going to continue our job. For me, that meant continuing to strengthen US-Israel relations, and it meant continuing to draft a peace plan in the hopes that one day it would be revealed with or without the Palestinian leadership on board. In the meantime, we would also try to improve the Palestinian economy, an outreach that ultimately led to a major conference in Bahrain in June 2019. And, of course, we were also heavily working on our approach in an attempt to forge separate, one-on-one relationships between Israel and Arab countries. I pressed this point in so many different ways in every meeting I had with Arab officials and leadership.

We were not going to let the Palestinian leadership in Ramallah stop us from doing our job, just as we were not going to let Hamas stop us. We wouldn't have started down this road if we were going to let discouraging things prevent us from moving forward.

Years ago, Secretary of State James Baker had issued a challenge of sorts to Israel when he felt negotiations had come to a standstill. He gave them the phone number for the White House switchboard and said, "When you're serious about this, call me."

I used that same line with all those folks who thought I ought to build a ladder for Abbas. I told them he had my number. I was available if anyone wanted to get in touch with me. Otherwise, I had work to do. And, indeed, I was as busy as ever. I was the lead on drafting a plan that our team felt made sense, that would explain the history of the conflict and the rationale for proceeding as we were. We had no idea when the plan would be released, perhaps not until Trump's second term, or perhaps even later, by someone else who would, just maybe, give it a look one day and say, "You know, this plan makes logical sense."

When President Trump had made his announcement about recognizing Jerusalem as Israel's capital, along with his decision to move the US embassy there, not a few old policy mavens suggested that we had accomplished something significant by just making the speech, and there wasn't necessarily a need to do anything else. We had put a marker down, so to speak, and that was important in itself. And besides, everyone knew it usually took years to plan and construct an embassy. It might not even happen while Trump was still in office. In the meantime, anything could happen. Delays could occur. We were still getting calls from foreign capitals urging Trump to reverse his decision, or at least attach some new, onerous condition on Israel before actually proceeding with the embassy project. In their minds, no doubt, this was our "ladder," our opportunity to climb down from our own tree. All we had to do was—nothing! We could just silently let the whole matter drop and gather dust. The important thing was to not follow through on what President Trump had said. Really, now, that wouldn't be so bad, would it? So many former presidents had said so many things about Jerusalem that they never ultimately carried through on. We certainly wouldn't be the first to renege on a promise—and politics being politics—we wouldn't be the last.

When the modern State of Israel was born on May 14, 1948, it had been nearly nineteen centuries since the Romans destroyed the capital that the Babylonians had destroyed some five hundred years before. After all those years of exile, of persecution and pain, the prayers for a sovereign Jewish State had been answered in 1948. On May 14, 2018, the seventieth anniversary of Israel's founding, America finally officially relocated its embassy to Jerusalem. David Friedman worked very hard to make that May 14th deadline so that President Trump could make good on his commitment to the Israeli people, indeed, Jewish people around the world, and the law of the United States of America.

The opening ceremony was held in what was the former US Consulate in the Arnona neighborhood in Jerusalem, a temporary location while we looked for something permanent. President Trump spoke by video link from the White House to a crowd of about eight hundred people. I counted myself fortunate to be among them. What 192 other United Nations members had always taken for granted—the right to pick the site of their own capital—was now Israel's as well. It was a good day to be a Jew. It was a good day to be an American.

CHAPTER 11

Bahrain and Bicycles

JUNE 25–26, 2019

In 1930, Albert Einstein gave his son, Eduard, some private advice that still rings true: "*Beim Menschen ist es wie beim Velo. Nur wenn er faehrt, kann er bequem die Balance halten.*"

"It is the same with people as it is with riding a bike. Only when moving can one comfortably maintain one's balance."

Today, nearly a century later, Einstein's famous observation has become an aphorism for the ages: "Life is like riding a bicycle. To keep your balance, you must keep moving."

Although we may not have officially adopted it as our motto, Jared, David, and I were certainly maintaining our activity level—and thus, our equilibrium—as we continued to press forward with our peace efforts in the Middle East.

Starting with no more than a bare outline in 2017, we had begun to put flesh on the bone of what ultimately became the Peace to Prosperity Plan with each new trip to the Middle East, each new meeting, each new bit of information that we gleaned from a wide array of sources both here and abroad. The hard copy of the plan was kept in a safe in my office—and the safe was always locked unless I was working on it. Not a week went by without me opening that growing document and adding things. There would be countless revisions, of course, but it slowly grew from a thin term sheet that was almost purely aspirational, as so many past plans had been, to something quite specific and detailed.

The Peace to Prosperity Plan was actually two plans—one political, the other economic. Although we had originally envisioned presenting the entire, two-part plan together, due to seemingly never-ending elections in Israel, which were necessitated by a notoriously fractious Knesset, the economic part ended up being presented ahead of the political framework in a conference held in Manama, Bahrain in June.

It was Jared's idea to try to mix things up and do something different, provocative, and unexpected—all in the service of getting people talking. He wanted to show the Palestinians, and the watching world the almost indescribable potential benefits of concluding a peace agreement with Israel. He wanted to let everyone see the dazzling package of economic development opportunities that were in store for the West Bank, the Gaza Strip, as well as Jordan and Egypt. It was something approaching the size and impact of a Marshall Plan for the Middle East—a thoughtful and comprehensive program to recreate a vibrant economy in that region, much like General George Marshall's plan had served to restore western Europe after the Second World War. The price tag was a jaw-dropping $50 billion. The political settlement we envisioned between Israel and the Palestinian leadership would finally be presented the following year, in January 2020, at the White House.

The framework of the plan I had been working on with the team started with a few long-ignored facts. Chief among them was dispelling the notion that Israel was the "bad actor" in all of this "drama," and that the Israelis were the stubborn and intransigent party. Even a cursory glance at history showed that Israel was not allergic to peace with its Arab neighbors.

Israel had made peace with the Arab Republic of Egypt in 1979 and it would go on to make peace with the Hashemite Kingdom of Jordan in 1994, two countries with whom the State of Israel had fought multiple wars and numerous border skirmishes. Israel has also exchanged sizeable territories for the sake of peace, as it did when it withdrew from the Sinai Peninsula in exchange for peace with the Arab Republic of Egypt. While Israeli citizens had suffered greatly over the years as a result of violence and terrorism, they still desired peace. These two peace agreements, now forty and twenty-five years old, had endured and bettered the lives of citizens in Israel, Jordan, and Egypt. The conflict between the State of Israel and the Palestinian leadership was not only an aberration in that peace narrative, but it had also kept other Arab countries from normalizing their own relationships and jointly pursuing what ought to be a more stable, secure, and prosperous region.

Unlike previous plans, we were acutely aware that the promise of security for Israel was not the same thing as security, itself. These heavily word-smithed but vague proposals that only included high-level concepts but no practical means of achieving their ends had not and would not work. It was as simple as that. Why was security so important to Israel? If you look at a map—and most especially if you actually see the territories in question for yourself—one thing becomes immediately obvious: Israel, both from a geographic and geostrategic standpoint, has no margin for error.

Even if a comprehensive peace agreement could be achieved between Israel and a new State of Palestine, the reality is that there would always be those—Hamas in Gaza immediately comes to mind—that would actively desire to undermine the safety, stability, and security of an Israeli State. This is no theoretical fear; Israel has had the bitter experience of withdrawing from territories in the recent past, only to see them used as a launching pad for terrorist attacks. We were extremely cognizant of this fact and designed the security provisions in our plan in what I would describe as a defensive manner. That is, while we hoped for the best, we assumed the worst. If the new Palestinian State was peaceful, and stayed peaceful, well and good. But if it did not, Israel would have, at long last, the security it needed to defend itself.

Our plan offered the establishment of an independent Palestinian State in Gaza and slightly more than 70 percent of the West Bank, nearly double the amount they currently had limited jurisdiction over, plus territorial compensation in Israel itself, and a capital on the outskirts of East Jerusalem. It envisioned that future Palestinian state connecting Gaza and the West Bank by a combination of modern roads and tunnels, very much like the bridges and tunnels that I crossed each day to and from my home in Teaneck, New Jersey, and my work in New York City before I began working at the White House. We felt that these new transportation corridors would create a cohesive sense of a single state by increasing general mobility from one place to another, greatly reducing the need for old-style checkpoints—long a sore point with the Palestinians—and greatly enhancing the quality of life and the opportunities for commerce and development.

Under our plan, no one would be uprooted from his home, which we thought would be a recipe for civil unrest and ran counter to the idea of two people living in mutual harmony. Thus, all of the so-called "settlements" in the West Bank would remain in place. Israel would retain sovereignty over all these settlements, for which the Palestinians would receive land in parts of Israel as compensation. Israel would also have control over the strategic Jordan Valley to ensure its adequate security.

As for Jerusalem, we divided our plan into two areas: religious and political. Our position was that, unlike so many other previous powers that had ruled Jerusalem,

Israel had safeguarded the holy sites of other religions instead of destroying them.

We recommended that all of Jerusalem's holy sites should be subject to the same governance regimes that had existed for the past fifty years—that Jerusalem's holy sites should remain open and available for people of all faiths. I also recommended that people of every faith, including Jews who were presently excluded, should be permitted to pray on the Temple Mount/Haram al-Sharif, in a manner fully respectful to their religion, taking into account the times of each religion's prayers and holidays, as well as other religious factors.

Politically, our view was that any division of Jerusalem would be inconsistent with the policy statements of the Jerusalem Embassy Act of 1995 of the United States. History showed that all former US presidents who had been involved in the peace process have agreed that Jerusalem should not be divided, but accessible to all. Our plan did envision a Palestinian capital that would be located outside—east and north—of the existing Israeli West Bank barrier in that part of East Jerusalem that encompassed Kafr'Aqab, Shuafat, and Abu Dis.

Our plan also called for disarming Hamas, as well as Palestinian Islamic Jihad and other terrorist groups, the recognition of Israel as a Jewish state, and the immediate termination of the "prisoner and martyr payments"—the notorious monies disbursed to terrorists and to the families of deceased terrorists by the Palestinian Authority—to be replaced by a true humanitarian and welfare program, based on need, not terrorist acts. We also required that Hamas return the bodies of two soldiers of the Israel Defense Forces—Hadar Goldin and Oron Shaul, and to return two Israeli civilians they were holding captive—Avera Mengistu and Hisham Al-Sayed.

We anticipated that our plan would not be warmly greeted by the Palestinian leadership, to put it mildly. Nevertheless, we thought it was an honest reflection of today's realities. We also thought it provided a very clear path for the Palestinians, who had never really run a national government, with a path to a dignified national life, along with the respect, security, and practically the unlimited economic opportunities that came with it. At the same time, we felt our plan, at long last, gave Israel real security, rather than just guarantees of security. It had its own land and military assets that made its security a reality rather than a promise. Palestinians would have the power to govern themselves as they desired, but not the power to continue to threaten Israel.

Both privately and publicly, several Arab countries would urge Abbas to accept the plan as a basis for negotiations. Netanyahu would call it an "historic breakthrough," equivalent in significance to Israel's declaration of independence in 1948. Abbas would accuse us of blatant favoritism toward Israel and had condemned the plan before it was even released, effectively walking away, as he had so many times before, with so many other proposals. But that was all in the future, and we didn't have a crystal ball handy in the West Wing. Indeed, when and how that peace proposal would be unveiled was scarcely our only concern. There were other commitments to keep and issues to address.

Back in mid-February 2019, we were the co-host of a conference, along with Poland, whose purpose, as described by Secretary of State Mike Pompeo, Tillerson's replacement, was to focus on "Iran's influence and terrorism" in the Middle East. This Warsaw Conference, as it came to be known, was both the consequence of a common recognition in the region that Iran was a "bad actor," and also reflected the increasingly warm relations between Israel and many of its Arab neighbors.

Iran predictably protested the conference, calling it a hostile move, as did the Palestinian Authority and Hamas, but sadly, many of our European allies seemed to agree that Iran was unfairly being picked on.

Federica Mogherini, the then-foreign policy chief of the European Union, boycotted the meeting. That was not a surprise, as she once walked out in the middle of one of my speeches at the AHLC at the United Nations (her aide later claimed she had a prior meeting). France and Germany also chose not to attend and Russia was a no-show as well. British Foreign Secretary Jeremy Hunt said he would attend, but only if the United States, Saudi Arabia, and the United Arab Emirates would agree to a sidebar on Yemen.

Vice President Mike Pence, who was leading the conference on our side, called out our European allies for essentially working to weaken the pressure President Trump was putting on the Iranian regime. Trump had announced in May 2018 his intention to withdraw from the JCPOA agreement reached in July 2015. The vice president warned that Iran was plainly pursuing "another Holocaust." And they were. And they are.

Although the Warsaw Conference was largely ignored and widely panned, especially in Europe, it marked something new in Middle Eastern affairs, something which Secretary Pompeo would later say he thought paved the way for the Abraham Accords a year later. I agree with him.

Vice President Pence certainly seemed to sense a sea change at the conference as well. In addressing the guests at a dinner at the Royal Castle in Warsaw's old town, he observed, "Tonight I believe we are beginning a new era, with Prime Minister Netanyahu from the State of Israel, with leaders from Bahrain, Saudi Arabia, and the UAE, all breaking bread together, and...sharing honest perspectives on the challenges facing the area. Poland and the US welcome this outward symbol of this gathering, a symbol of cooperation and a hopeful sign of a brighter future that awaits nations across the Middle East. Let us recognize that we are stronger together than we would ever be apart."

The US-Bahrain Peace to Prosperity workshop that followed the Warsaw Conference in late June was another opportunity for potential progress. It was made possible by that country's gracious host, King Hamad bin Isa Al Khalifa. Consequential as it was, the two-day event was unfortunately largely pooh-poohed or ignored by most media outlets in the United States. They were pre-occupied with domestic politics. But media elsewhere saw something both historic and extraordinary in it, and they covered it extensively.

There were more than three hundred delegates from thirty countries who came to hear about new ideas and new economic resources that could transform the long-postponed dreams of Palestinians into a living reality—that is, if the two participants in the Israeli-Palestinian conflict would agree to, well, agree. Mohamed Alabbar of the United Arab Emirates seemed to speak for many when he observed, "The younger generation will not let us continue (to be) trapped by our past. Palestinian people are our people...By generating jobs, income opportunities and filling gaps in delivering basic services, the private sector can help build momentum behind a fragile economy and instill hope in the people of the region."

This wasn't just aspirational happy talk. The economic development plan discussed nearly two hundred specific projects from electric and water systems to digital services, agriculture, manufacturing, and infrastructure improvements, such as a new, $5 billion high-speed highway linking Gaza to the West Bank. In a region where unemployment hovered at 31 percent, this would be nothing less than life-changing. In truth, Jared implicitly acknowledged—and challenged—those who had been mocking our peace plan, which had been dubbed "The Deal of the Century" by observing that this economic development plan could be "The Opportunity of the Century" if the regions' leaders had the courage to pursue it.

I thought it a shame that the Palestinian Authority chose not to attend and tried to convince others not to attend as well. They distorted our message and attempted to undermine our progress. But they did not succeed. Not for the first time, they missed a real opportunity. By drawing the curtain around themselves, and turning their back on friends and partners from across the world, they missed the opportunity to see what was on the other side of that curtain.

And what *was* on the other side? A brighter future for Palestinians and for the entire region, drafted by people willing to say that the status quo was not good enough. An alternative path with the potential to unlock a prosperous future for the Palestinians if they chose to follow it. An exciting economic vision, with real projects and programs, promising the potential to unleash sustainable, private sector-driven growth. A new life for the next generation of Palestinians.

The people who attended the workshop didn't shy away from problems because they too hard. They weren't discouraged by the conventional wisdom about the fate of the Palestinians. They didn't give up after hearing, in meeting after meeting, the same broken record of negativity about why progress cannot be made. Instead, global leaders and experts on investment came from all across the world to show that there was an interest, appetite, and willingness by the global community to help the Palestinian people in the right context—the context of a realistic peace deal—if the parties could achieve one.

Many of the participants at the Bahrain summit seemed quite taken with the economic development plan, including a contingent of Palestinian business-people who spoke encouragingly about how they were already working cooperatively with Israelis in various nascent business ventures. But this sort of "economic development" was decidedly not pleasing to President Abbas. When these Palestinian delegates returned home, many were arrested, their homes raided. After all, such cooperation with the "enemy"—Israel—was a heinous crime, indeed. I was sad that he had responded so harshly. I certainly knew that he had an unforgiving side. For example, he refused ever to be in the same room with our ambassador to Israel, David Friedman, and had once called him a "son of a dog." He had also given an infamous "history lesson" speech before the Palestinian National Council that claimed the Holocaust was not caused by anti-Semitism, but by the "social behavior" of the Jews, including money-lending and other vile and outrageous comments.

But he could show warmth as well. Once, at the conclusion of a rather tense meeting I had with him and President Trump on the sidelines of the United Nations General Assembly, I extended my hand to say goodbye, and he kissed me on the head and wished me a Shanah

Tova, the traditional Jewish greeting for a Happy New Year. Soon enough though, I was dealing with the other Abbas, the inflexible leader who would brook no dissent, no departure from the party line.

In their inimitable way, *The New York Times* editorial board wasn't any more congenial to our economic plan than Abbas. They called the proposal "a fantastical New York real estate promotion" that was "patronizing" in tone and which dealt "only in generalities." But their biggest complaint seemed to be that in premiering the economic development plan ahead of any political settlement, the whole exercise was ridiculous on its face. This was criticism of a curious sort. It was also an argument from silence. There had, in fact, never been a successful political solution to the Israeli-Palestinian conflict. If placing the political solution to the Israeli-Palestinian conflict first in line, before any other discussion, was the secret to success, how had success eluded everyone so far? This was, once again, an argument about process rather than results. And that old process had failed, and repeatedly so.

What we saw in Bahrain, however, was yet more evidence that the old political paralysis that had plagued the Middle East was, ever so slowly, being replaced by a new pragmatism. It might not come in the next few months, or maybe even in the next few years, but it would come. And we wanted to be ready for it.

After Abbas had reacted so badly to the Bahrain conference, I think I realized that he would not come back to the negotiating table. I'd held out hope, of course, that he would see the conference as our earnest attempt to help the Palestinian people. Boycotting the event was one thing, but arresting some of the ordinary citizens who dared to show up and jailing them for it was another. I knew any chance of reconnecting at this point was a fool's errand.

True, it was still more than a year until election day, but I felt that if Abbas had ridden us out this long, he had no problem in riding it out that much longer. From his perspective, if Trump lost, he could crow about how smart he was to stand up to us. If Trump won reelection, Abbas knew that he could ring our bell and come back again. He knew we were always ready to talk. Politically, it was a no-lose situation for him, either way it went.

At the same time, however, it was becoming more and more clear to us that, despite our present impasse with Abbas, we were increasingly within reach of a profound political inflection point. In every meeting, every interaction with an Arab leader or representative, and in every public event, we saw that the old way of thinking about the inside-out strategy—that is, nothing happens until the Israeli-Palestinian leadership problem is resolved—was changing before our eyes.

Something new and wonderful was about to bloom, like one of those exotic plants that only flowers once in a generation. We had been patiently watering that plant and fertilizing it, waiting and hoping. I would no longer work at the White House by the time that flower finally blossomed, but I would be invited back to see it. In the meantime, as Jared was so fond of saying, "The sands of the hour glass keep going down," and my "crowded hour," to pilfer a phrase from Teddy Roosevelt, would soon be at an end.

Before I departed, however, I wanted to make sure that I left Jared and David in good shape. That meant putting the final touches on the Peace to Prosperity Plan, as well as continuing to push for other agreements between Israel and its Arab neighbors, as we had been doing from the start. It would be up to Jared and David, going forward, along with Avi Berkowitz, Jared's longtime deputy and my soon-to-be successor, to keep watering that plant called "peace" and waiting for it to flower. Brian Hook, the State Department's special representative for Iran, had also worked closely with us on the Iran file, and would help as well.

I would miss this place and all the excitement it had brought into my life, but I missed my family more, and was eager to get back to them. I could only hope they would be equally glad to have me back.

CHAPTER 12

Dayenu: *Abraham and Beyond*

OCTOBER 31, 2019

One of most beloved songs during the Passover Seder is "Dayenu." It's one that's traditionally sung during the telling of the story of the Exodus. The song's stanzas list a series of kindnesses G-d performed for the Jewish people and each concludes with the word *dayenu*—"it would have been enough."

If G-d had just created Adam and Eve, you sing, it would have been enough. If G-d had freed us from slavery in Egypt, it would have been enough. If G-d had given us the Torah at Mount Sinai, it would have been enough, and so on. It's a song more than a thousand years old with seemingly as many verses.

It's also a song about being grateful to G-d for all the gifts he has given the Jewish people. The point of the song is that G-d keeps giving. Yet, if G-d had only given just one of those gifts, it still would have been enough.

As I took my leave at the White House, that was certainly how I felt.

It would have been enough to have been a top executive for The Trump Organization, a job I so enjoyed, so that I could provide a good life for my family. It would have been enough to have helped Donald Trump with his campaign for president. It would have been enough to be chosen as special envoy and help the Trump administration deepen its bonds with our cherished ally Israel. It would have been enough to see if peace could be achieved between Israel and the Palestinians and work toward that goal. It would have been enough to work deeply and closely with Israel's Arab neighbors to develop ties and relationships, and hopefully, peace.

It would have been enough to see Jerusalem recognized as Israel's capital—and the site of America's embassy. It would have been enough to see President Trump recognize the Golan Heights as part of Israel. Right after that announcement, President Trump called me to tell me he did that for me, my wife and our children. Of course, I knew there were real reasons for the announcement, including that it was the only realistic approach to the Golan Heights, and essential to Israel's security, though I was very flattered that he would call to tell me that he did it for us. It would have been enough to peel away the distortions, rumors, myths, and lies about the Israeli-Palestinian conflict and help change the conversation toward truth and reality. It would have been enough to have made multiple, honest, frank speeches, speaking hard truths to the UN Security Council in the footsteps of Ambassador Nikki Haley. It would have been enough to have had countless similar conversations with diplomats all over the world, shredding false narratives about Israel and the Israel-Palestinian conflict that somehow grew like poisonous weeds, full of sharp thorns.

It would have been enough to try to help millions of Palestinians have a prosperous future, if their leadership in Ramallah, and their so-called leadership in Gaza, were willing to lead them. It would have been enough to have had honest, respectful, positive, and surprising conversations about Israel throughout the Arab world over three years, in many cases so very different than many of the conversations I had with diplomats and leadership in the European Union and elsewhere around the globe.

It would have been enough to have worked for the United States, a country that has been incredible to my parents and my immediate and extended family over decades (G-d bless America!). It would have been enough to have been welcomed and respected as an observant Jew throughout the Arab world, from the leadership to all people I interacted with, including among Palestinians. It would have been enough to have helped build the infrastructure and helped coax, seed, grow, and nurture what would eventually become the Abraham Accords.

But I had been a part of all of that, and more. Ahead was a new life, a new reason to be grateful, a reason to say, "Dayenu."

It's not often that we make the time to take stock of where we have been, where we are, and where we are going. Today was one of those days.

Like any job, mine had certainly had its challenges and frustrations. But it had also provided me and my family with many, many blessings. I'd had the opportunity to work with an incredible group of people, people who didn't just want to make the world a better and a safer place, but people with the courage to try to *get it* done, and not just talk about it. People who had a clear vision for a more stable and a more prosperous world.

I like to think we brought a fresh set of eyes and open ears to the problems in the Middle East. We watched, and listened, and studied, and learned, and we challenged what we thought we knew.

My teachers were many. They were government officials and diplomats—Israeli, Palestinian, Arab, and international. They were ordinary Israelis, Palestinians, and other Arabs. They were people who suffered in this conflict—Christians, Muslims and Jews; religious and secular; children and adults. During my time at the White House, I experienced many emotional and heart-wrenching moments. This long-running conflict that we had inherited had been the subject of countless tragedies and an incalculable amount of grief. And yet, at the same time, I saw so much promise and potential amid those problems. I saw this among Israeli soldiers who tirelessly fight every day to defend the State of Israel, from many, ever-evolving threats. I saw it among Palestinians living under the brutal rule of Hamas in Gaza. I saw it among Palestinians who live in refugee camps, who have been used as pawns in a political game, and who should have been able to start new lives decades ago. I saw it among ordinary Israelis and Palestinians. Among many of them, I found the same values and hopes—and a healthy and unsurprising degree of skepticism about the prospects for peace.

On my journey, I had also found much that was less encouraging. In some places, I found bitterness and cynicism. I found some holding on tight to old resentments, refusing to let them go. I found some who told themselves the same stories that they learned decades ago as children, over and over again, so many times, and so loudly, that they were either unable or unwilling to listen to reason or be persuaded by facts. And among certain officials, I heard demands that were simply not achievable, and that were, and had been, unworkable for decades.

I met with optimists and pessimists, the curious and the naysayers. I met those willing to look forward and see what might be, and those who insisted on dwelling in the past. The optimists, the curious, and the courageous were willing to engage, to discuss, to see if a realistic solution to the conflict exists. The pessimists and the naysayers had a much tougher time trying to envision something different.

And then there was a third group who had made a home for hate in their hearts. They had refused to change and never would. Worse, they had no vision of something beyond that hate, nothing constructive that would build, rather than simply destroy.

In the thirty-three months and ten days of my tenure, I had welcomed constructive criticism and learned a great deal from those who shared their rational doubts, real concerns, and respectful questions. I had embraced their collective wisdom, their expertise, and their ideas, and I benefited from often spirited debates, both internal and external. Whether they were American, Israeli, Palestinian, Saudi, Emirati, Qatari, Bahraini, Omani, Moroccan, Jordanian, Egyptian, European—or from anywhere else—I listened. We did not always see eye to eye, but that didn't mean I plugged my ears to what they were saying.

I knew when I took on this task that there would be no magic wand that President Trump, Prime Minister Netanyahu, or President Abbas could wave to miraculously resolve this conflict. There were, and are, no easy answers or quick fixes. We were committed to honesty in negotiations, and we put aside the slogans and jargon of the past to deal with present-day realities. That approach upset some people. It certainly made many uncomfortable, but we believed it was the only way to make true progress.

Jared, David, and I had been accused of being undiplomatic at times, and perhaps we were, but our critics were rarely diplomatic in their messages to us. Still, that was merely an argument about tone, not about truth.

And the facts themselves proved it was impossible in the long run to improve lives without being truthful. You couldn't make things better by making false promises, raising unrealistic hopes, or proposing unworkable "solutions" that didn't solve anything. It's an axiom that "honesty is the best policy"—but that didn't mean that *dishonesty* was second-best policy—and, therefore, a viable option in diplomacy or the conduct of human relations in general.

The media reaction to the announcement that I was leaving the White House was the predictable and familiar mix of snark and speculation. The blue ribbon in the former category has to go to *New York Magazine*, which ran the headline: "Trump Somehow Replaces Unqualified Mideast Envoy With Even Less Qualified One." In that piece, the author scored a "two-fer"—slamming me as a "real estate lawyer" with "no serious foreign policy experience" with a similar swipe at Avi Berkowitz, a hard-working and dedicated member of the team, who was witheringly described as merely "a 29-year-old Jared Kushner friend who graduated from law school in 2016." Avi did a great job picking up the ball when I left, and continued to run it down the field with his teammates to help President Trump score the ultimate goal, together with the other bold, courageous leaders involved.

The hands-down winner of the prize for speculation, however, came from the executive director of the Arab Center in Washington, who wondered aloud:

What prompted this drastic and unexpected step by Greenblatt? Does his resignation reveal serious differences among members of the team, or between them and President Trump? More significantly, has the impending release of the political component of the Kushner plan led to the emergence of some serious internal disagreements about Israel's role or its anticipated response to the revised plan, pending the results of the Israeli election? Might these differences have made it difficult for Greenblatt to continue in his role of securing Israeli interests as he defines them? And finally, with regard to timing, why would Greenblatt resign just a few days before the dramatic "grand opening" of the show he has been directing for the past three years? No one seems to have complete answers to all these questions except Jason Greenblatt himself.

The only question this guy didn't ask is whether I knew where the Ark of the Covenant was. But he was certainly right about no one having answers to any of the questions he posed. Then again, I might have actually answered his questions if he had ever bothered to ask me.

The truth was that there was nothing at all "sudden" or "dramatic" about my decision to leave. The president and Jared knew all along that I had only planned to stay two years, and there I was, nine months into a third year. If I was going to be a proper father, husband, and family man, there was always going to have to be an end date. There's no question that I owed a great deal to my wife and kids. I couldn't have done my job without them sacrificing in all the ways that they did. Naomi had driven our kids from Teaneck to Washington so many times over the last two and a half years that we ended up naming the family dog "Delaware" in honor of the mid-journey rest stop break they made at the Delaware Welcome Center, ironically renamed the Biden Welcome Center in September 2018.

From time to time, my wife and I would evaluate whether I should stay on, and each time I had felt that too much was at stake to leave. But now my initial job was done—because the plan was done. Our team had carefully studied the conflict, and we had determined our proposed solutions. Perhaps just as importantly, we had changed the conversation in the Middle East. We could see that the relationship between Israel and its neighbors was on a positive path, and we had significantly strengthened the US-Israel relationship as well. In opulent, breathtaking palaces throughout the region I engaged in countless hours of honest, raw, welcome conversation and debate with the Arab leadership about Israel, its place in the region, and the future relationship between these countries and Israel.

The saplings of the relationships between Israel and its Arab neighbors had definitively taken root and were well-watered, tended to, and ready to grow, thrive, and prosper, including Israel's attendance at sporting events, an invitation to have a booth at the World Expo, and other good faith steps taken by some of these countries. I remember when each of these and other similar steps were thought of as remarkable, and at the time they occurred, they indeed *were* remarkable. I remember at the Bahrain conference, the win of getting Israeli press into Bahrain. And the minyan we had with Israeli reporters in a synagogue in Manama. We were all so happy. Each of those steps was great, but eventually, they coalesced into something so much better and bigger in the Abraham Accords. It was a natural breakpoint, and I felt good about handing off my duties to what I knew was a very dedicated group of talented and committed individuals—Jared, David, and Avi—and so many other dedicated people throughout the US government who had helped me over my time at the White House.

The real reason for my departure was that all of this was getting harder on my family; harder financially, harder emotionally because of my now nearly three-year significant separation from them. Now that the first part of the mission was done—the visioning, the architecture, the infrastructure, and the plan itself—I no longer felt that I was leaving the team in the lurch. While I hoped to be around for the launch of the plan, I needed to begin a transition back to my family and private life.

President Trump was so gracious about my decision to leave. On the day that I announced my decision, someone on the White House Communications team composed a very nice tweet for him to send out. I later came into the Oval Office to formally thank the president for the opportunity he had given me.

He looked at the tweet before hitting "send" and said, "Nah, this doesn't do you justice." He deleted it and composed a new one: "After almost three years in my Administration, Jason Greenblatt will be leaving to pursue work in the private sector. Jason has been a loyal and great friend and fantastic lawyer... His dedication to Israel and to seeking peace between Israel and the Palestinians won't be forgotten. He will be missed. Thank you, Jason!"

In my statement, I wrote: "It has been the honor of a lifetime to have worked in the White House for over two and a half years under the leadership of President Trump. I am incredibly grateful to have been part of a team that drafted a vision for peace. This vision has the potential to vastly improve the lives of millions of Israelis, Palestinians and others in the region."

I meant every word of it.

My life was suddenly going to be tremendously different from the way it had been for the last three years. Once again, I would finally be back with my family, in a house—our home—rather than living out of a suitcase. It all sounded positively normal and sane and predictable and, well, wonderful!

As for the prospect of our peace plan and that mission, the president, Jared, David, and Avi were like family to me. It went without saying that I would be around to offer advice or help, if it was needed. And I knew, if and when our plan was finally ready for prime time, that they would let me know. After all, I was only a phone call away.

Two months and twenty-nine days later, that call came.

JANUARY 28, 2020

It was like old times to see Israeli Prime Minister Netanyahu in that joint press conference at the White House, with President Trump, announcing the plan that I had spent so many months working to perfect with the team. Today, after so many delays, it was finally getting the debut it deserved. I was thrilled to be there with my wife and children. They got to see firsthand what I worked on for nearly three years, what they had sacrificed for when I lived apart from them. It was heartwarming to see the Emirati, Bahraini, and Omani ambassadors in the audience.

Like so much else that was inaccurately reported about the Israeli-Palestinian conflict, our plan had long been tagged by the media as the "Deal of the Century"—a catchy phrase that was supposedly coined by President Trump, a former business tycoon who was famous for doing big deals, and this was going to be his biggest yet.

Actually, the title of our plan was a good deal more, well, clunky. We had titled it, "Peace to Prosperity: A Vision to Improve the Lives of the Palestinian and Israeli People."

I don't recall if President Trump ever used the phrase, "Deal of the Century." From my perspective, I had actively tried to avoid using it. From the very beginning, I thought it was one of those slogans that was too slick by half, and the reaction to it was predictably dismissive, even derogatory. For critics, both in the media and elsewhere, the phrase became the subject of endless taunts and jibes. It was another bumper sticker bromide that opponents eagerly embraced to mock an earnest search for a solution to a very serious and long-running conflict.

Trump had given an interview to the *Wall Street Journal* shortly after his surprise (to some) victory in November 2016. At that time, he talked about the seemingly intractable conflict between Israel and the Palestinian leadership. He called it the "war that never ends" and said, "as a deal maker, I'd like to do...the deal that can't be made. And do it for humanity's sake."

According to an official "readout" from an April 3, 2017 meeting at the White House, Egyptian President Abdel Fattah al-Sisi told President Trump that he hoped his administration could find a "solution to the issue of the century with the deal of the century," but that was actually a glitch in translation. What he had really said was that he hoped the Trump administration could find "a solution to the problem of the century"—but without reference to the word *deal*.

Nevertheless, unfortunately, the phrase, "Deal of the Century" began to be widely used. By the time we recognized Jerusalem as Israel's capital in December 2017, it was a snide commonplace that had been attributed to Trump. It became a pithy epithet with which to simultaneously describe and deplore our approach to Middle East diplomacy—that is, as a real estate "deal" being brokered by a bunch of former real estate lawyers. Now, in describing our "Peace to Prosperity Plan," even the venerable "Gray Lady," *The New York Times*, had joined the chorus, along with the *Associated Press*, *Reuters*, and thousands of other media outlets the world over. They all agreed that "what the President has called 'The Deal of the Century'" was finally receiving its official unveiling.

In any event, once the Abraham Accords were announced, I thought the name "Deal of the Century" might be apt after all. The concept behind the Abraham Accords was built into the peace plan released by President Trump in January 2020 and was a part of that plan, or a potential Plan B if the Palestinians failed to seize the opportunity presented to them.

It was a phrase ripe for rebuke, and it came in like a flood. Abbas—who had long ago broken off all contact with the Trump administration and was still sitting up in his tree in Ramallah—called the plan "The Slap of the Century." Not to be outdone, Abbas's ever-loyal colleague, Saeb Erekat, tweeted out that the Trump plan was "The Fraud of the Century." From our friends across the pond at the *London Economist* came the equally judgmental headline, "Steal of the Century"—and there were many, many more.

It was a little like jazz musicians riffing on a well-worn piece of music at the Village Vanguard in Greenwich Village. Only this wasn't entertainment; it was, rather, an honest attempt to craft a solution to a problem affecting literally millions of people. Or at least it was to me. And I knew it was to the team and to President Trump as well. However, the sad truth was, the conflict between Israel and the Palestinian leadership *was* a form of entertainment to far too many people. It was, in its way, a sort of diplomatic "wonder of the world"—the unsolvable puzzle that was engaging precisely because it had never, and, according to many, would never, be solved. There were three things you could be sure of: the sky was blue, water was wet, and the Arabs would never make peace with Israel.

But then, six months later, another phone call. That once-in-a-generation flower that our team had tended for so long was finally about to bloom. The stars had finally aligned.

For decades, the relationship between Israel and the United Arab Emirates had been a cool one. But over the past few years, that had begun to change. Both countries had begun engaging in extensive, though unofficial, cooperative efforts in their joint opposition to Iran's nuclear program and its ambitions to dominate the region.

Over the past six weeks, Jared and Avi had been in almost continual talks with officials in both countries about the possibility, finally, of some sort of formal, public announcement of their desire to recognize this sea change in their relationship. Finally, after a critical, three-way phone call between President Trump,

Prime Minister Netanyahu, and the Crown Prince of Abu Dhabi, the de facto ruler of the United Arab Emirates, they agreed to go public. Hearing about that impending agreement, officials from the Kingdom of Bahrain called Jared and said, "We want to be next."

AUGUST 15, 2020

My son Noah and I were privileged to be among those gathered on the sunny South Lawn of the White House to witness what President Trump rightly called "the dawn of a new Middle East." It was the public premiere of the Abraham Accords—a name chosen to recognize and honor the patriarch of the three Abrahamic faiths and to promote interfaith and intercultural dialogue to advance a culture of peace among these faiths.

Israeli Prime Minister Benjamin Netanyahu called the moment "a pivot of history," one that "heralds a new dawn of peace."

Emirati Foreign Minister Sheikh Abdullah bin Zayed Al Nahyan, the brother of Abu Dhabi's Crown Prince observed, "Today, we are already witnessing a change in the heart of the Middle East—a change that will send hope around the world."

Bahrain's Foreign Minister Abdullatif Al Zayani concurred, saying, "We can see before us a golden opportunity for peace, security and prosperity for our region. Let us together...waste no time in seizing it."

Very soon, others would, indeed, seize the opportunity that the Abraham Accords represented. On October

23, 2020, Israel and Sudan agreed to formalize an agreement on reciprocal ties, making Sudan (home of the historic and deeply misguided Khartoum three No's), the third Arab country to set aside its differences with the Jewish state. And then on December 10, 2020, President Trump announced that the Kingdom of Morocco agreed as well to establish full diplomatic relations with Israel.

At the White House that August day in 2020, I was thinking about the myriad promising possibilities that the Abraham Accords could unleash. At the same time, I was reminded about a private conversation some three years before. I was thinking about the last time I would speak to my old negotiating partner, Saeb Erekat.

Saeb would not live to see Morocco's name added to the lengthening list of Abraham Accords signatories. Sadly, he died of complications from COVID-19 on November 10, 2020.

Not only in politics but also in personality, Saeb and I were polar opposites. By the time I met him in 2017, he had been the chief negotiator for the Palestinians for two decades running. Saeb was a master propagandist whose volatile temper could flare with an ill-perceived word or phrase. He was sensitive, emotional, and strident—qualities that simultaneously defined him, but also made him difficult to deal with at times.

I am the exact opposite. I try my best to choose my words carefully. No matter how emotional the issue, or perhaps precisely because an issue *is* emotional, I try to stay calm and logical and focused. I don't always succeed, but it is my golden rule. None of this is intended to paint a negative picture of Saeb. He was a passionate man, a Palestinian who had spent most of his life fighting for what he felt was right. I often vehemently disagreed with him, and many have said some very unkind things about him. I won't share my thoughts about Saeb here. He has passed away, and it would be disrespectful to share beyond what I have already said publicly while at the White House.

Saeb had been ill with pulmonary fibrosis well before I met him, but his condition deteriorated in 2017. That year, he had to come to the United States for treatment and underwent a lung transplant. At that time, tensions between the Palestinian leadership and the White House—and in particular with our peace team—had already intensified.

The Palestinians did not have an embassy in Washington, D.C. since Palestine was not recognized as a sovereign nation by the United States. However, their political organization, a former—some would argue not so former—terrorist group known as the PLO, or the Palestinian Liberation Organization, was permitted to open a mission in Washington. But there were conditions attached. Among these was a condition that they could not threaten to bring Israel before the International Criminal Court. The Palestinians were always looking for international organizations to make trouble for Israel and to try to gain an edge in their efforts to resolve the conflict without negotiations with Israel; the ICC was one such weapon they could use for that purpose. In the fall of 2017, President Abbas made a speech at the United Nations General Assembly. During that speech, he flagrantly ignored that stipulation, threatening to bring Israel to the ICC. Under US law, the predictable outcome of that threat by Abbas was that the mission was to be shut down.

The situation played out while Saeb was still in the United States recuperating from his lung transplant, and I took advantage of his proximity to pay him a personal visit. He and his wife, Neameh, invited me for lunch. They thoughtfully made sure to order me a kosher meal so that I could eat with them. We spent a long time enjoying our food and talking about their family, including their newest grandchild, who had recently been born.

As much as I did not want to introduce negativity into our visit, I felt that I had to tell Saeb that we were in the process of closing the mission in Washington. I knew it would provoke his anger and indignation, but I wanted him to hear it from me, rather than from a news outlet, and so I became the bearer of that bad news.

"Jason," he said, "If you do that, it's over. You will have failed. You are going to go home a complete failure."

I immediately thought of the young Israelis and Palestinians whom I had met throughout 2017 who deserved a better future. I thought particularly of the two million Palestinians in Gaza, suffering under the repressive regime of Hamas, going through life without the basic necessities, deprived of ample food, cut off from adequate healthcare and electricity because of their miserable, failed leadership.

I met his eyes, and spoke softly, but firmly, with the certitude of my conviction: "I will not have failed. I can go home. I will be with my family. We will live together under one roof, and we will once again enjoy one another and build wonderful memories. You are the one who will have failed, and the Palestinians will once again have failed."

I didn't say anything further, but Saeb knew what I meant. He saw me staring intently at the picture of his new grandchild. He knew I wasn't referring to the peace talks, whose demise had yet to occur, nor the escalation of tensions between our two governments. I was thinking of how Saeb and Abbas were failing, yet again, to create a better future—not only for Saeb's new grandchild—but for so many other children in Gaza and the West Bank. I also wanted him to know that I would never, ever, abandon my convictions or give in to a threat.

Saeb Erekat harshly criticized the Abraham Accords and the Arab leaders who signed them, including accusing them of stabbing him with "an Arab dagger—a poisonous dagger—in my back." Had Saeb been alive, I wonder if his view about the Abraham Accords would change over time. Would he continue to view it as a betrayal of the Palestinian cause, or would he see how this could be the beginnings of strong and prosperous alliances between Israelis, Palestinians, and those in the region around them? Would he eventually see how Palestinians could gain so much by working with the Abraham Accords and building on them for their own future?

I've learned that, as a diplomat, you need to be a pessimist, an optimist, and a realist all at once. My goal is always to be guided by the realist and fight every urge of letting the pessimist take over. But I admit, I am often, perhaps too often, an optimist. The optimist in me would like to think that deep in his heart, over time, Saeb would have viewed these Abraham Accords between Israel and its Arab neighbors with hope rather than hostility. I'd like to believe his thoughts were about his grandchild—and the future—as mine were now. I will never know the answer to that question. No one will. What the future will bring is a mystery, but for now, we have the Abraham Accords—and that is *Dayenu*—it is Dayenu—enough for today. My hope is that tomorrow, and in all the tomorrows yet to come, the Abraham Accords will blossom beyond our wildest imaginations, for the benefit of Israelis, Palestinians, and the entire Arab world.

CHAPTER 13

A Warning—and a Way Forward

In an age of increasingly poisonous identity politics and cultural chasms, a shallow and sensationalist national media, and the ascendancy of a permanent leftist punditocracy, the mere survival of the Abraham Accords is something of a minor miracle.

It says something important about the intrinsic viability and durability of the Abraham Accords that they have already outlived the political tenures of President Donald Trump and Israeli Prime Minister Benjamin Netanyahu, who did so much to foster and facilitate their birth.

In Washington, where practically the entirety of Trump's agenda has either been abrogated or repudiated, the Abraham Accords appear to be the sole surviving diplomatic link in a game-changing foreign policy initiative brokered by the Trump administration and inherited by the Biden administration. Despite the immediate benefits and the future promise they represent, the Biden administration initially has clearly been averse to acknowledging, much less uttering the term, "Abraham Accords"—insipidly referring to them for the most part as "normalization of relations agreements."

Finally, in what seemed to be a concession to the one-year anniversary of the Accords—and likely also as a result of criticism they received—the US Department of State began to use the name "Abraham Accords" instead of simply "normalization agreements." I hope that their original avoidance of the name was not an attempt to deny Trump the appropriate recognition for an obvious political "win," although I spent enough time in Washington, D.C. to know that this was a real possibility.

Meanwhile, the European Parliament marked the one-year anniversary of the Abraham Accords with a vindictive boycott of Expo 2020 in Dubai which was obviously designed to punish the United Arab Emirates for signing their landmark treaty with Israel.

The European Parliament resolution called on EU member states not to participate in the Dubai event, and for international companies to withdraw their sponsorship, ostensibly due to UAE's history of alleged human rights violations. That political body couldn't bring itself to even mention the almost hourly human rights violations of Hamas and Palestinian Islamic Jihad against Palestinians in Gaza, betraying a double standard that gives hypocrisy a bad name.

In the end, none of the dissembling or disparaging statements or petty political tirades really matter. Attempting to minimize the Trump administration's defining role in creating the Abraham Accords is far less important than what those agreements actually mean for Israel, its Arab neighbors, and the advancement of a more peaceful, prosperous, and politically stable Middle East.

If I've heard it once, I've heard it a thousand times: the Abraham Accords are not "peace treaties" in the classic sense, because the Arab countries that have thus far signed these agreements, or agreements based on the Abraham Accords, have never actually engaged in military conflicts with Israel. While this is certainly true, there is a world of difference between a lack of literal warfare between two countries and the positive "warm peace" that the Abraham Accords reflect and represent.

It's also commonly asserted by many diplomatic experts that the Abraham Accords are a diversion of sorts from the "real" issue in the Middle East, which they claim is a comprehensive solution to a future Palestinian state. I think those experts have it exactly backwards. The Abraham Accords prove that the creation of a Palestinian state isn't the sine qua non of greater Israeli-Arab cooperation, but its principle stumbling block.

In my view, the pressing question for the diplomatic community is: Why should the lack of a "perfect" Palestinian state forever forestall the slightest hint of cooperation between Israel and all the other countries in the Middle East? Or, to put it a slightly different way: Why should the Hamas terrorists in Gaza and PLO Chairman Mahmoud Abbas be the unquestioned arbiters over the lives and futures of more than 420 million people in the region?

Could it be that, for some, the continued fierce allegiance to a two-state solution in Washington, Europe, and the United Nations has more to do with personal pride than foreign policy objectives? Could it be that some diplomats are more worried about salvaging careers, based on a faulty premise, than they are in creating a more peaceful and prosperous Middle East?

Before President Trump arrived on the scene, the conventional wisdom in the United States and among our key European allies was that no progress could ever be made on Middle East peace until the Israeli-Palestinian conflict was first successfully dealt with. Such had been the official policy of both Republican and Democratic administrations for seven decades.

From Dean Acheson in the Truman administration to John Kerry in the Obama administration, the refrain was the same: Find the formula for the ever-elusive contours of a Palestinian state, and the Middle East would, somehow, be magically transformed. What we heard from the leaders with whom we spoke in the region led us in a different direction.

When I first came to the White House as a Special Envoy to the Middle East, I was confidently assured of many "facts" which, upon further inspection, proved to be either false on their face or to have been superseded by changing circumstances in the region. Cumulatively, the effect of these assertions tended to support an outdated and simplistic political narrative that I found to be largely misleading and ultimately unhelpful.

The first "fact" to fall was the contention that there existed a single, unified Arab perspective on the Israeli-Palestinian conflict. It just wasn't so. While Arabs take understandable pride in a religion that is shared by so many, as well as a common culture, there is no collective economic or political pan-Arab nationalism that exists much beyond the symbolic and superficial.

An unofficial Arab national anthem sung at sporting events is not a cohesive and compelling example of a fully-functioning pan-Arab movement. That's roughly akin to equating the lyrics of Francis Scott Key's "The Star Spangled Banner" to the United States Constitution and Bill of Rights. The first is a poetic expression of patriotism; the second is an encompassing legal document that sets forth the design for a national government. Within the Arab world, there is no such overarching governmental structure, nor even one state that is recognized by its neighbors as the undisputed leader in such a national movement. Truly common interests are few, while individual state interests routinely supersede any larger pan-Arab ones, as they should.

What I found, as I began my work in the region, was not a single, monolithic view of Israel nor of the Palestinian cause, but a varied collection of often diverse—even competing—opinions, interests, and goals. Some Arab countries viewed Israel with anger and suspicion, but others saw the Israelis as useful and beneficial strategic allies against a common foe, Iran, and a partner to charting a new future. Several of these nations had been pursuing under-the-table relationships with Israel for a decade or more. Still others wearily, albeit privately, complained that the Palestinians had proven themselves impossible to please, and they simply wanted them to negotiate a settlement and move on.

Another "fact" without any particular foundation was the contention that the so-called "two-state solution" was the indispensable predicate to peace in the Middle East. If nothing else, the conspicuous lack of any meaningful progress on the Israeli-Palestinian conflict over the last seventy years seemed to implicitly challenge the premise and credibility of that diplomatic paradigm. I felt instinctively that something else was at work here, and it obviously wasn't about creating a functioning Palestinian state.

In my extensive talks with Arab leaders, there were always the obligatory discussions about the many contentious issues surrounding the Israeli-Palestinian conflict regarding settlements, the so-called Palestinian refugees, and proposed land boundaries. But beyond these familiar and well-rehearsed issues, there was a readily apparent, and growing, tension between their sympathy for the Palestinian people and what had been, until then, a solid show of support for the Palestinian Authority.

These leaders didn't want to abandon the Palestinians themselves, but they were increasingly and deeply frustrated about the significant amounts of money their leaders had expended in supporting the "Palestinian cause" over the years. Time and again, some Arab leaders would complain about the billions of dollars that could have gone toward bettering their own countries, both in terms of critical infrastructure and on the advancement of their own people, that instead went to preserving a seemingly endless "crisis" that was never resolved.

It was increasingly galling to some of them that their financial generosity to the Palestinian leadership was not respected and that the money they gave was so often misused in careless and often corrupt ways. It might not have mattered to them decades ago when all that oil money seemed to be never ending, but conditions had changed. It mattered now.

Some of these Arab leaders were beginning to speak, behind closed doors, about their own national interests and how they needed to put those interests first. Although a final resolution to the Israeli-Palestinian conflict was an outcome they strongly desired, its relative importance often depended on the country and its current circumstances. What was still a political imperative to some was increasingly incidental or even inconsequential to others in the larger scheme of things.

It occurred to me relatively early in my tenure as an envoy that, at least to some diplomats and other professionals long involved in the peace process, keeping the conflict alive seemed to serve a political purpose more important than finding a solution to it. Certainly, this stifling status quo effectively blocked Israel's ability to work with other Arab countries—or they with Israel—except in the shadows.

Meanwhile, I couldn't help noticing there were twenty-two member states in the Arab League; perhaps some of them could be plausible partners with Israel. Even before my first State Department briefing, there was something about the lopsided logic of that age-old diplomatic arithmetic that didn't quite make sense to me.

One of the things I learned during my time in Washington is that negotiation can all too easily become an end in itself, rather than a means to an end. Concentrating on the Israeli-Palestinian conflict, to the exclusion of every other opportunity for Israel to reduce tensions and increase cooperation between itself and other Arab partners, seemed not merely stubborn and non-productive, but downright dangerous, especially given the stakes involved.

The putative "linkage" between the "Palestinian cause" and greater acceptance of Israel in the region may have once been compelling, but by the time we arrived on the scene that was no longer the case, nor had it been the case for years prior to that. Part of that change was due to the growing threat posed by Iran. But much of the reason for that change can be fairly laid at the feet of the Palestinian leadership and their legendary intransigence.

The Palestinians have been offered their own independent state, again and again, from the 1930s onwards, only to refuse to negotiate in good faith. There are any number of other peoples who immediately come to mind—the Uyghurs, the Kurds, the Tibetans, or the Chechens—who would give anything to be on the receiving end of such sustained solicitude by the international community.

By continuing to make perfect the enemy of the good, the Palestinian Authority had, slowly but surely, eroded much of what was once rock-solid political and financial support by its neighbors. For more and more Arab countries, it is was one thing to support the desire of Palestinians for a peaceful state, but it had become increasingly untenable to continue to make that cause a higher priority than the competing needs of their own citizens who both desired and deserved a more prosperous future as well.

The Palestinian leadership demanded that all the other Arab states refrain from any relations with Israel until their own conflict with that nation was concluded to their satisfaction. Once upon a time, all the countries in the region agreed with that strategy for a host of reasons that had as much to do with their own internal politics as it did the Palestinian cause. Over the years, however, that support had become increasingly strained and more conditional in nature. Cracks in the façade of Arab solidarity began to appear and public statements didn't always align with private actions. It didn't help matters that there was a large rift and bitter competition—many would say outright hatred—between the leadership in Ramallah and the so-called leadership in Gaza that, in many ways, seemed to dwarf that between Israel and the Palestinian Authority.

A relentless diplomatic focus on the old two-state "conflict" narrative had made it easier for opponents to blame Israel for the misery of the Palestinians in Gaza, but the real story was messier and far more complicated. In many ways, the Palestinians in Gaza were the pawns in a years-long political struggle between President Abbas's Fatah faction and Hamas, which had absolutely nothing to do with Israel. Hamas, for example, frequently refers to Abbas as a "traitor" for merely agreeing to security coordination between the PA security forces and their Israeli counterparts in the West Bank. Meanwhile, Palestinians who dare to "collaborate" with Israel in any way—merely working for an Israeli, or selling a plot of land to a Jew—are frequently the subject of imprisonment, and even death sentences. Abbas has tried repeatedly for years to put pressure on Hamas to relinquish control of Gaza, to little effect.

Hamas, meanwhile, continues to divert the massive amount of foreign aid meant to help the Palestinians in Gaza to construct schools, hospitals, and industrial parks for their own nefarious purposes. They use much of it to train their military, manufacture weapons and dig massive tunnel networks that are used to attack Israel. Today, it's estimated that 80 percent of Gazans live in poverty and unemployment there remains at a staggering 65 percent.

When Israeli authorities announced in October 2021 that a limited number of Palestinians in the Hamas-ruled Gaza Strip would be able to work in Israel, tens of thousands of defiantly brave Palestinians converged on the offices of the chambers of commerce throughout the Strip in the hope of obtaining a permit to work in Israel. Such scenes are the best evidence yet of how desperate Palestinians are for work in the country they are supposed to hate. It is also a deeply embarrassing commentary on the failure of Hamas and the Palestinian Authority to do anything concrete to improve the living conditions for their people. This, despite the billions they have received from the United States, the European Union, and the United Nations over the years.

If Israel is the proverbial "black hat" in the region, why do so many thousands of Palestinians want to work for them? Similarly, if Israel's "occupation" is the core of the conflict and a shared grievance, why hasn't the Palestinian Authority been able to reconcile with Hamas in this common cause? Why are average Palestinians threatened with long prison sentences, and even death, for cooperating with Israel? How is Israel supposed to deal in good faith with the same terrorists President Abbas can't control?

It always seemed to me that the problem here was not Israel, but Hamas. What bargaining chips, concessions, or commitments could Israel ever make to entice Hamas's homicidal hoodlums to not carry out their intentions? What objective facts would persuade anyone to believe that Hamas will suddenly decide to give up its terrorist tactics or its goal of Israel's total destruction? That Hamas and the Palestinian Islamic Jihad are directly supported by Iran, a foe feared and hated by other countries in the region, scarcely contributes to a sense of Arab solidarity around the idea of Palestinian statehood.

As I made my rounds in the region, I was struck, again and again, by how many countries were increasingly viewing the technologically savvy Israelis as their last best hope for successfully confronting the terrorist mullahs in Tehran and improving their economies. At the same time, for an increasing number of these countries, Palestinian statehood had begun to seem more like a dangerous distraction than a political necessity. Each time the Palestinian leadership would reject a new attempt to craft an acceptable deal, the suspicion grew that the Palestinian leadership did not, in fact, really want an independent state. If they did, surely by now, they would have found a solution out of all those formulated, that would have been acceptable to them.

The creation of a Palestinian State living in peace beside Israel has been an idée fixe of the international community for almost as long as Israel, itself, has existed as a modern nation. In that time, it is no exaggeration to say that virtually every possible permutation for creating such a state has been proposed, and subsequently rejected, by the Palestinian leadership.

Why did all those well-intentioned efforts on behalf of so many people fail to persuade the Palestinian leadership? Sheer stubbornness is certainly one factor, as is a general inability or unwillingness to face facts and changing circumstances.

And then, there's a third possibility. In negotiations that have now literally spanned a lifetime, what constitutes "success" is, more and more, in the eye of the beholder. It has as much to do with process as it does with outcomes. Simply keeping their cause alive has, itself, become a species of victory for the Palestinian leadership.

And yet, a fundamental question remains: Can any actual political settlement of the Israeli-Palestinian conflict ever suffice to satisfy the expectations that decades of ever-more extravagant promises and propaganda have engendered among the Palestinian people?

Step by ineluctable step, the negotiating process has become increasingly untethered from reality. For years now, Israeli-Palestinian negotiations have essentially ceased to be about realistic, mutual compromises that would lead to a satisfactory solution. From the Palestinian side, ever-expanding right-of-return demands for the children, grandchildren and great-grandchildren of refugees, the uprooting of Israeli cities, towns, and neighborhoods in areas claimed by the Palestinians, and the forced contraction of the Israeli state back to its indefensible 1948 borders are so farfetched that they represent little more than exercises in wish fulfillment. What the Palestinian leadership describe and demand are not the conditions for a real state but a dream state. It's a chimera, not a political possibility.

And so, instead of a solution, there is a continuing stalemate. Instead of a final victory, there is, instead, an open-ended grievance. There's a certain method to what otherwise seems like madness. After all, the flush of triumph soon wanes, but an appeal to a "cause" can build and sustain a fervent and continuing constituency of mythic proportions. Then, too, an actual sovereign state has very real problems that its leaders must take own-ership of and responsibility for. By contrast, the "dream" of a state is just that—an ever elusive, yet infinitely per-fectible, future in which all strife is erased, all obsta-cles overcome—and, as Hamas still hopes, all Jews will be eliminated.

In terms of political positioning, what may seem like an apparent failure of the Palestinian leadership to accept a final status agreement allows them to strike a heroic pose at home and abroad. It also keeps their cur-rent gravy train running at full throttle.

A self-governing and independent Palestine would mean that the billions in donations that currently pour into the coffers in Ramallah and Gaza—including annual aid from other Arab countries—would finally come to an end. What happens when the handouts stop and the hard business of actually governing begins? It doesn't appear that Palestinian President Mahmoud Abbas, much less his Hamas opposites in Gaza, are in any hurry to find out.

The obvious downside of this strategy is that, after seventy years of repeatedly saying no to a deal, the dream of an independent Palestinian State, which once had a universal claim on the conscience and cash of other countries in the region, is increasingly seen by other Arabs not as a cause for which they should con-tinue to sacrifice blood and treasure, but a con in which they are ever more the hapless victims.

Unlike the Israeli-Palestinian conflict, where no amount of concessions from Israel appear sufficient to prevent continued terrorist attacks, the Abraham

Accords proceed from the premise that each nation has something positive to offer the other, whether that be trade, tourism, technology transfers, or security initiatives and the like.

The Abraham Accords embody an almost infinitely flexible and reliable strategic framework, one that allows the United States and its greatest ally in the Middle East to no longer be a prisoner of a single and seemingly insoluble conflict.

The Abraham Accords were a recognition that successful, one-on-one agreements with Israel and its Arab neighbors could be shaped as long as the strategic objectives of both parties could be met.

The Abraham Accords have already begun to change the conversation in the Middle East. They provide a practical exit ramp of sorts from a cynical diplomatic circularity that thrives on procrastination and the systematic sidestepping of critical issues. For the sake of a more peaceful and prosperous region, it's a conversation well worth continuing.

The Biden administration needs to seize the moment and capitalize on the forward progress already made. There is every reason to believe that other countries in the region would come forward as additional signatories to the Abraham Accords if the United States indicates its willingness to commit itself to that diplomatic framework. Israel, its Arab neighbors, and indeed the entire world, are waiting to see what path America will choose. But in making that choice, our commitment must not be tentative or ambiguous. Only by taking an active and leading role can we make the significant strides necessary to achieve the goal of a peaceful, prosperous, and progressive Middle East.

From the very beginning, the Abraham Accords have been guided by the straightforward belief that the possibility of peace between Israel and its Arab neighbors should not have to wait for permission from the PLO, the Palestinian Authority, or Hamas. Despite seven decades' worth of intense—one might well say even myopic—focus by the US and the international community, the truth is, the Israeli-Palestinian conflict simply wasn't a major issue of the day for them anymore.

What *was* a major issue for these leaders—and what some of the most intense exchanges centered on—was their deep sense of betrayal by President Obama because of the Iran deal. By far, their gravest concern was what to do about a terrorist Iran in their midst and its hegemonic ambitions in the Middle East and elsewhere. Indeed, on this issue of an ascendant Iran, both Israel and its Arab neighbors were on the same page.

To put it mildly, the previous eight years of the Obama administration's many diplomatic overtures and outright giveaways to Iran had done nothing to signal to Israel or to the Arab states in the region that the United States was in the least serious about reining in this ever-growing Jihadi juggernaut. By contrast, both Israel's government and the Arab leaders I spoke with felt that President Trump was, finally, someone in the Oval Office who understood their common needs and interests. They felt he was a partner in fighting against extremism, terrorism, and just plain evil. It made sense to them that Israel had a right to defend itself against terrorism coming out of Gaza, just as Saudi Arabia, for example, had a right to defend itself from Houthi terrorists from Yemen.

It was, in fact, only in May 2018, when President Trump formally withdrew the United States from the JCPOA, and later in November of that same year when the president reinstated sanctions targeting Iran and the states that trade with it, that the mullahs knew there was a new sheriff in town.

Those sanctions led to a crippling decline in Iran's economy and a quadrupling of its annual inflation rate, resulting in internal protests from Iran's own people and simultaneously driving away formerly willing foreign investors. The sanctions would have had even more bite if some of our chief European allies had not valued profits over people. As it was, these nations quickly set up an alternative payment scheme that allowed international companies to continue to trade with that treacherous regime without facing US penalties.

While the Middle East is a very dangerous place, perhaps even more dangerous has been the illusion that the terrorist leaders in Tehran can, somehow, be bribed into becoming peaceful partners in the family of nations. Israel has long understood that such appeasement is futile.

Peace is rarely possible without a show of strength. At any rate, weakness, whether real or perceived, often invites war. Israel and the Gulf States can't afford to rely on lofty proclamations and promises from Washington that Iran won't attack them. They, after all, are in the direct line of fire and their survival can be measured in seconds.

But the Middle East is not just a dangerous place because of Iran's bone-deep commitment to violence. Far worse are the nations who look on, or look away, and do nothing to stop them in their murderous path. It was President Trump's determination that we would not be one of them.

We face a very real danger at this moment in history. The foreign policy success of the Abraham Accords can be significantly set back, or even undone, if the Biden administration is inattentive and neglects or pursues misguided policy objectives in the region. Regretfully, all of these things seem painfully apparent to the mind and eye of a careful observer. Chief among these is the current administration's publicly stated commitment to a perilous replay of the JCPOA negotiated with Iran during the Obama administration when Biden was then vice president.

History often has a nasty way of repeating itself. With respect to the first iteration of the JCPOA under President Obama, it was readily apparent that this was a disastrous deal from the start, as then-candidate Trump said repeatedly on the campaign trail. The agreement was one that both emboldened and enriched the most extremist anti-American sponsor of terror in the Middle East, if not the entire world.

Under the JCPOA's lavish provisions, Iran gained unrestricted access to tens of billions of dollars in previously frozen assets. It was free to resume selling oil on international markets and using the global financial system for trade. It was, at best, an unbelievably naïve arrangement. It allowed Iran to double down on its expansionist and destabilizing activities in a host of countries including Syria's Assad dictatorship, where hundreds of thousands have perished, as well as its attacks, either directly or by proxy, in Iraq, Yemen, Lebanon, Bahrain, Saudi Arabia and the UAE, not to mention its continued backing of terrorist organizations like Hamas and Hezbollah, which have both been directly responsible for thousands of deaths, including those of many Americans, civilian and military.

So far, the Biden administration has made no progress whatsoever in building on the Abraham Accords, preferring instead to pursue a perilous rapprochement with Iran while simultaneously attempting to coax Palestinian President Mahmoud Abbas to come down from his tree in Ramallah, where he continues to pout about his declining political relevance.

That said, I know first-hand that progress in the Middle East can be difficult. The Abraham Accords were the result of years of behind-the-scenes work that finally clicked into place toward the end of our administration. Perhaps the same is true of the Biden team. I certainly hope that's the case.

The seeds we planted among those who have not yet signed the Accords are lying in the soil. Some are dormant; others have green shoots already peeking forth, but they will require an incredible amount of tender nurturing to grow and blossom. Pursuing rapprochement with Iran, mistreating Saudi Arabia, a key friend and ally, and coddling the Palestinian Authority are unlikely to help grow those seedlings, and may well cause them to whither and rot.

A failure to embrace the Abraham Accords and make expanding on them a priority would represent a missed opportunity of significant proportions—one that appears to have rare, bipartisan support in an otherwise polarized Congress. Especially after his disastrous and humiliating withdrawal from Afghanistan in September 2021, President Biden would seem to desperately need a foreign policy success that expanding on the Abraham Accords could provide.

Even if the Biden administration fails to diligently work on the possibility of increasing the list of signatories to the Abraham Accords, Congress appears to recognize its possibilities.

A promising piece of legislation that seeks to capitalize on the Abraham Accords is the Israel Relations Normalization Act of 2021, sponsored by Democratic Congressman Brad Schneider of Illinois in the House of Representatives and Republican Senator Rob Portman of Ohio in the Senate. The bill calls on the State Department to assess how the Abraham Accords "advance prospects for peace between Israelis and Palestinians."

This legislation seeks to build upon the success of the Abraham Accords by explicitly stating that it is US policy to expand and strengthen these normalization agreements while requiring coordination throughout the administration. I wholeheartedly support this bipartisan legislative effort.

In introducing the bill in the House, Rep. Schneider observed that the Abraham Accords were "historic steps for a more peaceful, secure, and prosperous future in the Middle East" that the United States "must continue to nurture in the pursuit of regional stability."

The Israel Relations Normalization Act of 2021 would require the State Department to provide a strategy to strengthen and expand the Abraham Accords and other related normalization agreements with Israel through:

o An assessment regarding the future staffing and resourcing requirements of entities across the interagency for expanding and strengthening normalization agreements.

o An assessment regarding areas of cooperation such as economic, social, cultural, scientific, technical, educational, and health fields, as well as identification of potential roadblocks in these sectors to increase cooperation among states.

o An assessment regarding potential areas for further security cooperation as well as identification of potential roadblocks to future cooperation.

o As assessment of opportunities created by normalization agreements to advance prospects for peace between Israelis and Palestinians.

o A detailed description of how the US government will leverage diplomatic lines of effort and resources from other stakeholders to encourage normalization, economic development, and people-to-people programming.

The bill would also require a report on international efforts to promote normalization through:

o Identification of existing relevant investment funds that support Israel-Arab state cooperation and recommendations for how such funds could be used to support normalization and increase prosperity for all relevant stakeholders.

o An assessment of the feasibility and benefit of increasing the capacity of existing State and USAID-funded programs for developing people-to-people exchange programs for young people between Israel, Arab states, and other relevant countries and regions.

o Recommendations to improve Department of State cooperation and coordination, particularly between the Special Envoy to Monitor and Combat Anti-Semitism, the Ambassador at-Large for International Religious Freedom, and the Director of the Office of International Religious Freedom, to combat racism, xenophobia, Islamophobia, and anti-Semitism.

o A proposal for how the US government and others can use existing federal resources to counter

Holocaust denial and anti-Semitism abroad. An assessment on the value and feasibility of inter-agency support for inter-parliamentary exchange programs for Members of Congress, Knesset, and parliamentarians from Arab states and other relevant countries and regions, including through existing federal programs that support such exchanges.

Lastly, the bill would require a report on the status of anti-normalization laws in Arab states and other relevant countries and regions. The bill should be crystal clear that the anti-normalization activity directly and indirectly supported by the Palestinian Authority, the PLO, and others acting at their behest should be included in these reports. The report would include:

o Instances of prosecution of citizens or residents of Arab countries for calling for peace with Israel, visiting the state of Israel, or engaging Israeli citizens in any way.

o Instances of extrajudicial retribution by Arab governments or government-controlled institutions against citizens or residents of Arab countries.

o Steps taken by Arab governments toward permitting or encouraging people-to-people relations between their citizens or residents and Israeli citizens.

In my opinion, these reports, while a good beginning, are not sufficient. I think there should be real consequences for this sort of pernicious activity. This has traditionally been one of the chief ways that other views, supportive of closer relations between Palestinians and Israelis, have been silenced. It's long past time that the Palestinian people should be free to speak for themselves, without fear of imprisonment—or worse.

Promoting the Abraham Accords should not be a partisan project. America and Israel share a deep desire and mutual interest in working with others in the region. It's obviously in America's long-term strategic interest to help forge lasting ties between Israel and our Arab allies. Promoting those ties will allow them to work more closely than ever before. The relationships they develop will, in turn, help counter the Iranian threat they share. Such partnerships will also enhance regional stability and bolster their economies. A more stable Middle East means a reduced threat to America, our military, and our interests in general. The formation of a bipartisan Abraham Accords Caucus in early 2022 to support and promote the Abraham Accords, especially when Congress remains deeply fractured along party lines, is a step in the right direction. I hope we see more important efforts like this.

The Abraham Accords were not designed to remain the preserve of a single administration or a single political party. In fact, their survival depends on strong bipartisan support that is sustained across the periodic domestic successes or defeats of a particular president or party. These new relationships between Israel and its Arab neighbors—and the additional relationships that can be forged in the future—should be the common objective of Republicans and Democrats, indeed even among the progressive portion of the Democrats.

Just as a strong US-Israel partnership has traditionally been a bipartisan effort in the past, the goal of bringing our regional allies in the Middle East together in the pursuit of our common interests should be a shared objective in the future. It is, quite literally, in the world's interest that Israel concludes as many of these agreements with Arab leaders as possible. As more Arab leaders forge ties with Israel, they are not only expanding the opportunities for their people but also increasing the prospect for broader Israeli-Arab and Israeli-Palestinian peace.

A PEACE DIVIDEND

When Bahrain and the UAE signed the Abraham Accords in September of 2020 on the White House lawn, it marked a landmark shift for the region—the first time Israel had signed a major diplomatic agreement with an Arab country in twenty-five years. Before Trump's term of office ended, Sudan and Morocco also announced their intentions to establish full diplomatic relations with Israel.

The Abraham Accords turn a page in an ongoing story that is a new and modernizing Middle East. This new chapter heralds not just the cessation of hostility but the beginning of a new hope of peace and prosperity for the entire region. It's the starting point of new strategic alliances between Israel and its Arab neighbors that benefits them both.

The Abraham Accords foster economic development, but they also represent the beginning of an ever more powerful and united front in the face of threats from Iran, a common foe. And although the Palestinian leadership has rejected them outright, the Abraham Accords also provides a useful path to what can eventually be a warm and peaceful co-existence with Israel by all of its Arab neighbors, including the Palestinians.

The impact of the Abraham Accords, which was made possible by a strong US-Israel partnership that President Trump had rebuilt on the ruins of the previous administration, demonstrates that engaging with Israel creates opportunities for peace, prosperity, and progress.

Israel and its Abraham Accords partners have so far signed numerous diplomatic agreements to facilitate new cooperation in areas such as joint innovation, tourism, sports, culture, science, air transit, and technology.

To streamline travel, Israel and the UAE signed a visa waiver agreement, enabling Israelis and Emiratis to travel freely without a visa. Israel and Bahrain established the world's first bilateral agreement for COVID-19 vaccine passports.

Travel between Israel and its new partners has accelerated dramatically—some even jokingly refer to the Abraham Accords as "The Travel Accords" because of the huge increase in airflights for tourism and business. In just the first ten months since the signing of the

Abraham Accords, for example, 200,000 Israelis visited the United Arab Emirates alone. Commercial airlines have signed unprecedented flight and travel agreements with Israel, establishing direct flights from Tel Aviv to Dubai, Marrakesh, and Manama, though COVID-19 has understandably narrowed the volume of travel.

Just as important, Israel and its Abraham Accords partners are actively exploring defense-production and intelligence-sharing agreements to counter the mutual threat of Iran—something that enormously enhances regional stability.

For me, the Abraham Accords are a template of how progress can be achieved in the Middle East. It's a valuable way forward, and it represents a new way of thinking about things. The benefits are not confined to the Middle East, either; if that region is more peaceful and prosperous, that benefits the United States as well, both in economic and strategic terms.

The sea change from conflict to cooperation embodied in the Abraham Accords and other related normalization agreements with Israel portends significant socioeconomic prospects for Israel and the four current signatories to those agreements, the positive effects of which are hard to overestimate.

A recent Rand Corporation study forecasts nearly $70 billion in direct new aggregate economic benefits for Israel and its four partners in these separate Free Trade Agreements over the next decade and the creation of almost 65,000 new jobs. If all five partners, in turn, trade with one another in a plurilateral FTA, Rand calculates the additional aggregate benefits to exceed $148 billion and the jobs created to exceed 180,000.

If other possible signatories mentioned in the Rand report, such as Oman, Indonesia, Mauritania, Pakistan, Uzbekistan, and Saudi Arabia were to sign onto the Accords in a plurilateral FTA, Rand estimates that, over the next decade, new aggregate economic activity would exceed $1.3 trillion and would result in a job creation figure that tops 4 million.

In many ways, the Abraham Accords can be likened to the formation of the European Union in the late 1940s by its six founding members: Germany, France, Italy, Belgium, Luxembourg, and the Netherlands. The leaders of those nations envisioned a common economic and political association that would bind them together in a positive, shared future, and thereby put an end to the all-too-frequent wars between neighbors that had culminated in World War II. The Abraham Accords can serve much the same purpose in the Middle East, which has long been a poster child for bone-deep grievances and bloody conflicts.

THE UNITED ARAB EMIRATES

The UAE's deal with Israel is the largest success resulting from the Abraham Accords. Commercial ties between the two countries are robust and thriving. From the growth of kosher food offerings in Dubai (lucky me!) to a massive UAE investment in Israel's offshore natural gas industry, this is already a booming and mutually beneficial relationship. In 2021, the national rugby teams of the UAE and Israel held their first friendly game in Dubai, signaling a man-in-the-street level of familiarity that, for all their fame, the negotiations at Camp David or Oslo never achieved.

Equally symbolic and significant, Israel and the UAE are even collaborating on a joint space mission that could see the two nations' flags planted on the moon by 2024. The Beresheet 2 shared mission will carry a satellite jointly designed by students from both countries that will help pinpoint the precise time of a new moon—something important to both nations, since both Jewish and Muslim calendars, and the dates of their respective major holidays, are driven by the moon's cycle. As an observant Jew, I can thoroughly relate to this and appreciate this.

None of these things would have been possible without the Abraham Accords. And the Abraham Accords, in turn, would not have been possible without the political courage of UAE's leadership.

Sheikh Mohamed bin Zayed bin Sultan Al Nahyan, colloquially known by his initials as MBZ, is a unique leader. One of the most influential people in the Middle East, he also one of the most humble and thoughtful. Wise and extraordinarily open-minded, he knows the best way to plan for the future is to create it. UAE's Foreign Minister Sheikh Abdullah bin Zayed, known as ABZ, is likewise a forward-looking figure in his own right and a gentleman through and through. He was always thoughtful in his approach and willing to lend a helping hand. Ambassador Yousef Al Otaiba is quite simply one of the best ambassadors in the business. From my first lunch with him as White House Envoy, it was clear that if any progress were possible, he would be essential to it.

I remember when Sheikh Abdullah and Yousef first told me about the plans for The Abrahamic Family House in 2019, a year before the Abraham Accords came into existence. The concept took my breath away. Presently under construction on Saadiyat Island in Abu Dhabi, it will feature a synagogue, a church, and a mosque in a single complex that, like the Abraham Accords, derives its name from that Biblical figure who is universally recognized and revered by Jews, Christians, and Muslims alike. It's an architectural testament to an ancient covenant between G-d and man and the commonalties we share. It represents the continuing hope that we can ultimately bridge our differences and overcome the obstacles to cooperation and greater understanding among our three faith traditions.

These days, Emiratis and Israelis are hard at work expanding on the Abraham Accords in practically every commercial category, and Sheikh Abdullah is openly predicting that his country will meet or exceed $1 trillion in bilateral trade over the next decade. It's clear that the relationship between government officials in the UAE and Israel are growing to be warm and personal. Less public, but certainly no less important, Israel and the UAE are also continuing to explore common efforts to counter the security threat represented by a rogue Iranian state.

BAHRAIN

His Majesty, King Hamad bin Isa bin Salman Al Khalifa, was never shy about acknowledging that because the ways of the past did not work, he was open to hearing new ideas. His willingness to listen and consider new approaches was refreshing. King Hamad's decision to host the conference in Manama that launched the economic portion of President Trump's peace plan in 2019 was a very courageous thing to do, and an extremely important step in that process.

While the island nation of Bahrain, with a total population of just 1.5 million people, is far smaller than the UAE, it is nevertheless expecting to benefit from joining the Abraham Accords as well. To that end, Bahrain has been working to position itself as a center for online trading and global fin-tech—the computer programs and other technology that is used to support or enable banking and financial services. It's seeking to attract foreign investors by offering a zero corporate tax and in helping foreigners do business in the kingdom. With the help of one of its Abraham Accords partners, the UAE, along with Saudi Arabia and Kuwait, Bahrain has committed approximately $10 billion to that effort. Undoubtedly Crown Prince Salman bin Hamad Al Khalifa will play an important role in this economic growth. He too was willing to listen with open ears and an open mind.

According to Dalal Buhejji, the executive director of Investment Origination at the Bahrain Economic Development Board (EDB), this tiny island nation has the longest established financial center in the region and is already home to close to four hundred financial institutions. It's also the first country in the region to embrace "open banking," a banking practice that provides third-party financial service providers open access to consumer banking, transaction, and other financial data from banks and non-bank financial institutions through the use of Application Programming Interfaces (APIs).

Open banking allows the networking of accounts and data across institutions for use by consumers, financial institutions, and third-party service providers. By relying on networks instead of centralization, open banking can help financial services customers securely share their financial data with other financial institutions. From fraud protection to securing the best mortgage rate or business loan, open banking is the wave of the future.

When I first visited Bahrain, I was unaware that it had long housed a small Jewish community that dated back to the late 1800s, and I took the opportunity to pray at the synagogue in Manama. I remember how the fact that we held a minyan in the synagogue there was such big news; videos of us singing there made some waves across various social media platforms. Like so many other steps that were important at the time, they seem small in comparison now. I was also surprised to learn that Houda Ezra Ebrahim Nonoo, who is Jewish, served as Bahrain's ambassador to the United States from 2008 to 2013. She was also the third woman to be appointed as Bahrain's representative in Washington.

It's no surprise to me that Bahrain decided to enter the Abraham Accords. As much, and perhaps more than almost any other country, their views and values were wholly consistent with the spirit of those historic agreements.

MOROCCO

I must confess a sentimental fondness for Morocco as an observant Jew. Morocco was formerly a major Jewish population center, and consequently hundreds of thousands of Israeli Jews trace their lineage there. Unsurprisingly, Morocco has long considered Israel to be its second-largest diaspora, after France. And perhaps no Muslim leader in recent history is more beloved by Jews than Sultan Mohammed V, the third son of Sultan Moulay Youssef, scion of the Alaouite family, which has proudly ruled Morocco since 1649. Mohammed V was handpicked by the French to succeed his father when he was just seventeen years old. No doubt, they thought the young prince would be a compliant client in their colonial ambitions. They couldn't have been more wrong.

When representatives of Nazi Germany and Vichy France met with King Mohammed V during the Holocaust to discuss the issue of Jews in Morocco, he famously stated: "There are no Jewish citizens, there are no Muslim citizens, they are all Moroccans." King Mohammed V, as it turned out, took seriously his role as descendant of the Prophet and "Commander of the Faithful." As a consequence, the Jews of Morocco were not sent away to be systematically slaughtered in concentration camps and death camps like six million of their Jewish contemporaries elsewhere.

King Mohammed V's tradition of interfaith respect continues today with His Majesty King Mohammed VI who has said he interprets his title, "Commander of the Faithful" as "the Commander of all believers...(including) Moroccan Jews and Christians from other countries, who are living in Morocco."

Given that rich interfaith history between Jews and Muslims in Morocco, the Abraham Accords, in so many ways, formalizes ties between Israel and Morocco that have run deep for decades.

While many in the media took Morocco's decision to sign a trilateral agreement with Israel and the US in the spirit of the Abraham Accords as something in the nature of a given because of that country's long-standing Jewish connection, that was not the case. King Mohammed VI initially took a "wait-and-see" attitude about normalization with Israel. Among other considerations, the king was very conscious of his role in connection with the protection of Islam's holy sites and was committed to the Palestinian cause. The sovereignty of the Moroccan Sahara was a very important issue as well, and I was sympathetic to their cause. I believe President Trump made the right decision when he recognized

Morocco's sovereignty over that long-disputed territory. I had pushed for that in 2018, as it was the only realistic answer. But the time was not yet ripe. Morocco's foreign minister, Nasser Bourita, was a very helpful partner in this process, pragmatic and open-minded.

King Mohammed VI was courageous in entering into a trilateral declaration with Israel with the same spirit and the dynamics as the Abraham Accords. The friendship between Israel and Morocco, which is already evident, has the potential to grow enormously in the future.

Increased cultural and religious outreach aside, the Abraham Accords is expected to have a very significant effect on the economies of both Israel and Morocco. Direct flights between the two nations will boost the tourist trade in both countries, hopefully in both directions. The expected benefits for future economic development, trade deals, and technology transfers between these two nations are yet to come. The only limits on that cooperation—and the prosperity that flows from it—are our own imaginations of what is possible.

SUDAN

Signing the Abraham Accords was a big step for Sudan, although I was not personally involved in it. Their decision to do so occurred after my departure from the White House.

Sudan is a country that actually waged war with Israel twice, in 1948 and 1967. It was also, infamously, the location of the Arab League Summit in Khartoum that issued the "three no's": No to recognition of Israel, No to peace with Israel, and No to negotiations with Israel. Sudan is also the country which infamously played host to Osama bin Laden in the 1990s. And yet, precisely because of that history, a Sudan-Israel peace agreement is actually all the more meaningful.

Agreeing to normalize relations with Israel represented a sea change in how Sudan is perceived on the world stage. As part of the agreement, the United State removed it from the US list of states that sponsor terror.

One of the positive consequences of signing the agreement was a $1 billion bridge loan from the United States, which has had a positive effect on Sudan's shaky economy and has subsequently given it access to the World Bank for the first time in nearly thirty years. The hope for Sudan is that these signs of good faith by the United States, the World Bank, and others like the UAE will help them stabilize their economy and make long overdue improvements to their infrastructure that has deteriorated greatly over the past couple of decades.

While the transformation of this former Islamist state is still very much a work in progress, Sudan's addition to the roll of Abraham Accords is a strong and significant signal of sorts to other Arab countries that peace with Israel is something well worth contemplating.

There are several other Arab states in the region that fall into a category I'd like to optimistically call "not yet signatories to the Abraham Accords" such as Qatar, Oman, and Saudi Arabia. I believe the leaders in these countries may one day decide that a closer relationship with Israel is in their best interests.

QATAR

Qatar has quietly been working informally with Israel for many years. One could argue that Qatar was one of the earliest Arab countries to normalize its relationship with Israel in 1996 with the opening of a trade office and a visit by Israel's then-President Shimon Peres. Israeli athletes have participated at sporting competitions in Doha over the years, way before the Abraham Accords were a twinkle in anyone's eye. The relationship between the two countries is handled quietly, without fanfare, and it certainly has gone through its challenges over the years.

It is my firm belief that Qatar has nothing against Israel, and certainly not against Jews. The Emir of Qatar, Sheikh Tamim bin Hamad Al Thani, remains a staunch supporter of the Palestinian cause, yet I believe our meetings with the Emir were important and productive. I was also very impressed with Foreign Minister Sheikh Mohammed bin Abdulrahman Al Thani, who I always found to be a practical, sincere, straight shooter and was always available when called upon.

The level of professionalism from Sheikh Mohammed and others in Doha was impressive. Qatar indeed has its very clear red lines when it comes to Israel, but I found the leadership willing to try to get to a yes, or offer alternatives, if we respected those red lines.

Qatar is often accused of funding Hamas. I think it is important to recognize that during the time we were at the White House, the funds sent by Qatar to Gaza were done in coordination with the Israeli government. While not an ideal situation, and I certainly understand the concern of many, my view has been that if the Israeli government decided it was in their interest to work with Qatar on this, it was not our place to interfere.

Many in the United States, the Gulf countries, Israel, and elsewhere accuse the Qatar-based media behemoth *Al Jazeera* of being biased and then some. Indeed, I have wildly different viewpoints on *Al Jazeera* when it comes to so many things, especially and including its treatment of and reporting on Israel, and some of our other friends and allies in the region—the UAE, Saudi Arabia, Bahrain, Egypt, and others. While at the White House and after, I was often interviewed by *Al Jazeera* and was surprised by the strident nature of their questions and reporting. Yet, I believe that the way to introduce change is not to hurl criticism and do nothing else. Instead, I believe that to effect real change, we need to comfortable with the strength of our positions and bring them to networks and audiences that are not accustomed to hearing our views and help show them why they should think differently.

A formal recognition by Qatar of Israel is a bridge too far at the moment, yet it's my hope that the existing informal business and cultural ties will continue to grow until such a recognition is eventually possible.

OMAN

Among all the Arab states, Oman has perhaps been mentioned more often than any other state as a possible addition to the roll of Abraham Accords signatories. By comparison with its neighbors, Oman is notably moderate and out of necessity tries hard to maintain cordial ties with all the regional powers in the Middle East.

Recently, Eliav Benjamin, an Israeli foreign ministry official, told reporters that Oman was a country that Israel has had sustained, albeit low-level, relations with for the last three decades, leading many to speculate that Oman would soon sign an agreement with Israel. Since the late Sultan of Oman, Qaboos bin Said Al Said, who welcomed Prime Minister Netanyahu to Oman during the time we served in the White House, is no longer the policymaker, I am not certain which way that wind is blowing. But without betraying any confidences, I would say that, when the circumstances merit it, a formal relationship between Oman and Israel is not merely possible but likely.

SAUDI ARABIA

As White house envoy, my first visit to the Kingdom of Saudi Arabia was far different—in a very positive way—than I ever would have imagined. Saudi Arabia is a country on the move and the reason for that largely resides with Crown Prince Mohammad bin Salman (MBS). He is a truly visionary leader. I cannot possibly understand what then-candidate Biden was trying to accomplish when he said that he planned to make the "Saudis pay the price, and make them, in fact, the pariah that they are," and also when he said there is "very little social redeeming value in the present government in Saudi Arabia.

Aside from the fact that I strongly disagree with that view, what does it accomplish to alienate a key ally and friend of ours in the Middle East? If we have issues with our friends and allies, we should address them, but not in this way. This is not merely unhelpful; it is downright harmful.

While Saudi Arabia is a steadfast supporter of the Palestinian cause and has given massive sums of money to them over the decades, they also want the Palestinian leadership to use those funds wisely for the benefit of the Palestinian people themselves.

I believe that Saudi Arabia recognizes how folding Israel into the region as a partner and friend can be a very positive step for the region. I do think that while they support the Palestinians, they are not unyielding in their view of conditioning friendship or partnership with Israel or peace in the region on solving the Israeli-Palestinian conflict.

Saudi Arabia holds a special and revered place in the Middle East, and within Islam generally as the protector of the world's two holiest mosques: Mecca and Medina. Whatever the Kingdom does vis-à-vis a closer formal relationship with Israel will, therefore, be done thoughtfully, respectfully, and with a genuine regard for the feelings of Muslims, not only in the region, but around the globe. The leadership will need space to make their decisions about Israel. Whether they take small steps or one big one, they will do so in their own time and in their own national interests. But it is clear that they do not regard Israel as an enemy and recognize that Israel can be a great friend. I am thoroughly comfortable in my travels to the Kingdom and see significant progress in MBS's view on where he wants to take the kingdom with each trip I take. I look forward to the day, which I hope will not be long, when I can be sitting in a kosher café in Riyadh, Jedda, or Neom and feeling absolutely at home.

Then of course, there are two very important Arab countries who signed peace agreements with Israel years ago, Egypt, in 1979 and Jordan, in 1994.

EGYPT

Egypt has long played a key role in the Middle East, trying hard to balance an important relationship with Israel while continuing to strongly support the Palestinians. Without betraying confidences here, it's my sense that Egypt would like to see a warmer peace with Israel beyond the strong security relationship Egypt and Israel currently share. Both Israel and Egypt could benefit from this. Egypt has a tremendous amount to offer the region and, together with Qatar, plays a significant role when trouble flares up in Gaza. Egypt deserves to be treated as an important ally and friend of the United States. I hope the Biden administration focuses on this relationship in a positive, helpful way.

JORDAN

I found King Abdullah to be an ever gracious, yet frank and forceful supporter of the Palestinian cause. I cannot fault him and his team for fighting for what they believe is best for Jordan and for standing by the Palestinians, even though I disagreed with some of those key positions. We had challenging conversations with them indeed, but King Abdullah and his team were consistent with their positions and tried to be helpful where they could be. Still, it was also clear to me that, from a state perspective, Jordan generally welcomed the Abraham Accords and appreciated the fact that they "lowered the temperature," so to speak, in the Middle East generally. Although I know that it is the official position of Jordan that a resolution of the Israeli-Palestinian conflict must precede any closer ties with Israel, I hope they will decide to take that courageous political plunge toward a closer formal relationship with Israel and not wait, indefinitely, for a solution to that conflict that seems increasingly out of reach.

A PARTING HOPE—AND A PRAYER

In 1983, when I first traveled to the Middle East as a teenager, the prevailing stance of the Arab world, with the exception of Egypt, was, as it had been for decades, one of aggression and war with Israel. Nearly forty years later, however, there is a different reality in the region. Confronted by an increasingly emboldened, aggressive Iran outside their borders and populations, the vast majority of those in the Middle East are anxious to have allies to confront that danger. They are simultaneously eager to explore the many economic opportunities within their community. More and more of the leaders in that region understand now that Israel is not the problem. Indeed, they see more clearly every day that it can actually be part of the solution to their needs and desires for a better, more prosperous life.

For all the apparent economic advantages that they make possible, it is the nascent and strengthening bonds between Israel and its Arab neighbors that are the Abraham Accords' greatest benefit. This is especially the case with the rising generation in the Middle East, which has the largest youth population in the world.

The percentage of the population in the Middle East under the age of 25 ranges from 25 percent in Qatar to 50 percent in Oman. In the UAE it stands at 34 percent, while it is 35 percent in Bahrain and 46 percent in Saudi Arabia. One of the obvious questions is whether this "youth bulge" will be a liability or a blessing. A great deal of the global literature on youth paints a dismal socio-economic picture of high unemployment, instability, and conflict. But the Abraham Accords holds the promise of a more vibrant economic future where new jobs and new opportunities abound. Turning that promise into a working reality, in turn, depends on the education these young people receive.

All too sadly, over the past decades, most schools in the Middle East frequently featured a disappointing diet of anti-Semitism that, day by day, year by year, perpetuated vile stereotypes about Jews of the worst kind. I'm happy to report that is changing, and rapidly.

I'm especially excited about the changes I see in educational opportunities in the countries that have signed the Abraham Accords or agreements based on the Accords.

In the UAE, one of the signatories of the Abraham Accords, Sheikh Mohammed bin Zayed bin Sultan Al Nahyan, has reformed the school curriculum that had previously been authored by the Muslim Brotherhood. It is now quite remarkably different, teaching tolerance and peacemaking.

Similarly, in Morocco, a country that has entered into a trilateral declaration with Israel with the same spirit and dynamics as the Abraham Accords, King Mohammed VI has instituted the teaching of Moroccan Jewish history. Efforts like these are so important in changing the cultural environment in the Middle East. In part, thanks to the influence of the Abraham Accords, there is a new opportunity to engage with curriculum developers in the region.

Engagement and friendship with Jews, not merely tolerance, and the acceptance of Israel's peaceful place in the Middle East and the Arab world at large can become the "new normal" in education there—and in a region where so many impressionable minds are up for grabs—a more inclusive school curriculum has the power to change a culture of hate into one of hope.

The potential for the Abraham Accords to transform lives and expand opportunities for the rising generation in the Middle East is almost beyond calculation. Such progress and possibility are, in turn, the key to greater stability and the most reliable recipe for reducing the appeal of religious radicalism to young men with few prospects for employment and a better life.

To those who often mocked our team and scoffed at the notion that observant Jews could bring peace between Israel and its Arab neighbors, I want to end with a story.

My 92-year-old father passed away in early September 2021. Under Jewish law, I am considered a mourner for twelve months and for eleven of those twelve months I must say the Kaddish prayer during prayer services, ideally three times a day. This is the same Kaddish prayer that I spoke about in an earlier chapter of this book when I described how Bibi Netanyahu joined me to help make a minyan in his office so that I would be able to say Kaddish that day of the yarzheit of my mother's passing.

Recently I had been waiting for several weeks for the confirmation of some important meetings I was setting up for a client in the Middle East. One morning I was going to be stepping up to the podium to lead the services for morning prayers and a few moments after that, to say the Kaddish prayer. I noticed my phone buzzing on the chair next to me, and I could not help but look at the screen to see who was calling. I saw the name of the person whom I had been trying to reach for a while to confirm the appointment. He had been very difficult to contact, so I was faced with the choice of missing a very important call so I could lead the services and say Kaddish, or picking up the phone, having the conversation I was so anxious to have, but missing the Kaddish prayer.

I picked up the phone and told this Muslim gentleman, an important person in the country I was trying to get the meeting with, "Hello, I am so sorry to be rude, but I am at morning prayers right now, and about to say a very important prayer; would I be able to call you back in a little while?"

His answer might surprise some of you. He was so apologetic for disturbing my prayers. He must have apologized four times and told me he would make sure to be available for me when I called him after the prayer service. Why? Because he, too, is a descendant of Abraham. He understands the meaning of prayer and religion in one's life.

That conversation, that kindness from that person that morning was the same as I experienced with Bibi Netanyahu that day in 2017. A respect for religion and prayer and G-d's place in one's life. Muslim or Jewish, it did not matter. We spoke the same language.

I'd like to think that my individual story is a harbinger of something broader being born in the Middle East. Instead of our religions, and the observance of our religions, being a roadblock, I have always viewed these are positive traits, ones that could possibly help, and certainly not hinder, progress. Because we know how to respect what is important and dear to our hearts.

In Judaism, there is a "Traveler's Prayer"—or Tefilat Haderech—that is said as we embark on a journey. Reciting it helps to remind us that G-d is with us and that, in his care, we are ultimately safe, guided, and blessed. The foundational story of Judaism is, itself, the story of a journey. A journey of discovery in which we are forever on our way, and direction is more important than destination. Some of the airlines of the Arab countries from the Middle East broadcast the Muslim traveler's prayer at takeoff time. When I fly one of these airlines and I hear the prayer being recited, I am again reminded of just how similar we are, as I am reciting the Jewish traveler's prayer at the same moment.

While many challenges remain in the Middle East, I am encouraged by what I see so far. But this shared journey between Israel and its Arab neighbors is just a beginning, a first step on a shared path from yesterday to tomorrow. If America continues its responsibility to lead the way, if America continues to be engaged in encouraging this process, I am confident that the people of Abraham can walk a common path toward a better, brighter, and more tolerant future.

ACKNOWLEDGMENTS

Just as we all have been warmed by fires we did not build, I have been helped by a host of individuals without whose aid and advice my job as White House Envoy—much less this book—would never have been possible.

And so, in that spirit, I'd like to acknowledge and honor those who have given so much of themselves to help me along the way. The spark they ignited in me will always be there, encouraging me to make the world a brighter and more peaceful place for all of us.

Without Donald J. Trump, absolutely nothing I have done during twenty-five years of my professional life would have been possible. I am so grateful that Donald Trump trusted me to work with the small team entrusted with one of the most important missions of his presidency.

Jared Kushner is the best boss I ever had or will ever have—with the possible exception of his father-in-law—Donald Trump. His passion was infectious, his eternal optimism inspiring. No matter how difficult the day or daunting the issue, Jared's "can-do" attitude gave our entire team the confidence it needed to keep going in the face of near constant criticism.

David Friedman is the kind of person you hope will always be your ally and hope will never be your enemy. He was a forceful advocate for America's greatest ally in the region, Israel. I am so glad we are friends and loved being in the trenches with him on so many tough issues and on the many things President Trump accomplished for the Jewish State of Israel. A special shout-out to David's trusted deputy, Aryeh Lightstone, who worked hard and was always willing to roll up his sleeves.

Avi Berkowitz took the baton I passed to him when I left the White House and ran an amazing race to the end of President Trump's term. He was—and is—a talented individual who was an essential member of the team that enabled President Trump reach the finish line.

The most important honor and recognition for the tremendous victory of the Abraham Accords goes to these incredible, courageous leaders: President Trump, Israeli Prime Minister Bibi Netanyahu, Mohamed bin Zayed bin Sultan Al Nahyan, better known by his initials, MBZ, the Crown Prince of the Emirate of Abu Dhabi, Hamad bin Isa bin Salman Al Khalifa, the King of Bahrain, Mohammed VI, the King of Morocco, and Abdalla Hamdok, the Prime Minister of Sudan.

There were many others who helped me and the team along the way in so many ways, so I would like to publicly thank them as well. My deepest apologies if I left anyone off this list.

Unlike so many politicians who have a public and a private side, Vice-President Mike Pence was, refreshingly, the authentic article. What he *seemed* he *was*—and that was a man who was unflappable and unfailingly helpful, no matter the problem, big or small. Religion wasn't something Mike Pence put on or off like a piece of clothing. It lay at the core of his convictions and informed the way he lived his life, both publicly and privately.

Graduating from top of his class from West Point was only one of Mike Pompeo's many great accomplishments, and I very much doubt he's done accomplishing all he wants to do. As CIA director and later, Secretary of State during the Trump presidency, Mike was an invaluable part of our mission in the Middle East who simultaneously saw the "big picture" but also had a mastery of the details as well. Mike is another Trump "alum" who is clearly going places – but where he's already been would fill a set of encyclopedias.

Polished, wise, willing to fight when necessary (and knowing how to fight), and politely and tirelessly persistent, Ambassador Nikki Haley was almost certainly the United Nations' worst nightmare as the United States' ambassador—and the best advocate for America, Israel and the unvarnished truth to ever walk the halls of Turtle Bay. I cherished our time together and look forward to watching whatever this extremely talented friend does next.

I can't say enough about my wonderful White House colleagues Dina Powell McCormick, Josh Raffel and Hope Hicks. They worked without applause, and made it all look easy, but without them my job would have been far more difficult.

And I can't afford to miss thanking my three "right hands" at the White House and one of Jared's right and left hands while I was at the White House: Matt Saunders, Alex El-Fakir, Ari Einhorn, and Cassidy Dumbauld. Also very helpful in Jared's office was Charlton Boyd.

I could never have accomplished my task as White House envoy without the sage counsel, advice, wisdom and support of so many people in the Middle East, among them the Prime Minister of Israel, Benjamin Netanyahu; the Crown Prince of the Emirate of Abu Dhabi, Mohamed bin Zayed bin Sultan Al Nahyan; the King of Saudi Arabia, Salman bin Abdulaziz Al Saud, the Crown Prince of Saudi Arabia, Mohammed bin Salman Al Saud; the Emir of Qatar, Tamim bin Hamad Al Thani; Hamad bin Isa bin Salman Al Khalifa, the King of Bahrain; Mohammed VI, the King of Morocco, the King of Jordan, Abdullah II bin Al-Hussein; the President of Egypt, Abdel Fattah el-Sisi; the late Sultan of Oman Qaboos bin Said; the Crown Prince and Prime Minister of Bahrain, Salman bin Hamad Al Khalifa, the foreign minister of Qatar, Mohammed bin Abdulrahman Al-Thani; the foreign minister of Oman, Yusuf bin Alawi bin Abdullah; the foreign minister of Morocco, Nasser Bourita; the foreign minister of Jordan, Ayman Safadi; Adel bin Ahmed Al-Jubeir the former Saudi Minister of Foreign Affairs and the current Saudi Minister of State for Foreign Affairs; former Saudi ambassador HRH Khalid bin Salman bin Abdulaziz (who was brought back to Saudi Arabia to work on a broader portfolio, and replaced with the very talented HRH

Princess Reema bint Bandar bin Sultan bin Abdulaziz Al Saud); the Ambassador of Bahrain to Washington, Abdulla bin Rashid bin Abdulla Al Khalif; the Ambassador of Jordan to Washington, Dina Kawar; the former Egyptian Ambassador to Washington, Yasser Reda; former advisor to the King of Jordan, Manar Dabbas; Bishar Al-Khasawneh, the current Prime Minister of Jordan; Major General Abbas Kamel, the current Director of the Egyptian General Intelligence Directorate and Egyptian Foreign Minister, Sameh Hassan Shoukry. We may have disagreed over many issues, but your knowledge, dedication and willingness to listen and share was deeply appreciated.

A big thank you to my friends, Israeli ambassador Ron Dermer and Emirati ambassador Yousef Al Otaiba, two outstanding ambassadors, perhaps among the finest in Washington during my time at the White House. Ron was an incredible partner who I spent countless hours with; he worked tirelessly for the State of Israel on all aspects of the US-Israel relationship, including the Abraham Accords. Yousef was tremendous in representing Emirati interests at the White House and incredibly helpful to me with each step of building the path toward the Abraham Accords during my time at the White House and beyond.

I'd certainly be remiss if I didn't acknowledge Don Jr., Eric and Ivanka for twenty years of fun and excitement, which ultimately led to my role at the White House. Working with them over those years was a wonderful experience and they kept me on my toes.

I owe much to my dedicated National Security Council and State Department colleagues who did so much to educate this neophyte diplomat. They did exceptional work under often trying circumstances. National Security Advisor Lt. General HR McMaster and National Security Advisor Ambassador John Bolton always tried to be supportive and offer their wisdom. Other colleagues—Brian Hook played a very important role in enabling us to fold Iran into our overall strategy, Victoria Coates, David Milstein, Morgan Otagus, Heather Nauert, Yael Lempert, Connie Meyer, Eddie Vasquez, Ryan Arant, Amanda Pilz, Michael Ratney, Karen Sasahara, Donald Blome, Mike Hankey, the hard working team of the Palestinian Affairs Unit at the former U.S. Consulate in Jerusalem, and many others. I enjoyed working with you and learned from you (even those I heavily disagreed with—you know who you are). Also, a thank you to Sarah Sanders and the hard-working teams at the various communications and press offices who helped me along the way.

Each control officer in each mission in the Middle East that helped me manage all my trips—you were all awesome. At the risk of singling two out, I think Monica and Charles had to put up with me and my meetings the most!

I'd also like to thank my briefers from the intelligence community, although, unfortunately, I cannot share their names. I'd also like to thank my security teams in each country I visited, with a special thanks to those who covered me in Israel and the Palestinian territories.

Among those who shared their wisdom, advice and unvarnished conversations were Sheldon and Miriam Adelson, modern day heroes of the Jewish people. The late Sheldon Adelson was a superbly successful businessman, to be sure, but Sheldon's most important and lasting investments were in the Jewish people and the State of Israel. Sheldon, together with Miriam, have planted trees neither planned to sit under for the benefit of generations yet unborn. Their legacy will be a lasting one. I am deeply honored to have known Sheldon and also know that, despite his loss, Miriam will continue to carry on, alone, in all the important work she and Sheldon did together, for so long and so well.

I learned so much about Israel from a small army of people, among them current Israeli Prime Minister Naftali Bennet, current Israeli President Isaac (Bougie) Herzog, Yossi Cohen, Nadav Argaman, Meir Ben Shabbat, Yoav Horowitz, Dore Gold, Mike Herzog (now the Israeli ambassador to the United States), former ambassador Danny Danon, former Consul General Danny Dayan, Tzipi Livni, Nir Barkat, Israel Katz, Yarden Golan and others.

There are so many Palestinians I heard from and spoke with during my time as envoy. I cherished our time together. While many disagreed with our plan, I remain good friends with many. I would gladly include their names here, but for the sake of their own safety I will not do so here.

I am grateful to former British Prime Minister Tony Blair, Mohamed Alabbar, Hussein Agha, Nickolay Mladenov, Borge Brende, Tor Wennesland, and a host of individuals whose ideas and input were valued and appreciated. I also want to thank so many individuals in the think tank community. Most of you wanted to share your wisdom, experience and ideas, even if you disagreed with our approach. The small group of you who opted to attack us rather than help, well, you know who you are.

Journalists are vital to the functioning of a democracy and I was fortunate to interact with so many who do great credit to their profession. I had my tussles with some of the journalists, but you were all an important part of my work. I am sorry that I did not leak anything to any of you. Deep down, I know most of you respected that.

I certainly owe a debt of gratitude to Rabbi Shalom Baum, the Rabbi at Congregation Keter Torah in Teaneck, New Jersey who gave this lawyer-turned-globe-trotter some much-needed Jewish law guidance and perspective amid the frenetic world of Washington.

And there are those with whom I disagreed fundamentally, but, at least for most of 2017, engaged with me until they cut us off. Palestinian President Mahmoud Abbas, the late Saeb Erekat, Majed Faraj and Husam Zomlot. They made me think more deeply and more clearly about the issues involved in the Israeli-Palestinian conflict and helped sharpen and refine my own arguments and assessments of this prolonged struggle.

Finally, once again, I must thank my incredible wife Naomi, and amazing six children—Noah, Julia, Anna,

Sophia, Avery and Vera. Without your support, patience, understanding, encouragement and love, none of what I did or experienced would have been possible!